The Destruction of America

© 2014 by Eric Steele

ISBN-13: 978-1500908737
ISBN-10: 1500908738

The Destruction of America

TABLE OF CONTENTS

INTRODUCTION

Conservative white Americans worry that the influx of illegal aliens from south of the border and from Asia will threaten to destroy the Anglo-Germanic majority culture in the United States. Others worry that Islamic terrorists will succeed with additional attacks on our home front similar in scope to the 911 catastrophe. Some believe that a race war is inevitable, pointing to the stark economic disparity between whites and blacks. There are occasional urban riots when white cops shoot unarmed blacks, as police forces become more militarized with battlefield equipment and vehicles.

What people are overlooking is the gradual decay in the social infrastructure of America, where its great ideals of individual freedoms, tolerance, honesty, charity, and equality under the law are being supplanted by greed, corruption, predatory business practices, crime, and decay in the moral fiber of the populace. The destruction of America will not likely come from outside, but rather from the eventual collapse of its civility and respect for each other and its institutions. This path toward destruction can be stopped, if leaders and the electorate unite to solve long-standing problems before the weight of the shifting cargo tips the ship.

James Foley's beheading by an ISIS terrorist in Syria. R.I.P.

C1 - American Society Today

Policy makers have sought to understand trends among the populace that portends social change. Surveys and research projects attempt to gauge demographic differences and their changing priorities that are important to advertisers, product manufacturers, service businesses and government spending. Anticipating social change accurately can become a financial bonanza for entrepreneurs who recognize ever changing and evolving needs in society at large, and in social niches in particular. The sudden rise to wealth of relatively young founders of social network and many communications technology companies clearly demonstrate the power of social change that is reflected in consumer trends.

However, as promising as these virtual reality mega companies have become and the great paper fortunes that they have accrued, like all stock market gambles, they can collapse overnight and take down tens of millions of investors, retirement funds, and devastate the economy. We must understand what is real and the vulnerabilities that American society faces in modern times with instantaneous communications and computer programs that automatically make template decisions for our economy and society without weighing the possible unintended consequences of such far reaching decision making matrixes and its aggregate effects on society.

Social change as the topic of discussion in this book entails all aspects of what makes up our society. This book is not a simplistic discussion of social norms, fads or trends, but attempts to tie together the major aspects of social forces at work that either knit our society together, or act to tear it apart. All civilizations that survive and evolve must adjust to the sudden and dynamic social and political changes that result from economic, environmental, technological, military, religious and philosophical pressures. History has shown that peoples and cultures that could not adapt to those key changes have died off, either becoming absorbed by more pervasive, powerful, or efficient cultures or simply vanishing from the face of the earth like the Neanderthals.

Our great nation, the United States of America is relatively an infant of barely over 200 years old, as compared to civilizations, dynasties, kingdoms and empires that lasted a thousand or more years. As a people, we still have a lot to learn about getting along and overcoming historical prejudices and hostilities. Certainly, wise elected leaders have gradually challenged the divisive practices of the past, and now most of the offending "isms" are outlawed, or at the least swept under the carpet or kept locked in the closet as being politically incorrect speech and ideas. Those who have publicly expressed insensitive and offensive prejudicial speech and actions have earned their public humiliation and punishment, far more than the unmentionable words they spoke during unguarded public moments. Are attitudes really changing, or simply being muted in public?

Americans now face potential threats to the existence of America on many fronts. Many facets of society are now vulnerable to sudden catastrophic consequences. The Stock Market remains a ticking time bomb waiting for the next bubble to burst, taking down with it the lifetime savings of hardworking people and investors alike. Government borrowing continues to put our nation on the financial precipice of bankruptcy, where national debt now equals the annual GDP. Our friends and allies have become our global economic competitors, while our past enemies continue to improve their military postures while smiling during state-to-state meetings. Advances in technology, science, engineering, genetics, and communications will create great changes and opportunities for those positioned to benefit, but will also leave many behind who have not retooled their knowledge and career skills. Jobs are demanding greater levels of specific technical skills and knowledge not possessed by most college graduates as corporations continue to outsource jobs to low paying overseas populations. We need to deal effectively with these issues.

Al Qaeda and global terrorism is only one strategic plan to attempt to weaken The United States of America, our federal government, American culture, our freedoms, liberties, and way of life. The long-range goals of various anti-American conspirators are simple, as we are witnessing the results of its insidious plot, as our society continues to decay in all areas.

1. Social decay through propagating disunity among Americans.
    a. Fuel racism by blaming whites for all of society's ills, thus driving a wedge between minority races and the majority.
    b. Promote immorality and divisive cultural-ethnic-racial-sex-gender conflicts by legalizing homosexual marriages, pornography, illegal immigration, affirmative action, late term abortion, and encouraging degeneration through mass media, television programs, music, and popular culture.

c. Promote interracial conflict by creating ineffective minority hand out programs that pits one race against another.

d. Create disrespect for authority and government by gradually outlawing basic freedoms, and creating too much red tape.

e. Cause ethical and moral decay by outlawing reasonable corporal punishment of children for destructive conduct, when reasonable punishment by parents and teachers could keep certain students from lives of crime. Instead, disrespectful children later become rebellious teens who eventually spend much of their adult lives in prison, becoming subjected to highly violent environments that far exceeds the penalty of a loving spanking when it could have made a positive difference in their young lives.

f. Suppress and ridicule good citizenship and patriotism, while promoting sex, violence, and greed as a "cool" and desirable lifestyle.

g. Resist progressive changes to the education system, such as school vouchers. Mix all children into template classes, where disinterested and disruptive children ruin the class environment for students who wish to learn. Penalize the teachers by making them suspect for every frivolous and false accusation from dysfunctional students.

2. Political decay by the media and universities encouraging distrust of government, particularly the federal government.

a. Special interest groups and political lobbyists entice and corrupt government officials, politicians, and bureaucrats.

b. Alienate citizens from governance by making them feel disinterested and hopeless to positively change policies. When citizens no longer monitor government activities, there is greater latitude for corruptive influences to make significant inroads.

c. Persuade corrupted legislators and agency chiefs to make policies that favor special interest groups, while punishing citizens, thereby transferring citizens' money to special interest groups, corrupt corporate executives and economic elites.

3. Economic decay is evidenced by a strategy of wealth transfer from the working middle class to special interests elites.

   a. The U.S. A. is treated as just another consumer market for exploitation and wealth building by the elites, thus the ends justify the means, and patriotism is not a concern.

   b. Swindle retirees of their life savings and pensions through clever investment ruses and fraud. Enron, Arthur Andersen and Merrill Lynch corruption is only the tip of the iceberg. Law enforcement must identify, by using reverse phone trees and wire tapes, to obtain evidence to justify the round up of top executives from this conspiratorial network to prevent them from corrupting every person and corporation that they touch and bribe; otherwise, they and those like them will breed like cockroaches, and soon it will be near impossible to isolate and catch them.

   c. Use technology to replace American workers, to maximize corporate profits and compensation to greedy CEOs, CFOs and Board Chairs and Directors under the guise of necessity and competitive survivability, instead of admitting true wanton greed.

   d. Outsource manufacturing and white collar high tech jobs to cheap labor markets, even if the consequence is harmful to the U.S. economy.

   e. Concentrate control of strategic industries, raw materials, and consumer markets to MNCs whose executives have no loyalty to America, but only to personal wealth building.

   f. Destabilize the U.S. dollar, cause sudden massive monetary devaluations, and de-dollarize international trade when the monetary and trade imbalances makes currencies ripe for hedge fund speculation and attacks.

4. International relations decay by attempting to discredit, isolate and alienate our President and government leaders, the N.S.A., C.I.A. and our State Department on the world stage and among our supposed allies.

a. Implement anti-Bush, anti-N.S.A. and anti-American propaganda tactics.

b. Use elitist-owned or controlled domestic and international news media to foment anti-American and anti-C.I.A. sentiments through biased news editing, reporting, and commentary which is represented as factual news.

c. Foment international violence, conflicts and insurgency to test American diplomatic and military response, and to stretch out all of America's military resources abroad, thereby weakening the U.S. frontlines and logistics.

d. Criticize U.S. response as being either too little too late, too heavy-handed and unilateralist, or too insensitive, or whatever slant is necessary to discredit America's good intentions and good deeds abroad.

e. Foster anti-American sentiments to unify different political and religious camps by recognizing the U.S.A. as their common foe, by applying the "Your enemy's enemy is your friend" principle. This strategy is being used among Islamic states, anti-Semitic groups, and terrorist networks. A unified Europe, Sino-Russian rapprochement, and a unified South America all present potential hot spots in fomenting future anti-American sentiments around the world.

5. Military decay through compromise, overpriced military contracts, spying, contracting out to foreign companies, conflicts of interest among current and retired brass and civilian administrators, and wasting precious military funds on various kickback schemes, while American troops fail to receive the required equipment to protect their lives and to make them successful in their military missions.

a. U.S. dependency on foreign manufacturers, suppliers, and raw materials needed for military hardware and systems.

b. Spies and moles planted in sensitive government agencies and committees with oversight over intelligence, military technology, procurement, and operations.

c.   Government contracts and subcontracts that allow foreign corporations (thus governments) to monitor our military and government communication through service providers of email, phone, fax, hardware and software.

d.   Installation of "back door" and "trap door" computer chips or spy software in military and government computer networks and equipment, such as computers, planes, trucks, offices, and ships for spying.

e.   Integration of "override" chips or software programs into military weapons and communications systems to permit partial or complete take over, sabotage, or destruction of vulnerable military systems, such as virtual battlefield and the Joint Attack Fighter.

f.   Install spy technology into sensitive American facilities, buildings, vehicles, and offices through construction, art work, furniture, equipment, housekeeping and security contractors and suppliers.

People who doubt that these secretive agendas are in operation need only open their eyes to the decay that has inched its way into American society, laws, corporations, and culture since the end of the Vietnam War. We can not solve our nation's problems, protect our homeland and way of life, and restore civility, morality and ethics to our society until we recognize, rather than deny that a serious and grave set of problems exist that is being fostered by our enemies, both here at home and abroad.

Our nation and the world is awashed in perplexing, complex and persistent issues that seem to defy common sense solutions. Why? Are human beings genetically so selfish and conflictual that it is impossible for them to get along for very long? Let's consider a laundry list of human propensities that continue to persist and divide our nation's populace and nations around the world.

National and Global issues resistant to change:

- Elitism
- Classism
- Racism
- Sexism

- Ageism
- Poverty
- Oligarchs
- MNC's
- Political corruption
- Bureaucratic corruption
- Development
- Legalism
- Ecological devastation
- Labor exploitation
- Land ownership by banks
- World banking and debt
- Excessive greed
- Warfare and violence
- Power mongers
- Oil dependency

Human genetic propensities resistant to change:
- Hunting and killing instinct
- Predatory instinct
- Gathering – hoarding – greed instinct
- Planting – building instinct
- Destructive instinct
- Parasitic instinct
- Exploitation instinct
- Control compulsion
- Sexual urge
- Power urge
- Physical stimulation urge
- Emotional insecurities propensity
- Mental stimulation urge
- Spiritual balance need

- Art – music appreciation
- Entertainment and diversion
- Discovery and experimentation
- Exploration and risk taking
- Scientific knowledge
- Engineering – technology
- Escapism and recreation
- Humanitarianism
- Dependency
- Criminality
- Racism, sexism and hatred

As time marches forward, human societies advance technologically; however, the propensity for conflict traps people into complex webs of deception and confusion. Just why don't humans seem able to get along? How much is due to genetic predispositions and survival instincts, versus socially learned conditioned values? What contributes to the formation of attitudes which constitute beliefs relating to:

- Fear of the unknown or unfamiliar
- Territoriality, property and land ownership
- Differentiation, alienation, and segregation
- Hierarchical dominance relationships
- Protectiveness of loves ones & own group
- Affiliation with other familiar humans
- Jealousy, anger, envy and negative emotions
- Self-centeredness and selfishness
- Intolerance and rejection of differences
- Aggression, predatory and violent behavior
- Superiority versus inferiority
- Cultural, racial, and ethnic pride
- Class, race, sex, age, disability, ethnic, and intellectual discrimination
- Religious pursuits, beliefs, and superstition

- Group, peer, and media pressure to conform to norms
- Needing predictability in dealing with a matrix of needs
- Believing in authority figures, governments, schools, and the media
- Greed, hoarding, and competitiveness
- Desire for power and control over others
- Wastefulness, destructiveness, excesses, compulsiveness, and addition

The interaction and prevalence of human attitudes has resulted in the development of complex and apparently unsolvable problems. When human societies begin to focus on finding realistic answers to many of the following problems, there may be hope yet, that the human species may survive another century. What types of jobs will be eliminated by technology, outsourcing, and decrease demand for various products and services? What new jobs will be created as a result of technology, terrorism, and new consumer needs?

What are the negative consequences of globalization versus the positive results? How will globalization contribute to the rise of oligarchies, increased prices, manipulated supply shortages, decreased choices, and permanently lost occupations and jobs? What are potentially positive affects of globalization? Will it bring more efficiency, more coordinated and equitable distribution of resources and products, and minimizing wastage? Is nuclear proliferation, conflict, and global thermonuclear war likely?

How relevant is education as we know it? How can we improve it and prepare students for an unpredictable future? What are the purposes, goals, and transitions that education must endure to remain relevant as computers and high tech makes human knowledge broad and instantaneous? What areas of environmental protection are "essential" for the ecosystem, human survival, and quality of life? How do we control geometric world population growth?

What is the appropriate balance between personal privacy and the state's need to know to provide adequate homeland security and protections. What can be done to shrink government and the voluminous accrual of laws on the books that is a direct threat to individual freedoms? What is mankind's collective vision of the future of human beings?

How can world governments act in cooperation to "lift the tide" to reduce the great economic disparities between the rich and poor, to eliminate unequal distribution of resources and wealth, and to eliminate poverty and disease? What new "survival paradigm" versus the "hard work & zero-sum game" paradigm would more appropriately address future trends and changes? How can the cycle of gangs, poverty, and violence be broken?

How can we improve social interactions, relationships, and civility? How can the justice system become more "just" and efficient? How do we adequately provide for the elderly, infirmed, and disabled? How do we provide adequate low and reasonably priced housing? How can we eliminate terrorism before it eliminates civilization? How do we encourage teens to develop more responsible attitudes for their own lives and that of others? What are the solutions to the abortion, right to life, assisted suicide issues?

How can government bureaucracy become more efficient and effective? How can corruption be weeded out from government and corporations? How can legislators make more sensible and appropriate laws that serve the public interest instead of special interest? How can people become more content, self-accepting, and happy? What events are likely to cause human extinction within a few centuries? How can we improve human contact and relationships? What is fantasy versus reality nowadays? What would happen if everyone decided to be completely honest? What benefits can we obtain from space exploration and travel?

Topics come up on a daily basis to attack our senses and sensibilities. Here's an abbreviated list of just a few of the concerns that are inundated our minds.

1.	education	2.	crime	3.	warfare
4.	pollution	5.	pornography	6.	drugs
7.	immigration	8.	quality of life	9.	health
10.	excessive greed	11.	unemployment	12.	racism
13.	sexual slavery	14.	sexism	15.	exploitation
16.	sexual harassment	17.	deception	18.	stupidity
19.	lying	20.	dishonesty	21.	civility
22.	white power	23.	anti-Semitism	24.	Zionism
25.	Iraq ambushes	26.	special interests	27.	politics
28.	consumption	29.	employment	30.	career

31. ethnic pride	32. citizenship	33. patriotism
34. intolerance	35. overpopulation	36. disabilities
37. abortion	38. suicide	39. immorality
40. reproductive rights	41. sexual preference	42. alcohol abuse
43. smoking	44. social norms	45. media bias
46. homeland security	47. poverty	48. diseases
49. privacy rights	50. violence	51. technology
52. space exploration	53. destructiveness	54. energy costs
55. age of consent	56. alternative energy	57. death penalty
58. incarceration	59. credit problems	60. work ethic
61. rude & toxic people	62. prison sentences	63. 3 strikes law
64. escapism	65. recreation	66. rest
67. relationships	68. loneliness	69. alienation
70. sexuality	71. spirituality	72. religion
73. freedom of choice	74. freeway traffic	75. justice
76. fairness	77. court system	78. UFOs/ETs
79. zero-sum game	80. police brutality	81. police chases
82. gang violence	83. bureaucracy	84. boredom
85. winning	86. losing	87. cheating
88. money	89. gambling	90. lottery
91. sex	92. emotional needs	93. child abuse
94. creation/evolution	95. elderly abuse	96. threats
97. spousal abuse	98. science and reality	99. rage
100. uncertainty	101. aggressive driving	102. infinity
103. blood pressure	104. dieting	105. appearance
106. stem cell research	107. genetic engineering	108. g.m. foods
109. cloning	110. new world order	111. globalization
112. unemployment	113. parking space	114. end times
115. teen rebellion	116. IMF	117. WTO
118. WMDs	119. TEOTWAWKI	120. terrorism
121. mind control	122. witchcraft & sorcery	123. prophesy
124. religious conflict	125. television programs	126. email
127. banking	128. post office mail	129. family
130. shopping	131. grocery store strike	133. transit strike

134.	wardrobe	135.	bills and payments	136.	work & job
137.	auto repairs	138.	crazy people	139.	fees and fines
140.	government taxes	141.	parking tickets	142.	entertainment
143.	balance checkbook	144.	overdrawn fees	145.	tiredness
146.	being in a rush	147.	stressed out	148.	anxiety
149.	frustration	150.	depression	151.	anger
152.	eating choices	153.	social contact	154.	avoidance
155.	political correctness	156.	comparing oneself	157.	enjoyment
158.	current events	159.	investments	160.	death

Our minds are subconsciously running subroutines and we think and dream about many of these persistent and unresolved issues. During the past decade, 10% of these topics did not exist. It seems that every year, there's more topics that clutter our minds, hearts, and lives. One hundred years ago, there were 100 less topics of concern, because they didn't exist. Anything over 10 topics of concern per day has the potential of creating extra stress, distraction, and defocuses our lives from the more important issues. During simpler times, people probably only had to deal with half a dozen issues each day, such as tending the crops and animals, going in to eat when called, fetching water for bathing, resting and sleep, and family. Is that six? People were probably happier during those simpler days, and less preoccupied about so many extraneous issues that plague us today. We can't wait for scientist to discover how to send us back in time to simpler days. Oftentimes, it seems that living in the 21st century America is turning into a big rip off...

1. You can be ticketed for not wearing your seatbelt and jailed for almost anything
2. You can lose your job as a teacher, even when falsely accused
3. Credit card companies rip you off with a myriad of fees, penalties and usury
4. Whenever they want to raise gasoline prices, they conveniently burn down or close a major refinery (last time it was the Arco plant, now, Tosco)
5. Soon, average working people won't be able to afford driving to/from work, so they'll be out of work
6. Soon, average people won't be able to afford turning on their air conditioners
7. Soon, businesses will go bankrupt when they can't afford high-energy bills

8. Soon, people will get so stressed and pissed off again, they'll be rioting in the streets during the summer, burning down the symbols of greed and oppression...

9. Government unemployment statistics are underestimated by around 50% for political reasons by eliminating the long-termed unemployed, homeless and impoverished.

10. Are we headed for a police state, suspension of democratic processes, and the imposition of martial law, leading to the incarceration of political dissidents and other groups deemed undesirable by the government?

History has shown this emerging pattern might be the case. It all started in pre-ww2 Nazi Germany, and now it's showing its insidious head in America with law enforcement groups finding it necessary to purchase military surplus arsenals, including armored vehicles, assault rifles, and other equipment designed for use on foreign battlefields, but being deployed in domestic urban battlefields, such as in the riots occurring in Ferguson, Missouri, a small racially divided city of 21,000 people.

C2 - CONFLICT

Imagine if everybody in the world were genuinely honest, considerate and nice. There would likely be no significant levels of violence in society. We all go through life and are forced to deal with people one way or another, whether we want to, need to, like it or not. Generally, as we stumble through our life's path, we tend to meet primarily two types of people to various degrees on the continuum of behavior. On the positive side of personality expression are nice people, but on the opposing extreme are aggressive mean people. A comparison of these two types of personalities shows the obvious contrast between how nice versus mean people treat each others and their core character. If you find a person displays half a dozen of these behaviors and attitudes, be aware that it's likely part of the character pattern that makes nice people and mean people polar opposites. It's very difficult for nice people to be mean, and vice versa, mean people can "fake it" and be nice for only a short period before their true character shows itself through their demanding, aggressive, deceptive, manipulative, inconsiderate, insensitive, and mean manner.

NICE PEOPLE

(often referred to as **suckers**, **wimps**, and described as being **emotional weaklings**, when in fact, it takes much more sacrifice, tolerance, emotional maturity, mental stability, ability to withstand suffering, perseverance, and spiritual strength to be a nice person than to be an abuser)

1. considerate
2. compassionate
3. humble
4. selfless
5. cooperative
6. giving and charitable
7. fearful and anxious

MEAN PEOPLE

(usually regarded as **alphas**, **leaders**, users, and **emotionally, physically and mentally tough**, when it fact it is easier to be inconsiderate, self-centered, demanding, intolerant, rigid, emotionally mentally unstable, aggressive, pain avoidant, abusive and mean)

1. inconsiderate
2. cold-hearted
3. arrogant
4. selfish
5. dictatorial
6. demanding and taking
7. fearless and aggressive

8.	innocent		8.	predatory
9.	insecure		9.	over-confident
10.	under-achiever		10.	over-achiever
11.	open-minded		11.	opinionated
12.	approval seeking		12.	credit/recognition seeking
13.	guilt complex		13.	blameless and guiltless
14.	self-deprecating		14.	self-righteous
15.	courteous		15.	rude
16.	moralistic		16.	immoral or amoral
17.	sacrificing		17.	opportunistic
18.	apologetic		18.	ass kicking
19.	helpful disposition		19.	obsessed with winning
20.	kind		20.	stingy
21.	honest		21.	deceptive
22.	mellow and easy-going		22.	angry and driven
23.	patient		23.	impatient
24.	accepts blame		24.	blames others
25.	supporting		25.	leading
26.	status quo maintainer		26.	competitive or destructive
27.	goes with the flow		27.	it's their way or the highway
28.	feels used and unappreciated		28.	feels never enough just due
29.	worries about others		29.	worries about self
30.	a friend you can trust		30.	just another user asshole
31.	ethical conduct		31.	unethical
32.	peaceful resolution seeking		32.	violence prone
33.	loyal		33.	disloyal
34.	open-minded		34.	rigid and opinionated
35.	willing to admit mistakes		35.	self-righteous
36.	tolerant and accepting of others		36.	intolerant and prejudice
37.	sincere		37.	manipulative and insincere
38.	trusting		38.	distrusting
39.	dependable		39.	unreliable
40.	predictable		40.	unpredictable
41.	trustworthy		41.	takes advantage of trust

42.	creative and supportive maintainer	42.	destroyer
43.	forgiving	43.	revengeful
44.	loving and kind	44.	angry, hateful and miserly
45.	accepting of differences	45.	racist and prejudice
46.	sexually considerate	46.	promiscuous & aggressive
47.	facts are interpretive	47.	facts are absolute
48.	intelligence is developed	48.	intelligence is inherited
49.	freedom is to avoid external controls	49.	control is operative power
50.	good health is prevention and practice	50.	health is inherited superiority
51.	money is pragmatic and functional	51.	money is control and winning
52.	accepts aging process rationally	52.	wants to live forever
53.	being average is acceptable	53.	elitist attitudes
54.	wealth is desirable but unlikely	54.	wealth is desirable and attainable
55.	religious intolerance is undesirable	55.	religion is organized hypocrisy
56.	beauty is only skin deep	56.	beauty is a commodity
57.	say what is appropriate for situation	57.	say what I whatever I want to say
58.	do what is legal and appropriate	58.	do what I want without penalty
59.	eat enough to satisfy hunger	59.	eat whenever and whatever
60.	sex is expression of love and intimacy	60.	sex is power and recreation
61.	go where and when it's affordable	61.	go wherever and whenever
62.	rules should restrain natural urges	62.	rules don't apply to me
63.	avoid trouble by knowing limits	63.	push the limits and make trouble
64.	persuade others to cooperate	64.	outsmart and command others
65.	be humble in achievement	65.	win at all cost, then brag about it
66.	conserve something for a rainy day	66.	get other people's share for self
67.	living is a prudent gamble everyday	67.	gamble on high risk behavior
68.	be fair and reasonable	68.	attack and conquer
69.	other's welfare is also important	69.	no body else matters except self
70.	plan for the future and act cautiously	70.	react forcefully to dominate

Observation: Mean people seek out nice people because they tend to be users, abusers, and predators. They possess a more pronounced hunter instinct that's hereditarily akin to animals. These **alphas** define, drive, and destroy our world, which otherwise would be too nice. Nice people desire peace, freedom, brotherhood, family, love, civility, human dignity, human rights, and prefer to obey the law. Mean people want power, control, money, exploitation of others, self-centeredness, materialism, and don't like following society's rules, as they desire to be above the law. Following is a real example that distinguishes nice versus mean people:

There are many significant difference between people who prefer by choice to be nice and considerate versus those who often get their way by being mean, demanding, and selfish. Here's a description of a person, whom you may recognize among your associates or family members. This person may appear to be fictional, but the illustration is factual of the heightened tension and drama that personifies many **mean-spirited** people. Oftentimes, nice people may feel the following describes people who are **crazy** or **bi-polar**, but whatever euphemism is used, the actions are similar and fall into the **pattern of meanness.**

Description of behavior and attitudes of a mean person:
1. Makes decisions impulsively and impatient for gratification.
2. Insists on self-correctness and doggedly defends position, stubborn.
3. Changes mind on direction of action depending upon mood and impulse.
4. Insults people if their views are in opposition, calling others stupid.
5. Repetitious of certain favorite stories or phrases from their life experience.
6. Self-indulgence in everything, and highly self-centered.
7. Sometimes complements, but negates it with more negative criticism.
8. Blames others if things don't work out their way.
9. Takes contrary view, or criticize other people's positions, just to find faults.
10. Expects people to say and do things according to their expectations.
11. Intolerant of interruptions, as what they say is always more important.
12. Challenges other people's facts as conjecture and suppositions, while imposing their personal views and perspectives as factual.
13. Takes a historical view without futuristic or broad view of the world.
14. High risk behaviors and risk seeker, seeks action, contest, and competition.

15. Fearless when having the upper hand.

16. Revengeful and aggressive.

17. Obsessive and compulsive.

18. Triggers to high verbal volatility and aggressive profane barrages.

19. Disinterested in other's views, which are considered unimportant or stupid.

20. Competitive, if personally affected, and wants to win at all cost.

21. Racist view of world, interpersonal relations, and social economic order.

22. Punitive; threat oriented when feeling in charge, control freak.

23. Resist expressing positive emotions as sign of weakness.

24. Contradictory morality or immoral.

25. Rebellious against others who attempt to exercise influence or control.

26. Leaves fate blowing in the wind and will try anything if in the mood.

27. Doesn't give a damn, even if the worse consequences are possible.

28. Not compassionate, it's other people's own fault for bad things happening.

29. Manipulative, and will befriend if potential benefits in various ways.

30. Disloyal to family and loved ones, and unfaithful to lover; opportunistic.

31. Secretive, tells you what she wants you to know or think, not the truth.

32. Highly calculating and manipulative of immediate environment.

33. Highly exploitive in diverse and changing situations and opportunities.

34. Realistic and pragmatic view and approach to using people for self gain.

35. Inability to feel guilt, and or to love deeply.

36. Attracted to superficial appearances, people are like candy in a store.

37. Able to withstand high degree of physical pain to get self-benefits.

38. Feels they are superior and deserve to be a served and kiss-up to.

39. Desires total freedom and no commitments to others.

40. Persistent, compulsive, obsessive, extreme, and determined at all cost.

Ironically, both nice people, as well as mean people are attracted to nice people. Nice people enjoy being around nice people because it's a time for sharing, caring, communications, relaxation and enjoyment. Mean people want to be around nice people in order to be served, to take advantage, boss others around, get nice people to do things they are either too lazy to do, or don't feel like doing. And when mean people don't get their way immediately, they tend to yell, insult, and express rage like spoiled brats who never grew up emotionally. Unfortunately, those who rise to the top of organizations tend to be these mean-spirited and driven ass-holes because they refuse the alternative of going along with others, instead of always getting their own way.

These mean-spirited predators feel no shame or guilt in back-stabbing competitors, associates, friends, or family if anyone gets in their way of achieving their compulsive goals. Often, they get so used to others giving in to their demanding manner, that they don't even think they're being inconsiderate or mean. It never crosses their mind that they are the source of conflict and discomfort to others, because most people are willing to let mean people have their way, just to avoid all the unnecessary drama and conflict, usually over stupid and unimportant issues. And even when aggressive people realize they are being jerks, they enjoy the feeling of having power and control over others, making others run around like trained dogs. The feeling of power and invincibility is an aphrodisiac that reinforces mean people's rude behavior, and therefore it would be very foolish of nice people to ever expect mean people to change their stripes because they gain too much benefit from their instinctive predatory behavior.

The best thing nice people can do is to avoid mean people, to deprive them of their predatory ways. If all the nice people could someday band together and force mean people to change their ways, to be more humane and less despicable, the societies in the world would be a much nicer place, where people could become more fulfilled and happy. Unfortunately, it's the mean people who rule the world, own the world's resources, command governments and militaries, and enforce laws that keep them in control of the world's nice and meek people. The historical world paradigm has not been one of **survival of the fittest**, but instead, **survival of the meanest**. And perhaps that paradigm will never change in our lifetime because nice people will always give in to mean people, if for no other reason than to avoid conflict, and have some peace of mind away from dramatic, demanding, and aggressive mean people.

When confronted, mean people will often claim they were not aware how people viewed their behavior as being demanding and mean-spirited. Mean people become accustomed to getting their way by being inconsiderate of the needs of others. By being demanding of others, they get others to do the difficult part of work, while mean people stand around to criticize and give orders, then call that leadership. They will justify their behavior by saying they have high expectations, and want to push people to their highest potential – when in fact, these bosses probably don't have the knowledge and skills to achieve what they expect of others. It is the typical CEO or "boss" mentality to exploit workers labor, to do things that bosses can't often do themselves. Mean people often feel compelled to push and bully others out of their way, disregarding other's rights and needs, and will attempt to cut in line, even though others have patiently waited for their respective turns. Mean people feel comfortable using others to obtain personal gain, glory, and credit that would otherwise be due to others who actually accomplish the work. Of course when things don't go the way mean people want, they're the first to accuse and blame others for mistakes, wrongdoings, and crimes while attempting to exonerate their implicit knowledge and responsibility for the outcomes. They jump at the chance to claim credit for any achievement, and hide behind the otherwise good name of an underling who would be sacrificed to protect the bosses against penalties.

Why is the world still a dangerous and violent place? Is it because we have too many nice people? Or is it because mean people create conflict, violence, exploitation and abuse? It takes about 100 really nice people to neutralize one mean person. Now, if you were to count all the nice people you know (hopefully starting with you), versus the mean people, it would be very difficult to name 100 nice people for every mean one that crosses your path. That's too bad, because it dooms humanity to its primal Stone Age instincts, which prohibits enlightenment and humanitarian progress that is yearned for all over the world. With the coming advent of total economic and political globalization coupled with the rule of despots in developing countries, the future looks rather bleak for the world's majority of nice people.

Undoubtedly, nice people will again become the cannon fodder, and the exploited class of low-wage laborers for the foreseeable future. The only alternative is for nice people to stand up and refuse to do the bidding of mean people, but that's a spiritual revolution that comes with great penalties, pain, and punishment for nice people. And getting embroiled in conflict, violence, and anger does not describe the type of environment and mindset that fulfills nice people's lives; however, mean people seem to thrive on negativity and conflict. Mean people certainly have a clear advantage in the system of things in human societies and civilizations. And it's unlikely this paradigm will change anytime soon. Mean people are genetically prone to enjoy the challenge of creating conflict to give them ample opportunities to exert power and dominance.

C3 – A Culture of Violence

The United States of America was born of armed insurrection against their common ruler, the King of England. Subsequently, expansionism resulted in armed conflict and the genocide of indigenous Native Americans. Brothers and divided families fought a bloody and traumatic Civil War, supposedly to free Black slaves, but arguably large segments of the Black population are worse off now than had they remained on the Southern plantations of some benevolent owners. Historically, the South felt vulnerable and threatened by the North's economic and industrial strengths. To understand why Southern states found themselves in conflictual relations with the North, we look to historical facts that created the precedent and unequal pattern of North-South economic relations. We must also ask, "why" does the South feel vulnerable? Certainly a sharp economic and philosophical division on the question of slavery that led to the bloody American Civil War has left generational wounds that still continue to be open sores in the fabric of American society. Why do they feel threatened by the North? Who creates conflict, and why does conflict persist between the most people in the traditional anti-slavery states of the North and southern states of the South?

Historical precedents and patterns still persist in both overt and subtle economic strategies to dominate the national economy through an economic rationale for democratic movements toward modernity and capitalism, served by ideological justification and political legitimization, enforced by the hegemony of liberal thought and organization typical of the North Atlantic states. The creation of the NGO (non-governmental organization) known as the Federal Reserve Bank and handing it the power to regulate our national currency and monetary values further vested the financial power to the North, as the "northern strategy" of economic exploitation of the South occurred in four distinctive stages:

1.   The federal imperialism era was characterized by aggression and through military confrontation and conquest through warfare, as the North defeated the South their control of natural and human resources, destroying native economic infrastructures and supplanting it with wholesale resource exportation and the abolition of slavery that was essential for Southern farmers to build wealth from their plantations.

The forces of development and modernization combine to destroy traditional rural life in Southern counties, resulting in a constant impetus to emigrate from rural areas. Economic conditions determine whether the potential migrant selects an internal or external destination. The condition of the population of any state is determined by its social system and the political and economic conditions prevailing at home.

2.	The colonial post-war reconstruction period justified financial exploitation and dominion over the cultures of the South through the renouncement of such twisted concepts and principles as "Manifest Destiny", and later by population relocation strategies proposed by Northern intellectuals, and ethno-centric political "idealism" such as "national security interests". The North installed their own financial colonial governments, or placed governance under the control of puppets and surrogates in various the conquered lands of many Southern states, creating a class of local elites whose duty was to control, extort, coerce, and exploit their own people, to the economic benefit of the North.

3.	Post Civil War inequities and exploitation continued in the South, until it became too expensive to maintain political surrogates amidst increased resurgence of Southern cultural nationalism and renewed separatist sentiments in resentment of Northern agendas. As the South attempted to rebuild after the ravages of what was essentially a Northern civil war. In order for the North to maintain economic control of the South, it supported and/or installed corrupt elitist bankers and politicians who agreed to step in place with northern edits.

4.	Contemporary market stratification and structural agreement programs driven by Northern bankers whose greed and power lust continues to exacerbates economic imbalances between the North and South into present times. The Northern banking system coerced Southern states to accept high rates of interests, and worse, harsh structural adjustments that acted to dislodge traditional economic, social, cultural, and political infrastructures of the South. In place of values, traditions, and social systems native to the South, the banks forced Southern debtor states to accept economic austerity as its destiny, and a steady diet of new Northern-based political economies in the South.

The crisis of the postwar financial colonialism was profound and threatened to redraw the existing system of Southern states. The people of the South felt vulnerable and distrustful of Northern motives due to a clear history of economic exploitation by the North. As the Northern strategy for economic dominance of the South shifted through the four eras summarized above, the common theme remained the same: maintenance of the status quo of Northern superiority and control over the South's wealth, both exploitable and untapped. As social (e.g. religious/ethnic) and economic elites wield great power, their abilities to gain influence over a state's future depended on capturing and holding the political machinery. Coalitions organized around shared self-interest combined either to exert pressure on the Southern states or to dominate it, and the express purpose of these activities is to generate laws that divert social surplus to special interests.

In the current international environment, nations of the South (non-whiteThird World Nations) continue to feel threatened by surreptitious and deceptive Northern (the West – the USA) strategies. The North had been known to make offerings to the South in the name of humanitarian and economic assistance programs, only later do Southerners discover the reality of Northern banking's Trojan Horse strategy has always been to wrestle control of means of production from Southerners through indebtedness and conditional grants. The South has been forced to open its eyes, to recognize that anything the North supports is designed to serve the self-interests of the North, and must not be accepted simply as Northern altruism that benefits the South. No matter how many neo-liberal reforms were instituted internally in Southern states by federal mandates, an undercurrent of resentment, hostility and hatred is harbored by many Southerners who still to this day feel the South was unjustly attacked and its economy destroyed, and its people killed, using the philosophical abolition of slavery as an excuse to put Northern bankers in charge of the South's economy.

This undercurrent of conflict and hostility between the progeny of Southern slave states versus the Northern banking establishment festers to this day. It is evident based on voting trends that voters in the Republican majority "red states" have clear philosophical differences from those liberal majorities in the large cities that have substantial non-white voters. Generally, the white population maintains a majority in rural states in the mid-west and parts of what was known as "the Deep South" that is comprised of formerly Confederate States during the American Civil War. Both coasts and the previously industrial North Atlantic states with large cities are fertile voting territories for liberal whites and minorities… with some exceptions. While it's unpopular to publicly state racially prejudiced stereotypes and to use racial slurs, no doubt its typically done in private among friends. Race hatred still exists, and it is highly likely that the white population would prefer only to associate and live among their own… other white people in their own enclaves.

C4 - DEATH

In order to understand a society's attitudes and deep-rooted beliefs about its own survival... of choosing life over death, it is essential to discuss its cultural values about death and the avoidance of death. Consequently, government, religion, politics and social norms have insisted on the sanctity of life and forbade individuals from the right to either take their own lives, or that of others. Beliefs about living cannot be rationally considered without the inclusion of death as the opposing and balancing aspect of the eternal equation of survival. The right to live, or the right to die is the *essential* question. The right to die and the right to live issues have been embroiled in legal and moral confusion, where in some states, the courts and law makers have become executioners, in others, saviors; and still others as protectors of free choice by women.

It is high time for the U.S. Congress to enact legislation that would provide uniform standards that make sense, providing adequate protection of privacy, freedom of choice, right to die and right to live across our gloriously almost free and almost democratic nation. The issues are basic and simple, and should answer several fundamental questions:

1.   Do persons possessing legal capacity have the right to terminate their own lives at a time and in a manner of their own choosing; and is it legally permissible for physicians or other designated persons to assist in a humane suicide?

2.   In cases where a person does not possess legal capacity to decide issues of life and death due to disabilities or incapacitation, does a legal or court-appointed guardian have the authority to terminate a human life, and if so, under what specific circumstances?

3.   What entails artificial life support that could legally be terminated, when cessation of technological equipment would certainly lead to patient death?

    a.   Heart-lung machine
    b.   Kidney dialysis machine
    c.   Pacemaker
    d.   Feeding tube
    e.   Trachea tube for breathing
    f.   Appropriate medication, e.g. to prevent heart attacks

Certainly, in each case, denial of the assisted means of survival could be equivalent to a "de facto" death sentence, as surely as the denial of food and water would result in death.

4.   Would denial of food and water to a disabled or terminally ill person be considered cruel and unusual punishment, if the same standard were to be applied to persons who would otherwise be in good health, e.g. "normal people"?

5.   In the case of late term abortions, where the fetus would otherwise survive outside of the womb, does a woman have the right to abort and kill the fetus - infant? A proper C-section could, in most cases, save late term abortion fetuses, which could survive as most premature births do nowadays. If a life could survive on its own, then no one, not even the birthing mother has a right to terminate another human beings life.

The answer to these controversial questions should be based on a standard of sensibility and understanding of science, and strike a moral balance between the right to choose, and the sanctity of life that could survive without "extraordinary measures." In the first instance, persons possessing legal capacity should have the right to commit suicide. To presume that life is worth living for every person, who after all was born without choice into circumstances not of their choosing, is presumptuous. Many people who suffer extreme physical and/or emotional pain would rather die than to prolong their pain. There are extraordinary circumstances where, despite medical, psycho-therapeutic, pharmacological, and technical assistance, a person may choose to commit suicide due to terminal illness, emotional or mental disorder, philosophical or spiritual commitment, or simply a profound dissatisfaction with life or their circumstances and environment.

In addition, the presence of medical professionals or laypersons to assist in the administration of humane methods of euthanasia, free of suffering, injury or trauma should be allowed. The alternative forms of suicide are the horrific, violent, and traumatic actions such as gunshot, stabbing, car crash, jumping off tall buildings, home electrocution, carbon monoxide poisoning by running car engine in closed garage, natural gas explosion in one's house, drug overdose, cutting wrists, and other bizarre methods only desperate people would do when severely despondent or in terrible pain.

In cases where incapacitation does not permit a person to insist or communicate their final wishes, and a legally enforceable living will does not exist, the court or legal guardian should be deemed the authority to terminate life, where extraordinary means must be employed. Extraordinary means would entail elaborate and expensive technological assistance that artificially prolongs life, such as heart-lung machines. All other technological low tech methods, equipment, or apparatus such as pacemaker, feeding tube, trachea breathing assistance, medication, or kidney dialysis should be considered "ordinary means" to "assist" life sustenance, which must not be withdrawn.

Consequently, the denial of food and water, which is basic to survival of all living beings, must be prohibited regardless of a person's disability, incapacitation or terminal illness, where the person or the legal guardian has made a choice to live. The denial of basic sustenance is a form of cruel and inhumane punishment (though it is not unusual in our world due to poverty and famine), and should be considered an immoral and illegal killing.

In cases of late term abortion, or where ordinary means would permit a fetus to survive on its own, termination of life should be illegal. This does not address the morality issues regarding a balance between a woman's freedom of choice versus the point of inception of a separate life. Scientific facts indicate that independent life begins when an entity is capable of its own survival, without attachment to a host entity, and without extraordinary medical or technological means.

If society, law makers, and the courts fail to apply a sensible uniform legal criteria to issues of abortion, euthanasia, assisted suicide, right to die, and right to live, then citizens will not enjoy the full protection of the U.S. Constitution, as life and death should not be a states rights issue, but instead our government should set a national and universal definition and standards. It is inherently unjust for life and death issues to be subjected to jurisdictional differences, where any citizens' chance of life or death depends upon location instead of uniform lawful principles.

C5 - EDUCATION

It has always been politically correct to tout the trite phrase that our children are our future and consequently their education must be our national priority. As a dozen of the world's developed nations and developing nations have already surpassed American children in basic academic achievement as measured by math and science test scores, we continue to spend more money on a relatively less competitive educational system model than that spent by most other nations who have demonstrated far more productive results.

Perhaps part of the ineffective educational paradigm in America can be traced to a changing educational terrain where the current modern educational design and pedagogy is proving to be less effective than the old school model that continues to be utilized among our competitors. Let's examine the positive aspects of the old school methodology versus the new watered down, politically correct and socially driven educational paradigm.

Are we overloading our student with too many irrelevant subjects due to the liberalization of curriculum by social scientists whose agenda has been politically motivated, rather than based upon the urgent need to teach our children the knowledge and skills they will need to be competitive in the future world that will be highly dependent upon technology? Do we need sex education in elementary school more, or do we need more introduction to science and discovery courses? We need to examine whether school curriculum actually prepares our children for adulthood with useful knowledge, or whether rote memory of trivia questions and answers best prepare them for television quiz shows.

Following is a comparison of the old teaching methodology versus the current rubrics:

Old School	New Pedagogy
A. Purpose	
1. Educational purpose	Politics and money issues
2. Elective coursework	Basic 3 R's, few electives
3. After school programs	Few school sponsored programs
4. School clubs and activities	Few school sponsored activities
5. Organized sports	Few school sponsored teams
6. Physical education	Few school provided classes
7. Emphasis on learning	Emphasis on testing performance
8. Sensible curriculum	Greater quantity of useless subjects
9. Moral lessons in material	Short on analysis and moral values
10. Positive results	Low retention and test scores
B. Attitude	
1. Respect teachers & officials	Disrespect teachers and administrators
2. Get along with classmates	Dislike and hate certain classmates
3. Listen intently	Daydream and talk instead of listening
4. Follow teacher's instructions	Disregard instructions, then ask again
5. Raise hand, ask for permission	Blurt out and interrupt teaching
6. Quiet while studying	Talk to friends instead of studying
7. Student's personal responsibility	Complain that the work is too hard
C. Techniques	
1. Classroom management	Reacting to student behaviors & moods
2. Punishment for disruptions	Time outs, reasoning, pleading with students
3. Detention for misbehavior	Few after school detention programs
4. Parental participation	Parental disinterest; reliance on teachers
5. Parental supervision	Parental abrogation; reliance on teachers
6. Religious release time	Sectarianism; no mention of God
7. Integrated approach	Special education classes for dysfunctional
8. Multi-tiered pace of learning	Herding of variant abilities into standardized

9.	Modeling – positive examples	Graduated step learning, uninspiring models
10.	Hands on participatory learning	Limited support materials for hands on study
11.	Inspiration & motivation	Boring material taught in uninspired manner
12.	Expertise & excellence	Lack luster knowledge and mediocrity
13.	Recognition for achievement	Few school-wide reward programs
14.	Grading based on learning	Grading based on test taking ability
15.	Homework	Either no homework, or too much busy work
16.	Simplicity & honesty	Complexity when simplicity would suffice
17.	Straight forward approach	Confusing and contradictory materials

D. Support

1.	Patriotism- flag salute	Illegal to salute flag, corny and insincere
2.	Community and school pride	Pride? Whatever… few people care
3.	Classroom and school safety	Students and teachers are "at risk"
4.	Suspension not rewarding	Students act out to get out for free time
5.	Expulsion not rewarding	Students don't care, same program wherever
6.	Political support for education	Political positioning for illusion of support
7.	Legal support of teachers	Teacher's have few "rights" and protections

E. Teacher Qualifications and Mindset

1.	Commitment to education	Money; it's a flexible job
2.	Excited and rewarding	Time off, good benefits
3.	Neat and professional dress	Blue jeans and wrinkled tops
4.	Honest, fair, moral, and impartial	Personal lives imitate TV sitcoms
5.	Serious, mature, helpful, friendly	Disinterested, stressed out
6.	Engaging, inspirational, helpful	Disinterested, bored, lazy
7.	Dedicated and knowledgeable	Reliant on teachers' editions
8.	Thorough in depth information	Unsure of large data base
9.	Salaries on par with trades	Below trade standards

F. Why can't Johnny…

1. Read and comprehend complex material
2. Correctly complete math operations and applications
3. Write sensibly, legibly, and concisely

4. Think creatively, rationally, and positively

5. Analyze patterns, abstractions, and associations

6. Make logical and good decisions based on situations

7. Act appropriately and respectfully

8. Speak intelligently; articulate and communicate

9. Remember, recall, repeat, and summarize

10. Compare and contrast data and form examples

11. Listen and following instructions and directions

12. Desire to learn; satisfy a sense of curiosity

13. Ask well-formulated questions

14. Consider plausible options and alternatives

15. Get along with others

16. Respect authority figures

17. Be trustworthy and dependable

18. Accept personal responsibility for results

19. Obey school and classroom rules

20. Desire to succeed and strive for potential

G. Contradictions between values taught in school versus the real world

Success values taught in school	Real world success strategies
1. A good education leads to a good job.	Good connections gets good jobs.
2. Listen and follow directions.	Reward creativity and independence.
3. Authority determines the standards.	Define personal standards & goals.
4. Compare yourself to others.	Do your own thing & be happy.
5. Conform to the norm.	Go your own way; choose your path.
6. Excel in performance & testing.	Work smarter and not harder.
7. Don't socialize in class.	Popularity translates into big money.
8. Don't talk while learning.	Multi-task; adjust to distractions.
9. Be serious and don't joke around.	Levity improves group dynamics.
10. Don't be a class clown.	Humor is a rewarding attractant.

H.   Urgently Needed Educational Reforms

1.   Class size

2.   Classroom management

3.   Computer applications

4.   Visual aids

5.   Tiered learning groups

6.   Diagnostic assessment

7.   Student behaviors

8.   Protecting teachers

9.   Curriculum reforms

10.   Standardization

WHO IN THEIR RIGHT MIND WOULD WANT TO BE A TEACHER NOWADAYS?

It doesn't pay to be a teacher nowadays. Dangers lurk from threats, assaults, and career ending false accusations from disgruntled students and dysfunctional parents. Take the recent case of a high school coach in Los Angeles, who luckily was acquitted of charges he had sodomized a high school basketball player. Now his parents want to file a civil suit against the school district. In recent decades, there appears to be a marked increase in the percentage of people who are willing to destroy good teachers' lives so they can sue school districts for the big bucks. How many good teachers are falsely accused and convicted by the system? Surely some who are convicted on circumstantial evidence and false testimony are innocent.

Teachers are being blamed for the ills of society. Their careers are always in a tenuous position. Their pay is relatively low, stress often high, and their classrooms can be dangerous and sometimes life threatening places. Five years of college and one year of internship starts teachers with a salary that is often less than that paid to police officers, who also have dangerous jobs. More than ever before, teachers find themselves being unfairly cornered into the dubious position as scapegoats for society's failures and subjected to subterfuge by both students and parents. Teachers need to learn how to better manage staff and students, and to read the nuances that are present in classroom relationships that can result in distrust, misunderstanding, and conspiracy.

The teaching profession is filled with potential traps, legal "catch 22's", relationship distortions with staff, students, and parents that can lead to misperceptions and complaints. The liability aspects are great, and the potential for false accusations is always present. Teachers are expected to be responsible for parenting and character building in addition to procuring higher test scores from their diverse student populations. Yet, teachers are impotent to affect much of anything if students, parents, and staff are not cooperative. Teachers are held legally, criminally, and financially responsible for the outcomes of activities, known or unknown to them, in their classrooms, and they are held to a higher moral code than parents, politicians and the police.

Being a teacher nowadays requires a certain degree of "gumption"... dedication, courage, patience, persistence, and forgiveness. Teachers now occupy an occupation that is constantly criticized, evaluated, microscopically monitored, subjected to undue financial and legal liabilities, public suspicion, and occasionally unsympathetic and unreasonable administrative and political pressure to create high achievement from children of dysfunctional families in a failing civilization. Teachers are being assaulted on many fronts, physically, mentally, and emotionally, and they are becoming the scapegoats for society's ills and faults, while politicians shift the blame for the consequences of poverty and racism to teachers.

Why do teachers need to do a better job? And what can we realistically expect teachers to embrace as their responsibilities for the mental, emotional, and moral development of our children? First, teachers need administrative, procedural, and legal protection from misbehaving and overly aggressive students, and irrational and dysfunctional parents. Teachers must be shielded from false accusations and resultant litigation, and even criminal charges that result when police are called unnecessarily and unfairly to taint the good reputation of teachers just because a few notorious examples of teacher misconduct have been in the news. Teachers are not molesters!

School administrators owe it to the teaching profession to diplomatically handle all complaints that question teacher professionalism, and should come to the defense of teachers, rather than to abandon them, or to disassociate when media attention is focused on their schools. Every year, countless numbers of teachers have to endure incidents where they become victims of violence, verbal and physical abuse, false accusation as perpetrator of all sorts of misconduct; from yelling at students, verbally threatening students, inappropriately touching students, ineffective teaching strategies, insensitivity to demanding parents, and the list goes on. This is a very disturbing trend in America, where teachers are subjected to lingering doubts about their personal reputations as they are under constant suspicion and often have little defense against total fabrications besides the admission by accusers of errors, misinterpretations, misperceptions or outright lies. And how often do false accusers admit their wrong doings? Rarely is it a crime.

Teachers need to be advised and warned not to be so forthright in their classrooms, and to withhold examples of personal opinions and experiences. To preventing potential mistakes in class that may set them up for future allegations and litigations, teachers should document any potentially controversial remarks they might make in the course of getting through the day. They must be able to come to class each day with a clear state of mind so they may give their best effort as teachers to help our children to improve their mental and emotional development, even though it's unfair to expect teachers to provide a completely safe classroom environment due to the lack of respect, and aggressiveness that many students display toward teachers and authority nowadays. It's not fair for society to expect teachers to be parent, police, and psychologist.

Many classroom situations cause high anxiety not only for students but for teachers. These occupational conditions contribute to setbacks in teacher's physical and mental health due to high levels of responsibility and liability their classes, including disruptive students who may be emotionally disturbed, who create stress and drama for everyone. Teachers often don't feel safe in their own classrooms due to unstable environmental factors such as unpredictable student actions and behaviors. Consequently, teaching demands a new emphasis on dealing with the behavioral peculiarities and needs of students, parents and staff that takes away from the focus on helping children to learn. Even the most patient and humble teachers can get hurt due to the lessening of positive circumstances in the teaching environment where they can enjoy a sense of safety, accomplishment, and fulfillment. Teachers seek confidence in the trenches where there is a constant level of challenge, lost of respect, and distractions to their effectiveness due to a lack of support and understanding of the current teaching environment by politicians, parents, and administrators. Rarely if ever is the issue of problems confronting teachers mentioned in the news media or by politicians, and are rarely dealt with in teaching credential programs and unions.

Especially in the field of special education, behavioral problems are often exacerbated by staff. In cases where instructional aides are used, too often they are rarely trained and may have developed the habit of yelling and triggering students to "act out." It's challenging enough that many students are often anxious due to the unpredictable environment of being at school, in classes that are potentially "explosive", often changing (students are transferred in and out), and where they are expected to be "mainstreamed" to keep up with the "regular" students in both academics and behavior for the entire school day. These expectations oftentimes exceed the individual emotionally disturbed student's ability to retain self-control, and one consequence is they explode into various inappropriate behaviors.

Having these types of students in the same environment magnifies the probability of negative behaviors, as one student sets off another, and at times, when staff contributes to heightening the emotional temperature in the classroom, the results are predictable... chaos. We see this principle occurring among the "normal" population, as frustrated and angry citizens riot in the streets when authority is used excessively. In the classroom, the same microcosm exists. When teachers and staff attempt to apply authority excessively, there's a tendency for rebellion against order because teens need and want a sense of control over their lives due to their own confusion, uncertainties, and insecurities. While they may need more structure, too many in the teaching profession confuse "structure" with "authoritarianism", resulting in the creation of classroom environments that are not conducive to learning and growth. Fortunately, the vast majority of teachers and para-educators are sensitive and sensible in their desire and approach to helping students, but occupational frustration with changing attitudes in school often takes its toll on the patience level required of teaching staff.

The majority of para-educators are aides instead of teachers because they tend to have little training and education. They attempt to do their jobs based primarily on their experiences in life and with raising their own children. How can we expect aides to parent emotionally disturbed or disabled children when their own parenting practices may be inadequate? A requisite for teaching special children is to be very patient, and to speak softly; using directive questioning that clearly defines the alternatives of decision-making choices to ensure that students are making desirable mental and emotional connections. People who deal with special children need to realize that they're special for many reasons, and to be more sympathetic. Instructional assistants can improve, hinder, or disrupt the teaching effort in the classroom. Many "veterans" are overly protective of their turf and routines, and they tend to resist direction from teachers, especially new teachers to "their" classroom. Teachers oftentimes find themselves trying to teach not only the students, but also instructional aides who may not know how to act, and whose interactions may be detrimental to the emotional health of students.

Those courageous and dedicated souls who remain in the teaching profession from true desire to make positive contributions to the development of children should receive all the support that the "system" can give; from parents, administrators, politicians and students. Certainly, the job is not an easy one; the pay is mediocre, responsibilities and liabilities are great, and gratitude is more often a personalized phenomenon rather than displays of appreciation from others. Who will speak out for teachers? So far, no charismatic leader has taken up the causes of teachers, and until legislators begin to think more pragmatically rather than politically, teachers will continue to receive less respect, gratification and support, and instead will continue to be blamed for our society's misgivings and for the shortcomings in their profession. Anyone who has the heart to continue teaching should be commended. All others beware the traps of being a teacher.

I had to take a sabbatical from the teaching profession to safeguard my life, freedom, and sanity, not because of the kids, but due to a conspiracy of three teaching assistants who felt I was a threat to their comfort zone and program of kicking back, shoving students around, yelling, and setting them off. They were people who were collecting checks because they lacked other marketable talents, in my opinion. I suspect more teachers will decide to leave teaching careers, further exacerbating an already serious teacher shortage that will be accentuated by Proposition 98, and impending retirements within the next five to ten years, while a relative few opt to tackle the challenges of teaching.

Who can justly blame teachers for leaving an increasingly politicized and demonized profession that is rife with potential litigation and personal liability for alleged criminal and civil acts or omissions? And how fair is it to blame teachers for pervasive low test scores from dysfunctional and demotivated children from hostile and negative environments, especially where poverty, crime, and lack of adult supervision is prevalent? It's not fair, and teachers who are fed up are quitting by record numbers, while teacher tenure rapidly decreases in response to the growing environment of disempowerment, political and bureaucratic manipulation and societal insensitivity and blame. My hat's off to all dedicate teachers who can survive. As for me, I threw in the towel by the end of the school year. And the sad fact is I believe the vast preponderance of the children who I've attempted to teach genuinely liked me, though I've been warned by staff not to treat them so nice, or they'd take advantage of me. But from my perspective, I got more cooperation from children by giving them kindness, than by being a demanding authoritarian. In fact, the students in one of my classes loved me so much, I could not visit the school site because they would run out of their rooms to hug me, disrupting their school day.

I cannot visit them, because it would give them false hope that the system will change any time soon. Perhaps we need to teach more kindness in university teacher preparation programs. If we cannot instill love and concern in those who are entrusted to guide our future generations, then our civilization is doomed, even without the scourge of terrorism. I am very disheartened by the state of our teaching profession, as I feel we're turning out novices who are ill prepared to deal with the hard knocks that face them. At the least, we owe them a warning.

PERSECUTED TEACHERS

With the advent of the new millennium, the increased attacks against teachers and the blaming of teachers for society's ills has made the teaching profession a dangerous occupation from a career and personal legal liability perspective. Teachers, especially substitute teachers are expected to quickly evaluate student cultures in classrooms, and to maintain classroom control while lacking legal authority. Teachers are expected to pursue educational standards created by so-called curriculum specialists, who have rarely experienced classroom environments first hand.

The demands and expectations on substitute teachers are particularly unfair, as they are often abused by both students and administrators; behavior problem students who see the absence of the regular teacher as an opportunity to disrupt classroom quorum, and principals who expect substitute teachers to automatically continue "business as usual" in some very challenging classroom environments. Oftentimes, substitute teachers find themselves "babysitting" students who refuse to accomplish classroom assignments, and who would rather use class time for social interaction, with the full knowledge that substitute teachers in particular have no clout, no power, no authority, and less expertise regarding any topic than their regular teachers. Students also know that if they act up, it is highly likely the substitute teacher will not return to their class, so there is little or no consequence for misbehavior.

Following is an example of the exasperating circumstance that faced a substitute teacher who was usually a favorite among students, regular teachers, and school districts. This is only one of several "war stories" that happened unexpectedly over the course of five years of trying to teach students when their regular teacher was absent. Some principals are not competent and do not appreciate teachers as being the core of the educational program.

Contesting Negative Evaluation

I must admit that I was rather surprised by the completely negative evaluation that I received from the principal at [deleted], and disappointed at her overreaction, excessively punitive orientation, abuse of her position and power, and her disinterest in due process. You will notice my signature was not present on the evaluation form because I didn't know there was a problem of this perceived magnitude, as certainly I was not asked to confer with the principal. In fact, for over a week, several sites under her jurisdiction (or should I say "control"), requested my presence, and I fulfilled those requests very satisfactorily.

I surmise you've seen evaluations made of other substitute teachers, and I know when someone doesn't have even one good thing to say about another person, that it's highly likely those views are biased, prejudicial, and unreasonable. If another person were to read the negative report made by principal [deleted], one would tend to automatically conclude that I must be a bad person, or a block of wood, or from another planet. Far from the truth!

In all fairness, I encourage you to make at least a cursory investigation, as I plan to request the same of my union representative. For starters, please note that I successfully discharged my duties at the [deleted] on seven separate occasions since the start of 2002, as summarized in *Appendix 1*, attached. In addition, I hope you will talk to para-educators and teachers who have requested me in the past, such at off site locations, also listed in *Appendix 1*. I will stand on my record, and while I never claimed to be perfect, or a nominee for Substitute Teacher of the year, I feel I've served our children with compassion, concern, and commitment.

Now, I would like to explain what happened on the day in question, which in retrospect, I should have never taken the assignment, because it was a extremely difficult population that I had never encountered in the past, and involved a para-educator that was instigating complaints, and a principal who was rude, unprofessional, and unhelpful, who was disrespectful and biased. Let's take a look at the evaluation, and address each of the negative comments:

1. *Did the substitute arrive on time?* It would really help if the substitute finder computer would give the correct address of the work site, as it sent me to [deleted school] and NOT to the [deleted] address. Check for yourself, for [deleted] unless they've recently changed the recording. I had a personal emergency, and was 15 mins. late returning from a 1/2 hour lunch period, and I called in to let her   know, and to inform the class assistants. Otherwise, I almost always report to my worksites on time, unless the computer gives me the wrong addresses, which happens 20% of the time. And I never deliberately abuse my lunch breaks.

2. *Did the substitute follow the teacher's lesson plans?* I sat at the teacher's desk and tried to find something that may have resembled a lesson plan, and didn't find one. I was going to rely on the 4 assistants to clue me in, but two sat on their butts and read magazines, criticized me, and pointed at the door every time a child ran out, so I would have to chase them down to bring them back.

3. *Did the substitute actively participate in class activities?* Well, constantly telling pubescent boys to take their hands out of their pants, to stop grabbing people's butts, to stop smelling other student's asses, and other inappropriate behaviors that should have been extinguished long before I dropped into that class was a lot of work. In addition, chasing down students because two of the aides just sat, read magazines, and chatted instead of getting up to help me demonstrated that I had worked extra hard. I finally had to stand for two hours in front of the door to direct traffic, while half of the assistants helped out with students.

4. *Did the substitute maintain proper classroom control?* No one fought or tried to hurt each other. At one point, I had to try to keep an eye on 9 kids, with one assistant (others were out to lunch, with the instigator who complained to the principal about my abusing the lunch period actually took a one hour lunch instead of a half hour). Yet, I was able to keep them from acting crazy, while the remaining assistant sat on her rear and read a magazine.

5. *Was the substitute prepared for the assignment?* I must admit, I've never had such a bunch of strange pubescent masturbating males all in one class, where half the assistants didn't lift one finger to help. When a student smelled like he had a bowl movement, I had to mention it to two separate assistants, who rudely quipped, "Then why don't you change him, that's what you're paid for!" I've been   to many schools, and the professional para-educators will at least suggest, "Okay, we can change him together." Finally, the older assistant took the student into the restroom alone, and I overhead her say, "OH MY! YOUR DICK IS HARD!"

    I would be foolish to try to change an adolescent male, who had an erection, and enjoyed smelling other children's asses, while masturbating. Why was this child's inappropriate behavior not already extinguished through proper behavior modification? When I asked one of the assistants who enjoyed sitting around, she responded that they were going through puberty, and they're just that way all the time. Unacceptable! I spent a lot of time telling the boys to stop the inappropriate behaviors. If had I specialized in this type of group, I would have known what to expect, and I could have been more prepared, by requesting the child psychologist's help!

6. *Did the substitute interact appropriately with students?*   Well, if trying to get students from exhibiting strange, bizarre, and inappropriate sexual behavior was appropriate, then I did my job. These kids were in their own mental zone, and were mostly out of touch with reality. They were just vegetating. Now, is that my fault?   I'm a substitute for one day, and I'm supposed to solve all the problems that full-time regular staff should be addressing on a daily basis? Get real!

7. *Did the staff cooperate with the staff and administration?* Besides Scott, the helpful assistant, the other staff members were rude, unhelpful, and tried to instigate conflict between me and the principal by constantly complaining to her. What did I do wrong besides report to work? Five minutes into the work day, I was told to stay in the room by the older assistant, while she went to the buses to get the kids, as I needed to be in the classroom to supervise the students. But where were the other assistants? I was sitting down, trying to find the lesson plan, when a lady, who I had never seen in my life (who turned out to be the principal) came into the room, and without even the courtesy of a welcome or introduction, told me in a rude tone of voice, "You can't be sitting down! This is a hard class, and you have to be on your feet!"

I was on my feet for the rest of the day, while two of the assistants sat, read magazines, chatted, and criticized me that I didn't have control of the classroom, while the students were mostly kept in order and were safe. I found the staff (except for Scott) and the principal to be very unprofessional, unhelpful, and rude. They failed to show me any respect or to demonstrate any desire to advise me, or to help make the situation better. All they did was complain, without offering one positive suggestion or good idea. I give them a failing grade on their lack of humanity, compassion, and professionalism. I felt like I was in juvenile detention or jail, being verbally attacked by the head jailer and the snitches. It was a very unpleasant experience that I don't plan to repeat ever again.

8. *Did the substitute leave the room in an orderly condition?* I was instructed to help take certain kids to the buses, and to wait on the bench with them. The room appeared to be in a similar condition to what I saw when I first entered the room in the morning. Let's face it, it's not a good example of how an exemplary class room should be set up or look like. It's one of the worse I've seen in the District, from all the places where I've served diligently, and there have been many.

9. *Would you want this substitute to serve your school again?* Thank you. Please don't do me any more favors. From the times that I've served at this school, I can see many problems. The staff is generally unhappy, in my opinion. But as the world turns, what comes around goes around, and if anyone were to confidentially interview the school staff, I think you will find a high degree of frustration and dissatisfaction with how things are run by the principal. I will never serve at that school again until they clean up their own house first.

10. Overall rating of unsatisfactory. That's how I see that school site.

In regards to cell phone use, I notice that staff at almost all sites use their cell phones or the room phones from time to time. Even the various specialists who go to visit sites use their cell phones. I was looking at my cell phone, once all the students were sitting and behaved, and I was reading a text message that just came over, when the principal barged into the room (probably because one of the lazy assistants complained about me), and she in a very rude, disrespectful, and demanding tone, with a highly negative emotional demeanor, almost yelling at me, stated, "YOU CAN'T USE A CELL PHONE IN CLASS! IT'S AGAINST MY RULES!" Well, it's the first time I've heard of such a rule, and I had to take an emergency call from my cousin, who told me to get home to give medicine to my 75-year-old uncle, who was recently in a roll over car accident (do you want to see the CHP report, medical records, and emergency helicopter bill?)... which explains why I was a little late getting back.

I complied with her order and put away my cell phone. But I'll admit, I had to take just one more call later, when I was guarding the doorway from runaway teen boys, but I kept my eyes on them, and was supervising. It's not like I had my back turned to them (I know better, because one of the boys had already grabbed my ass earlier when I happened to walk by), and it's not like I can't talk and see at the same time for a few minutes. If there's a system wide policy against the use of phones or cell phones, then let's apply it to everyone equally, and not be capricious and biased.

The comment about being "told to interact" was never uttered. Maybe the principal had planned to make that her positive comment, suggestion, and pearl of wisdom for the day, to help me to become a more motivated and better substitute teacher... but what came out her mouth was harsh, rude, and unprofessional. She needs to learn how to talk to people with a little more respect and kindness. As for the newspaper, I don't remember having one, as I walked into the class without anything in my hands. Perhaps I was reviewing something I found on the teacher's desk, which I had hoped was a detailed lesson plan.

Certainly, I've heard occasional stories of substitute teachers who sit at their desk and read a book or newspaper all day, while the para-educators interacted with the children. But if you look at your own records, how many of them are banned from an entire district? I interacted with staff, children, and did my job as best as I knew how for a difficult population, for which I now realized I was not adequately equipped to understand, nor was I provided even the minimal support from two of four "aides" assigned to the class, nor were adequate lesson plans available, nor did the para-educators volunteer to inform me of the typical day's lesson plan, nor to assist me with designing and implementing an ad hoc plan (why, because maybe they don't normally have one?). Is it fair to ban me from an entire district? What are the criteria in place to warrant being banned from an entire district? Capriciousness alone is not a legal or justifiable criterion, and I don't believe it is either fair or warranted. The principle and I both agree on one thing; her school site is not a healthy one for me; however, I insist that *banning me from all off site locations is a terrible abuse of power.* And if I had ever planned to be a full time teacher, this experience has certainly taken the wind out of my sails.

At five minutes into the school day, the principal who didn't even have the courtesy to introduce herself so I didn't know who she was berated me. I presumed she was an "aide" who was having a power trip and a bad day. Now I realize that they were making their bad day into my bad day. Actually, the principal did me a favor, because I had decided that I never want to work at "her" school anymore, while she remains "in charge." But I do feel very badly that all the children and staff in "her" offsite locations will never have the opportunity to interact with me again, because unless I'm blind, and they're all lying, then we really enjoyed each others' company, and had very good days indeed at other off site locations.

I hope you'll recognize that nothing is a simple as it first appears. Administrative insensitivity and poor leadership has been one of the major common complaints made by teachers through their unions. I must admit, this has been my first experience with such administrative audacity in my two and half years with the school district, but perhaps I've been too blind and forgiving to recognize it. It's such a shame that substitute teachers never get a pat on the back, or a good note placed in their files for all the good and sacrifices they make in doing a good job with very difficult and diverse populations. All we usually hear are the negatives.

At any rate, I accept your decision to honor the principal's request to exclude me from all of the sites under her control. You won't get any complaint or trouble from me on this dead issue. I won't even bother to file a personnel grievance against that principal on the grounds of unprofessional conduct. Other than filing a copy of this letter with my teachers' union, I'm going to drop this issue and move on in a positive path, so I may continue to be of service to students. .

Thank you for reading this rather lengthy response; however, in all fairness, I felt it was necessary to balance the playing field, and not allow myself to be victimized by what I feel has been a highly prejudicial evaluation, and conduct unbecoming of a professional principal. I'm also attaching a copy of an essay that I've sent to our elected officials, teacher unions, and to teacher advocacy groups. You will find a concise list of reasons why few people are seeking a career in teaching. Personally, after seeing what the teaching profession has become, I withdrew from my teaching credentials program to earn a Masters degree in public administration by November of this year, which I hope to parlay into a position that implements educational policies to correct the many wrongs that I see in the public education system. I'm a committee member on the Teacher Preparation Committee at [University], and I plan to make my input to address various problems in the teaching field. In addition, as a member of the Graduate Studies Committee, I plan to recommend additional curricula that focus on the field practice politics and nuances of the teaching profession. In the future, I plan to run for the school board of a large district like LAUSD because there are many wrongs in public education, and I might as well start with trying to fix this one.

The relationship between teacher training and academic achievement on students has been rehashed many times. Most studies have concluded that low use of teacher strategies is directly correlated with low academic achievement. Students who exhibited some strategies will have moderate academic achievement. Finally, students who exhibited a high number of teacher strategies had increased improvements in their academic achievement. The general conclusion is student academic achievement is directly correlated to and a statistically significant consequence of effective teacher training programs.

Researchers for some time have examined the role of teacher training and the outcomes of youth. Teacher training has been defined as Trainers needing to access the state of knowledge or information in the information base of trainees. Studies have shown that teacher's beliefs influence the acceptance and uptake of new approaches, techniques, and activities, and therefore play an important part in teacher development. Other studies have revealed that teacher training is affecting the academic achievement of language minority students. Teachers themselves are not satisfied with the hands on preparation they are getting in Teacher education programs and feel insufficiently prepared to manage classrooms on their first day of unsupervised teaching.

There also appears to be a significant difference between the learning styles of black and white students. White students showed to have applied more styles of learning than blacks, and blacks had more independent styles than whites. These findings suggest that changes need to be made in the curriculum for teacher training programs to better address the needs of diverse student populations, as the one shoe fits all traditional teaching pedagogy appears less effective with various groups from different socioeconomic cultures. Studies also found that teachers attitudes about their students and the types of methods that they use can contribute to the academic success or failure of their students. Consequently, teachers who harbor various racial or cultural stereotypes may contribute to a lower level of motivation to teach minority children.

In addressing classroom management, whether teachers are perceived as having control of the classroom, less than half of low achievement students felt the teacher was in charge. However, between 70% and 80% of moderate and high achievers opined that teachers were usually good classroom managers. Low achievement group students typically answer, "I seem to get in trouble a lot, teachers are always yelling at me because I don't pay attention." Or, "Teachers are always picking on me in front of everybody. I hate when teachers do that so I misbehave more." No wonder teachers of low achieving classrooms encounter greater classroom management challenges... more students are disinterested in learning and are more unruly. Consequently, teachers of low achieving students who are more prevalent in lower socioeconomic settings need to learn student motivation and coping strategies, that are usually not taught in Teaching colleges. It's no wonder new teachers may feel anxious, unprepared and perhaps even a bit overwhelmed on their first assignment to difficult low achievement schools.

Parents should make an appointment to visit their children's classroom at least once each semester to personally witness the classroom situations that pose challenges to teachers on a daily basis. Appointments could be arranged through school principals, as each school may have a different policy on parental visitations where overall District policy permits parental observation when not disruptive to classroom instruction. Following is a list of school emails.

Regular School Websites	School Districts
www.abcusd.k12.ca.us	Norwalk Cerritos
www.aadusd.k12.ca.us	Acton-Agua Dulce
www.alhambra.k12.ca.us	Alhambra
www.avc.edu	Antelope valley
www.avdistrict.org	Antelope high
www.ausd.k12.ca.us	Arcadia
www.azusausd.k12.ca.us	Azusa
www.bpusd.k12.ca.us	Baldwin park
www.bassett.k12.ca.us	La Puente
www.busd.org	Bellflower
www.bonita.k12.ca.us	San Dimas/Foothill
www.burbank.acityline.com	Burbank

www.castaic.k12.ca.us	Castaic
www.cerritos.edu	Cerritos
www.cousd.k12.ca.us	Covina
www.cvusd.k12.ca.us	Covina Valley
www.ewcsd.k12.ca.us	East Whittier
www.emcsd.k12.ca.us	El Monte
www.emuhsd.k12.ca.us	El Monte high
www.erusd.k12.ca.us	El Rancho-Pico Rivera
ayusem@garvey.k12.ca.us	Rosemead
www.glendale.k12.ca.us	Glendale
www.glendora.k12.ca.us	Glendora
www.hlpusd.k12.ca.us	Hacienda Heights
www.lcusd.k12.ca.us	La Canada
www.littlelake.k12.ca.us	Santa Fe Springs
www.lbusd.k12.ca.us	Long Beach
www.monrovia.k12.ca.us	Monrovia
www.montebello.k12.ca.us	Montebello
www.mountainview.k12.ca.us	El Monte
www.nlmusd.k12.ca.us	Norwalk-La Mirada
www.pasadena.k12.ca.us	Pasadena
www.pusd.org	Pomona
www.rowland-unified.org	Rowland Heights
www.rosemead.k12.ca.us	Rosemead
www.sgusd@aol.com	San Gabriel
www.san-marino.k12.ca.us	San Marino
www.spusd.net	So. Pasadena
www.walnutvalley.k12.ca.us	Walnut
www.wcusd.k12.ca.us	West Covina
www.whittiercity.k12.ca.us	Whittier
www.wuhsd.k12.ca.us	Whittier High
www.esgvrop.k12.ca.us	East San Gabriel
www.lpvrop.org	La Puente
www.pusd.org	San Antonio
www.tcrop.k12.ca.us	Whittier

C6 – FREEDOM

The United States of America has marketed itself as a free and democratic nation that is the world policeman for human rights. Sounds great, and an examination of the U.S. Constitution certainly provides a list of guarantees and rights granted to the federal government, states, and to individuals. But realistically, how FREE are Americans? Certainly with the scourge of global terrorism, we are less free. The U.S. Patriot Act has made limitations on many personal freedoms necessary to provide avenues to collect intelligence on potential terrorists. Technology has become so pervasive and invasive that we have more to fear about losing our privacy and identities to hackers, criminals, corporations and Internet service providers than we need to worry about from government in general. It is very difficult to count on both hands activities that are still legal, besides purchasing products or services from legitimate businesses.

A ranking of the most free to the least free states is excerpted from an Internet article, *An Index of Personal and Economic Freedom* by **Jason Sorens** and **William Ruger**, June 7, 2011.

Purpose of the Index

This project develops an index of economic and personal freedom in the American states. Specifically, it examines state and local government intervention across a wide range of public policies, from income taxation to gun control, from home schooling regulation to drug policy.

Measuring Freedom & Government Intervention

We explicitly ground our conception of freedom on an individual-rights framework. In our view, individuals should be allowed to dispose of their lives, liberties, and properties as they see fit, as long as they do not infringe on the rights of others.

Fiscal Policy

We divide fiscal policy equally into spending and taxation subcategories. These subcategories are highly interdependent; we include them both as redundant measures of the size of government.

Regulatory Policy

In this study, regulatory policy includes labor regulation, health-insurance coverage mandates, occupational licensing, eminent domain, the tort system, land-use regulation, and utilities. Regulations that seem to have a mainly paternalistic justification, such as home- and private-school regulations, are placed in the paternalism category.

Paternalism

In deciding how to weight personal freedoms, we started from the bottom up, beginning with the freedom we saw as least important in terms of saliency, constitutional implications, and the number of people affected, and working up to the most important.

Ranking & Discussion

By summing the economic freedom and personal freedom scores, we obtain the overall freedom index, presented in table 5. New Hampshire and South Dakota again find themselves in a virtual tie for first.

Conclusion

Although we hope we have demonstrated that some states provide freer environments than others, it would be inappropriate to infer that the freest states necessarily enjoy a libertarian streak, while others suffer from a statist mentality.

State Profiles

The state profiles (found through the above map) highlight some of the most interesting aspects of each state's public policies as they affect individual freedom. In preparation for this year's edition of Freedom in the 50 States, we conducted a survey of free-market policy analysts at think tanks associated with the State Policy Network (SPN).

Effects of the Federal Stimulus on State & Local Governments

This section assesses the consequences of the American Recovery and Reinvestment Act of 2009 (stimulus) for individual freedom, as affected by state and local policies. While the stimulus was passed immediately after the period covered by this study, we can use findings on the effects of federal grants on state policies to infer what the long-run consequences of the stimulus will be.

Comparison to Previous Indices of State-Level Economic Freedom

This project remains the only effort to code both economic and personal freedom in the 50 states. Other studies compare economic freedom or "competitiveness" in the states but do not treat other critical aspects of individual liberty or selectively subsume a few non-economic issues within economic freedom concepts.

Construction of Index

We started by collecting data on state and local public policies affecting individual freedom as defined above. All of the statutory policies are coded as of January 1, 2009, the fiscal data are coded for the fiscal year 2007–2008, the law-enforcement data cover the entire year of 2008, and all data are also back-coded consistently to January 1, 2007 (FY 2006–2007). We omit federal territories.

Data Appendix

This data appendix contains a description of each variable used in the study and its location in our spreadsheets on the website, as well as a hierarchical summary of category, issue subcategory, and variable weights.

About the Authors

William Ruger

William P. Ruger is an affiliated scholar with the Mercatus Center at George Mason University. His primary research interests include international politics, security studies, civil-military relations, U.S. foreign policy, ethics and international relations, and political theory.

Jason Sorens

Jason Sorens is an affiliated scholar at the Mercatus Center at George Mason University. His primary research interests include fiscal federalism, secessionism, ethnic violence, and comparative federalism.

The overall order of states, from most free to least free, with the study's numerical values (based on 1.0 being absolute freedom), were:

1.	New Hampshire	0.432
2.	Colorado	0.421
3.	South Dakota	0.392
4.	Idaho	0.356
5.	Texas	0.346
6.	Missouri	0.320
7.	Tennessee	0.284
8.	Arizona	0.279
9.	Virginia	0.275
10.	North Dakota	0.268
11.	Utah	0.250
12.	Kansas	0.210
13.	Indiana	0.208
14.	Michigan	0.206
15.	Wyoming	0.193
16.	Iowa	0.183
17.	Georgia	0.146
18.	Oklahoma	0.143
19.	Montana	0.125
20.	Pennsylvania	0.102
21.	Alabama	0.092
22.	Florida	0.068
23.	North Carolina	0.019
24.	Nevada	0.013
25.	Mississippi	-0.004
26.	Delaware	-0.008
27.	Oregon	-0.009
28.	Nebraska	-0.018
29.	Arkansas	-0.023
30.	South Carolina	-0.040
31.	Alaska	-0.071

32. Kentucky	-0.082
33. West Virginia	-0.097
34. Louisiana	-0.110
35. Minnesota	-0.111
36. New Mexico	-0.150
37. Wisconsin	-0.199
38. Ohio	-0.205
39. Maine	-0.214
40. Vermont	-0.217
41. Connecticut	-0.225
42. Illinois	-0.238
43. Massachusetts	-0.242
44. Washington	-0.275
45. Hawaii	-0.304
46. Maryland	-0.405
47. California	-0.413
48. Rhode Island	-0.430
49. New Jersey	-0.457
50. New York	-0.784

C7 - GUN RIGHTS

According to http://www.numberof.net/number-of-guns-in-america/, in America there are between 238 million and 276 million privately owned firearms. The exact number is unknown as the criminal networks and many 2nd Amendment advocates and gun enthusiasts don't register their weapons that they purchased at gun shows and over the Internet . There are unauthorized illegal arms like machine guns and grenade launchers that are smuggled in undetected and there is no federal gun registry for the legally owned firearms, as each state has different laws, rules and regulations regarding the legal ownership and registration requirements for guns. A wikipedia article speaks to the Constitutional guarantees for private ownership of firearms.

From Wikipedia, the free encyclopedia:

As passed by the Congress and preserved in the **National Archives**:[32] A well regulated Militia, being necessary to the security of a free State, the right of the people to keep and bear Arms, shall not be infringed. As ratified by the States and authenticated by Thomas Jefferson, then-Secretary of State:[33] A well regulated militia being necessary to the security of a free state, the right of the people to keep and bear arms shall not be infringed.

Second Amendment to the United States Constitution

United States of America

This article is part of the series:
United States Constitution

The **Second Amendment (Amendment II)** to the **United States Constitution** is the part of the **United States Bill of Rights** that protects the **right to keep and bear arms**. It was adopted on December 15, 1791, along with the rest of the Bill of Rights. The right to bear arms predates the Bill of Rights; the Second Amendment was based partially on the right to bear arms in English common-law, and was influenced by the **English Bill of Rights of 1689**. This right was described by **Sir William Blackstone** as an auxiliary right, supporting the natural rights of self-defense, resistance to oppression, and the civic duty to act in concert in defense of the state. **Academic inquiry** into the purpose,[1][2] scope,[3] and effect[4] of the amendment has been **controversial**[5][6][7] and subject to numerous **interpretations**.[8]

In *United States v. Cruikshank*, 92 **U.S. 542** (1875), the Supreme Court ruled that "[t]he right to bear arms is not granted by the Constitution; neither is it in any manner dependent upon that instrument for its existence. The Second Amendment means no more than that it shall not be infringed by Congress, and has no other effect than to restrict the powers of the National Government."

In *United States v. Miller*, 307 **U.S. 174** (1939), the Supreme Court ruled that the amendment "[protects arms that had a] reasonable relationship to the preservation or efficiency of a well regulated militia". This ruling has been widely described as ambiguous,[9][10][11][12][13][14] and ignited a debate on whether the amendment protected an individual right, or a collective militia right.

In *District of Columbia v. Heller*, 554 **U.S. 570** (2008), the Supreme Court ruled that the Second Amendment "codified a pre-existing right" and that it "protects an individual right to possess a firearm unconnected with service in a militia, and to use that arm for traditionally lawful purposes, such as self-defense within the home"[15][16] but also stated that "the right is not unlimited. It is not a right to keep and carry any weapon whatsoever in any manner whatsoever and for whatever purpose". They also clarified that many longstanding prohibitions and restrictions on firearms possession listed by the Court are consistent with the Second Amendment.[17]

In *McDonald v. Chicago*, 561 U.S. **3025** (2010), the Supreme Court ruled that the Second Amendment limits state and local governments to the same extent that it limits the federal government.[18]

Once again, the NRA has won the battle to restrict the possession of assault weapons subsequent to the public furor over the Sandy Hill massacre and attempted assassination of Congresswoman Gabby Giffords. It's no wonder. America as a nation was forged on the battlefields where the Minutemen and other partisan militias played an instrumental part in using their firearms to defeat the British and German mercenaries (the Hessians) during the American Revolutionary War. The American Republic was created through a violent armed struggle, and again restated in a bloody Civil War, and from those marquee wars (to the exclusion of fighting foreign wars), a large number of Americans believe they must retain their right to possess and use military style weapons to defend their homes and communities from each other, and any imaginary future foreign invasions. Unfortunately, domestic armed conflict almost always kills our fathers, mothers, sisters, brothers, children, relatives and friends.

In an article by **Max Fisher** Jul 23 2012 in the on-line version of *The Atlantic*, entitled, *A Land Without Guns: How Japan Has Virtually Eliminated Shooting Deaths.* IN PART BY FORBIDDING ALMOST ALL FORMS OF FIREARM OWNERSHIP, JAPAN HAS AS FEW AS TWO GUN-RELATED HOMICIDES A YEAR. A Tokyo "gun" shop owner, who mostly sells air rifles, displays one of Japan's relatively few licensed rifles. (Reuters)

I've heard it said that, if you take a walk around Waikiki, it's only a matter of time until someone hands you a flyer of scantily clad women clutching handguns, overlaid with English and maybe Japanese text advertising one of the many local shooting ranges. The city's largest, the Royal Hawaiian Shooting Club, advertises instructors fluent in Japanese, which is also the default language of its **website**. For years, this peculiar Hawaiian industry has **explicitly targeted Japanese tourists**, drawing them away from beaches and resorts into shopping malls, to do things that are forbidden in their own country.

Waikiki's Japanese-filled ranges are the sort of quirk you might find in any major tourist town, but they're also an intersection of two societies with wildly different approaches to guns and their role in society. Friday's **horrific shooting** at an Aurora, Colorado, movie theater has been a reminder that America's gun control laws are **the loosest in the developed world** and its **rate of gun-related homicide is the highest**. Of the world's 23 "rich" countries, the U.S. gun-related murder rate is **almost 20 times** that of the other 22. With almost one privately owned firearm per person, America's ownership rate is the highest in the world; tribal-conflict-torn Yemen is ranked second, with a rate about half of America's.

But what about the country at the other end of the spectrum? What is the role of guns in Japan, the developed world's least firearm-filled nation and perhaps its strictest controller? In 2008, the U.S. had over **12 thousand** firearm-related homicides. All of Japan experienced **only 11**, fewer than were killed at the Aurora shooting alone. And that was a big year: 2006 saw an astounding *two*, and when that number jumped to 22 in 2007, it became a **national scandal**. By comparison, also in 2008, 587 Americans were killed just by guns that had discharged accidentally.

Almost no one in Japan owns a gun. Most kinds are illegal, with onerous restrictions on buying and maintaining the few that are allowed. Even the country's infamous, mafia-like Yakuza **tend** to **forgo** guns; the **few exceptions** tend to become big national news stories. Most Americans would probable have no problem with banning gun ownership if criminals also don't have access. Unfortunately, criminals can always obtain guns.

C8 - HOMELESSNESS

The problem of homelessness has become greatly exacerbated by the recent economic recession, the return of emotionally damaged, crippled and relatively unskilled Iraq and Afghanistan veterans, increasing number of families in poverty, and an ever increasing elderly population whose Social Security benefits are insufficient to keep up with rent increases and the cost of gasoline and other life necessities in addition to food costs. The following homelessness questionnaire attempts to evaluate what happens to otherwise productive people who somehow find themselves fallen into the lost crevices in our socioeconomic structure.

HOMELESSNESS QUESTIONNAIRE

First Name:

Age:

Gender:

Ethnic Background:

Legal Marital Status:

Number of Custodial Children:

Number of Non-custodial Children:

Educational Level:

THE PAST:

1. How long have you considered yourself "homeless"?
2. What was your last job before becoming homeless?
3. How long was the period between your last job and becoming homeless?
4. What caused you to stop your employment?
5. What was your income level at the time you became homeless?
6. Why do you think you became homeless? Lack of money, alcohol, drugs, etc.?
7. Did you ever think that you could or would become homeless?
8. Who lived with you at the time before you became homeless?
9. Describe the process of losing people from your life as you became homeless.

Loss of spouse, children, parents, and friends?

10. What was your emotional state in reaction to questions #4 and #6, above?

11. Was there anything you could have done to prevent becoming homeless?

THE PRESENT:

1. What family members and friends do you still talk to, see and visit?
2. Where are your "loved ones" nowadays, who you no longer contact?
3. What is the general attitude of your family and friends toward you?
4. What positive things have you experienced in being homeless?
5. What aspects of "living on the streets" do you like?
6. What negative things have you experienced in being homeless?
7. What aspects of living on the streets do you dislike?
8. What do you miss most about your previous life style?
9. If you could change your life now, what are the 5 things you would do first?

THE FUTURE:

1. What are the chances that you will "get back on your feet someday?
2. Who do you think can help you to get going again?
3. What do you think you will be doing one year from now?
4. What advice would you give to others who may be facing a similar predicament to what you faced before you became homeless?
5. How can other people avoid becoming homeless?

No one in their right frame of mind wants to be homeless, just as no one in their right mind wants to be imprisoned, or a slave, or victim of crime. Statistics indicate that almost three-fourths of American workers are living month to month, with insufficient savings to last an entire month without employment. Of the fourth who have savings in the bank, two-thirds have insufficient funds to last more than 6 months unemployed.

REMEMBER... most Americans are only one paycheck away from becoming homeless!

C9 – IMMIGRATION REFORM

The primary purpose of permitting immigration should be based upon the needs of the American society, and U.S. borders must not be an open invitation for illegal immigration. Sensible immigration policy should foremost answer the question, "Will permitting this person to immigrate serve our national interests or society at large?" If not, then deny permission to enter our nation.

As with any other nation, the USA has limited resources, which are being strained by upwards of 10 million illegal aliens who obtain educational and health services, cash grants, food assistance, social services, and law enforcement interdictions at a heavy cost to American taxpayers. As a group, illegal immigrants cost our economy far more than they return in taxes from their menial unskilled jobs, criminal enterprises, consumption of products and services, and unemployment status. America would be better off without them, and almost all nations on earth would not tolerate the unchecked and uncontrolled immigration that typifies our national borders.

The United States of America should not be the dumping ground for Mexico's or China's poor, uneducated, criminal, and unskilled people, no more than Mexico or China would tolerate the emigration of all our homeless, criminal, unskilled, uneducated, and mentally ill populations across the border to Mexico. Mexico must fix their own economic, social, and political problems, and should no longer be allowed to sweep their problems across their border to America. Keep Mexicans in Mexico! While sound immigration should not penalize any particular nation due to enforcement of rules and procedures, it is evident that the U.S. population increase in the past decade has been predominantly due to illegal Mexican immigration.

A sensible immigration policy must address and prioritize our nation's need (if any) for immigrants according to areas and categories of need, and a specific quota must be established for the number, type, and national origin of immigrants desired by the American society and economy. In an ideal world without borders where sufficient wealth exist and there is more sensible distribution of resources, it might not matter how many people might reside in any jurisdiction. Now, in our not so perfect world, if the United States were to allow anyone to come in to partake in social services paid for by hard working taxpayers, we'd soon have more people in America than currently reside in China and India combined. America would become broke, as it is; most Main Street Americans are actually broke if they had to settle all of their credit card and other debts within a day.

What are some sensible and practical justifications for legalizing certain types of immigration?

Economic Justification:

- Immigrants who create employment for Americans through the purchase, investment, or start up of commercial enterprises valued at one million dollars or more, which employs at least 5 people.
- Immigrants who possess technical or professional skills necessary to fill shortages in industry or government.
- Immigrants who commit to serve at least 3 years in a branch of the U.S. Armed Services, and who pledge loyalty and allegiance to the U.S.A.
- Farm workers, who are temporary guest workers in seasonal employment programs.
- Other seasonal jobs, where there is a significant shortage of American workers who are willing to fill the positions, such as hotel maids, gardener assistants, seamstress, and janitors.

Political Justification:

- Asylum for pro-U.S., pro-democracy intellectuals and persons attempting to escape tyrannical or communist regimes, who are willing to pledge allegiance to the U.S.A.

- Foreign nationals who have dutifully served U.S. agencies, military, and corporations, who can be sponsored by their employers for continued employment in the U.S.A.

Social Justification:

- When a shortage arises in specific regions, and a need arises to import certain categories of persons to improve society, selective immigrants will be sought and admitted for permanent residency. For example, granting immigration to Dutch South Africans, Argentines, and white Russians to help balance the ethnic population mix in various states, while providing additional capital and skills to help our states rebound from its economic crisis.
- Family members of U.S. citizens born or residing in foreign countries.
- A sensible "amnesty program" where undocumented immigrants who have been employed in America, have children born in the U.S., have no criminal record, and possess the skills that enhance America's economy may be considered for permanent residency if they can prove the above for at least a ten year period prior to applying for "conditional amnesty" with NO PATH TO CITIZENSHIP.

All other forms of immigration would therefore be illegal, and any law enforcement official, school official, and public health official must be required to report any and all known cases of illegal immigrants to the INS. All illegal immigrants detained by law enforcement for the commission of a crime must be deported to the custody of their country of origin's authorities, except in cases of the most serious crimes, when the court of local jurisdiction may elect to adjudicate the case.

Round Up:

Law enforcement may question and detain any individual who can not prove their legal status to remain in the U.S. If any individual cannot prove their legal status, they may be arrested and turned over to the INS for status determination or deportation proceedings. Periodic neighborhood "sweeps" by INS agents and other appropriate law enforcement agencies to round up groups of illegal alien nationals who tend to congregate at certain public parks and right of ways, causing a nuisance or intimidating citizens. All illegal immigrants deported by the INS must first have a GPS locator chip implanted in their bodies where it cannot be removed, to prevent them from ever re-entering the U.S.A.

Conclusions:

Only through reasonably pro-active immigration policies and procedures can America become safer from potential terrorists, criminals, non-productive dead beats, and unemployable or lazy illegal aliens who suck up public services and cause an expensive and negative impact on the economic infrastructure of America.

The first priority of a revamped immigration policy must be the expelling of all illegal immigrants, whether they be Arab students who overstay their visas, or Mexicans who sneak into the U.S. across our borders, unless they qualify under a "guest worker" or "conditional amnesty" program, or other exceptions listed above. The deportation of illegal immigrants will automatically save hundreds of billions of dollars annually, and in additionally reduce the overload and negative impact on our overcrowded public schools, emergency rooms, freeways, and jails.

Continuing to do nothing, or to label such constructive attempts to control immigration as being racially or ethnically motivated is to play into the neo-liberal political agenda and propaganda, whose purpose is to make America the dumping ground for all of the world's deficient and poor. Having summarized this "compromise immigration reform" proposal that permits law-abiding "illegal aliens" to remain in the U.S., subject to various conditions and qualifications, without a path to citizenship.

Can we really blame Republicans for sticking their fingers in the immigration dike to try to hold back an inundating wave of Hispanic voters within the next generation? Why speed up the process by putting 12 million undocumented Hispanics on the path to U.S. citizenship? It neither makes political or economic sense to the good ol' boys whose fundamental interest is to try their hardest to maintain a white majority so the fates of white people won't be determined by non-whites who don't understand white culture. They send token white face Hispanics like Cuban born Rubio who is considered white of Hispanic descent to take conservative stands against dark skinned Hispanics and Mexicans, but he does not sympathize or identify with the liberal views and issues of most impoverished or working class Hispanics.

Republicans are all about the white way and are exclusionary. They have all white elitist clubs where a non-white has never set foot… except perhaps butlers, maids, and cooks. It's always been that way and they want to go back to "them good ol' days." But wake up GOP and Tea Partiers… them days are numbered. If the GOP continues to depend on racial politics to put their troops into office, then it's just a matter of time before troop attrition will make the GOP less relevant to national politics. Better they begin to include more dark-skinned people who could buy into their economic prominence and capitalistic philosophy to balance the Democratic social policies that attempt to redistribute wealth from the greedy and privileged to those who are unfortunate and less fortunate.

C10 - JOBS

American society, as in the societies of almost all nations on earth, and in the history of mankind, is structured along hierarchical class system. However, in capitalistic societies such as the USA, upward and downward socioeconomic mobility depends in great part on individual effort as summarize in THE HABITS OF LOSERS, SUCCESSES, AND THE WEALTHY.

. Our society, as in most modern societies, judge a person's worth by its cultural definitions of value. Why is one person perceived to be worth more, or a better person than another? Usually, the common litmus test is gauged in monetary accumulation. This chapter attempts a superficial look at what traits separate these three groups of people, based upon the general stereotypes that are operative in most societies.

Individuals must accept the responsibility for their own outcomes. There are no guarantees in life besides homelessness, poverty, illness and destitute. Any improvement to that basic subsistence paradigm must come with personal motivation and effort to lift oneself up from the bottom rungs, to stand on ones own two feet and learn to run with what can be learned and applied rather than what one can take and carry.

Following are comparative descriptors of those who by social definitions are losers, versus those who succeed through hard work to earn their successes, and finally the fortunate ones who through talent, ability, perseverance, luck and creativity manage to score in the big leagues.

Broke Losers	Solid Successes	Washing in Wealth
(low classes)	(middle/upper classes)	(1% elitists)
1. lazy to the bone	hard working	doesn't need to work
2. stupid	practical	clever & crafty
3. procrastinators	planners	plotters
4. escapist	pragmatic	recreational
5. addictive	obsessive	compulsive
6. physical	emotional	mental
7. borrow, steal and beg	earn and save	invests OPM
8. chump change	a thick wad	lots of digital zeros

9.	drug and alcohol abuse	workaholic	wary of others
10.	envious	protective	bothered
11.	users, cheaters, liars	honest and ethical	exploitive
12.	inconsiderate	considerate	oblivious
13.	insecure	secure	superiority complex
14.	false pride	proud	arrogant
15.	signs applications	signs checks	signs autographs
16.	dies on the streets after	dies in hospital without	dies on television
17.	police chases	police presence	with police escort

We often hear about how to emulate the habits of successful people. The reality is we can learn more about success by looking at the habits of failures and losers. The people who make the most money actually do very little work, as they just sign papers a lot. What they do is the opposite of what is done or not done by losers. It's really as simple in principle as that... only a lot more difficult to implement due to the nature of competition, financing, luck and consumer appeal.

Another simple fact is consumers drive the economy and are responsible for an average of 70% of the GDP, or gross domestic product – a measure of the state of the national economy. In order for consumers to afford buying the products and services that businesses have to offer, they must have jobs that pay sufficiently for them to afford to be customers of American businesses.

Let's discuss some of the salient issues on how to generate more American jobs to boost the economic output of America by putting more Americans back to work.

A. THE ECONOMY

Building consumer confidence

1. Protect the integrity of the free market system through appropriate government regulations, laws, incentives and treaties
2. Markedly reduce corporate corruption and excessive executive compensation
3. Regulate and annually audit/decertify cheating accounting firms & corporations
4. Monitor and regulate monopolies and oligarchies to prevent price manipulation
5. Emphasize practice of organizational and executive ethical code of conduct
6. Mandatory university classes on ethics, corruption, legal aspects of business

7. Provide highly effective homeland security
8. Rethink "the ends justifies the means" paradigm to eliminate excessive greed
9. Develop a clear political, economic, military, foreign relations vision and strategy that is rational and consistent
10. Greatly reduce unemployment and outsourcing
11. Reign in exorbitant credit card rates & fees
12. Reign in exorbitant bank card penalty fees
13. Increase consumer funds and savings
14. Full employment targeting
15. Reasonable pay rates (living wage)
16. Control inflationary forces in housing, energy, banking, and insurance industries
17. Tax breaks to strengthen specific segments of the economy suffering downturns
18. Affordable housing and rents based upon assessment of community standards
19. Low interest rate loans for consumer purchases and credit cards
20. Development of new consumer-oriented industries and products

B. Decreasing unemployment fears and anxieties
- Job creation incentives to business sector
- Job training and retraining tax credits to Individuals and employers
- Severance matching pay program for displaced employees
- Review excessive executive compensation
- Review excessive casualty insurance rates
- Increasing net exports and decreasing imports

C. Optimizing supply and demand equilibrium
1. Partnerships between government and universities to provide accurate and reliable economic analysis, projections, forecasting, and trend planning
2. Computerized models on Internet to provide public with useful data & trends
3. Balancing distribution through integrated real time computer reporting of supplies

4. Identify supplies and demands by specific regions, towns, cities, and MSA's.

D.   Bring back the business by improving our climate
- Tax incentives for hiring, especially in low economic areas
- Remove tax disincentives and bureaucratic hurtles
- Reform and reduce workers compensation system by reducing insurance premiums
- Place reasonable "cap" on civil injury recoveries awarded by juries
- Reform the "for profit" HMO system to reduce premiums and to provide better services
- Control energy expenses by imposing limits on the rate at which prices may expand in "non-emergency" periods, where increases can note justified, to prevent gouging
- Encourage investment in alternative energy for public buildings, and incentives for private sector and residential properties
- Give tax incentives to attract foreign investments, if low domestic investment
- Tax penalties for outsourcing jobs abroad,
- Except in allowable industries
- Increase homeland security expenditures
- To small businesses and local governments
- Corporate tax breaks and subsidies for
- Investing in new products and employment
- Tax incentives and subsidies for new
- Technology and human capital development

E.   Developing new jobs in cities and towns through more small business assistance programs
- Community responsibility tax for large corporations that destroy local businesses; paid to community reconstruction trust fund
- More federal sub-contracts to small towns
- More federal contracts to cities with low income in excess of 10% of population

- Corporations required to reinvest 5-10% of profits earned back into business operations

F. Capitalism with social responsibility

- Businesses required to hire at least 10 percent of employees and contracts from community/city where business is based
- Corporations to pay for higher percentage of city/town infrastructure as fees
- Technology as job maker versus job destroyer
- Implementation of new technologies must also present plan to detail how many new jobs are being created to replace losses
- When job loss from technology application exceeds 25% per year, company to pay into company unemployment fund equal to 25% of salaries saved through job terminations to supplement company's displaced workers
- Balancing outsourcing of America's economic base
- Penalties for outsourcing manufacturing jobs; withdrawal of tax incentives, and limits to 25% added outsourcing per year
- Penalties for outsourcing high-tech jobs, same as above
- Prohibition from outsourcing government contracts or sub-contracts
- Companies who outsource must pay state and local taxes on savings of payroll taxes resulting from domestic reductions
- Outsourcing without penalties approved for fields not negatively impacted or endangered, as determined quarterly
- Controlling wanton greed and price gouging
- Hey buddy, can you spare a dime? Pay it forward incentive programs
- Tax incentives for corporations who purchase from low income businesses
- Government grants for impoverished citizens to purchase successful established small businesses

G. Changing economic imperatives; the *horn of plenty* versus the *zero sum game* by exploring new options rather than being limited by old ideas that limit creativity and concentrate money into the hands of the few clever manipulators of the system.

- Deterring corporate corruption
- Criminal penalties for all cheaters
- Clean up stock market phony ratings
- Clean up investment banking kickbacks
- Outlaw hedge funds and shorting stocks
- Limit executive compensation to ten times the annual taxes they pay to the IRS
- Deterring *Wall Street* swindles
- S.E.C. needs to regulate, not kiss up to stock manipulators
- Brokers and executives bank accounts are frozen subject to investigations for malfeasance, stock manipulation, and conspiracies to defraud investors.
- Mandatory prison time for CEO's, CFO's and investors who deliberately collapse the stock market and threaten national security through economic collapse.

II.   THE BUDGET DEFICIT

A.   Balancing the budget without raising taxes (no increase to personal income tax, taxes on businesses and corporations, inheritance, capital gains, or gifts)
1.   Eliminate government duplication and waste consolidate/restructure departments eliminate "pork barrel" programs that are political pay-offs, unless beneficial to the nation and it's overall plans
2.   Eliminate social programs that don't work
3.   Reform prisons & outrageous public pensions
4.   Weed out corruption; embezzlement, bribery, kickbacks, and sweetheart contracts reform public education
5.   More effective/efficient technology use to reduce services for undocumented aliens
6.   Subsidize educational television to teach academic standards and testing for advancement; can advance to college at age 16

7. ***AUDIT EVERYTHING*** to discover waste, inefficiency, and corruptive practices
    a. Monitor the added costs of special interest legislation; get them off Political "pork barrel" coat-tails
    b. Privatize certain federal property (subject to 10/20/20/40/50 year lease-back agreements at rates stated by law)
    c. Tax incentives to American investors who purchase federal properties (25-50% reduction in future capital gains taxes for qualifying properties)
    d. Bring the *bucks* home from abroad
    e. Discount to foreign investors buying treasury bonds
    f. Discount to foreign investors investing in purchasing state property, but no special capital gains reduction as for Americans
B. Restore and maintaining public faith and trust in the American and global capitalistic system
C. Enhance anticipatory economic effects through accurate data collection and trend forecasting.
    1. Objective and factually based analysis, forecasting, rating, and transactions
    2. Realistic economic/employment outlook; lag effect, multipliers, equilibrium levels
    3. Applying technology and exploration for unlimited development of resources
    4. Intelligently managed distribution to minimize waste, and maximize conservation
D. Increase investment in the infrastructure and small businesses to increase the GDP.
    1. Tax incentives for foreign investments in certain sectors of low employment
    2. Tax breaks for small businesses to reinvest and employ American workers
    3. Corporate tax breaks and subsidies for reinvesting in products and employment
    4. Tax incentives and subsidies for new technology and human capital development
E. Increase discretionary consumer funds and savings.
    1. Full employment targets above subsistence pay rates (living wage)
    2. Control inflationary forces in housing, energy, banking, and insurance industries

3. Tax breaks to strengthen specific segments of the economy suffering downturns

4. Affordable housing and rents based upon assessment of community standards

5. Low interest rate loans for consumer purchases and credit cards

6. Development of new consumer-oriented industries and products

F. Decrease unemployment fears and anxieties

1. Job creation incentives to business sector

2. Job training and retraining tax credits to individuals and employers

3. Severance matching pay program for displaced employees

4. Corporate health assessment of executive compensation & insurance rates

5. Control the unjustified spiraling increases in the cost of insurance premiums

G. Increase net exports and decrease international debt and balance of payments

1. Decrease price in large quantity contracts for key exports; no tariff treaties

2. Track the amount of cash, stocks, bonds, and corporate assets owned by foreign nationals and governments; strategies to balance trade & assets

3. A weaker dollar against the Euro and Yen

4. Enforce new rules on large amounts of cash transferable or redeemable per period

5. Control or outlaw international hedge funds investing and speculating in U.S. dollars

6. Improve relationships with international trade partners

H. Improve government efficiency through contracts, privatization, and contracting out where needed

1. Centralized real time computerized tax collection with discount incentives

2. Privatize certain segments of bureaucracy with adequate agency oversight

3. Contract out inefficient government service functions

4. Improve bureaucratic effectiveness, efficiency and responsiveness through interdepartmental competition and incentives for cost-savings

I.   Optimizing supply and demand equilibrium
   1.   partnerships between government and universities to provide accurate and reliable economic analysis, projections, forecasting, and trend planning.
   2.   computerized models on Internet to provide public with useful data & trends
   3.   balance distribution through integrated real time computer databases that identify supplies and demand by specific regions, towns, cities, and MSA's.

These suggestions are by no means exhaustive, and hopefully will encourage our nation's leaders to "think outside of the box" to explore new solutions that are not apparent from "business as usual thinking." A few of the suggestions will generate some controversy due to sensitivities about illegal immigrants, but ask yourself this question: Would you feel obligated to house, feed, educate, and provide medical services to any stranger who sneaks into your home? Isn't America OUR HOME? I think so, even with all its problems, THERE'S NO PLACE LIKE HOME SWEET HOME!

THE TRANSFORMATION OF AMERICAN WORKERS

America is being raped by the corporate greed of the international pirates that include the leadership of the largest multi-national American, European, and Japanese conglomerates. American executives now earn in excess of 100 times the wages of the average worker, during a time of mass lay-offs, large corporate losses, and bankruptcies. The European and Japanese executives earn 10 to 20 times the wages of their average workers, and they are succeeding, for now. The global community is regressing to a stage of feudal nation-states, where the economic disparity between the ruling classes and the masses once again becomes legitimized by its institutions, where the rich minority exercises domination over the majority poor, and the primary purpose of the consumer classes is to provide a vehicle of profit for the wealthy equity holders.

Despite so-called experts who perpetually disagree with each other, the economy can be explained in rather simple terms and concepts. There are four basic components of any economy; first, natural resources; second, manmade goods and services; third, distribution; and finally, value that is created by demand. When any of these economic elements become unbalanced, the economy skews toward those who controls any of its elements. When any particular group controls the first three components, they develop a virtual monopoly on the fourth. Different political systems utilize laws to alter the natural relationship between these four elements of economy to shift wealth from its unprotected classes (the poor and consumer classes) to its protected classes (the economic and political powerful).

If left alone, without governmental restrictions, except that transactions should be based on a doctrine of mutually fair exchange of similar value (of whatever equivalent method of trade), economic systems would naturally tend to become balanced systems. If you don't believe it, name one person who you know who would knowingly consent to a barter situation where his own interests becomes secondary to making a profit for the other guy. If so, let's just give away the store. But in reality, with the legitimization and collusion of special interest government, the economic interests of the average citizen is subrogated to the self-perpetuating interests of the power brokers who attend to the economic interests of the ruling class, and depend on special interest support to maintain their positions.

Institutionalized inequities are more apparent in certain industries than in others; however it pervades the entire economic structure of America, and is legitimized by government, and is taught in universities as the way things should be, further perpetuating a system that primarily serves the will of the wealthy. We will discuss some of the more obviously maligned areas of our economy, and propose some potential solutions to bring a real economic balance to America.

THE MIDDLE CLASS, OR SOCIETY'S NEWEST SQUATTERS?

A redistribution of wealth from the rich to the poor, socialism, returning to a basic barter system, or any revolutionary change in the economy is not suggested. Positive changes should develop in prudent, predictable, and incremental steps to minimize the systemic shock that invariably results in great suffering for the vast majority of people. We should not dismantle all the positive institutions and systems that exist, but instead improve and encourage the development of a more motivated, productive, and wealthy middle class to ensure a diverse economic foundation that can survive in the global economic markets. Strengthening the middle class creates consistent markets for more products and services while providing the wealthy class greater opportunities to amass even greater fortunes. The larger tax base enables government to provide needed infrastructure improvements, funds to reduce the federal debt, support of social, national defense, and technological advancement expenditures. The shrinking middle-class can have a devastating effect on the economic survival of our nation, and decreases opportunities for both domestic and international businesses. While many cash fluid rich can increase net worth a hundred folds during a recession or depression by their ability to buy property at highly discounted prices from those who are cash starved, the long-term devastation of a recession or depression actually decreases the amassing of fortunes when compared to performance during economic boom periods.

The real causes of economic recession are the imbalances that are created when vast sums of money leaves the country from an imbalance of trade, the exporting of American jobs by both American and internationally-owned companies, and the uncontrolled runaway debt incurred at all levels of the economy, from individual to corporate and government. Presently, the total net worth of all the property in America has been estimated at $55 trillion. The gross productivity of the economy (GDP) is approximately $17 trillion per year, and the federal budget about one-fourth of the GDP. The national debt is slightly over $18 trillion. Federal, state, local taxes and user fees now account for about 40% of the average household's expenses.

The top 1% of the population owns one-third of all the wealth in America (the top 5% owns almost two-thirds), the bottom fourth owns less than 3% of America, and the middle-class owns the balance (30%). America is rapidly becoming a two-class society, of the rich versus the poor. Mankind's history is filled with examples of civilizations whose governments were eventually toppled by the poor after the disparity between rich and poor become obscene and inhumane. Let's hope corporate America isn't going down that slippery slope.

The federal government has now incurred over $18 trillion in national debt, and pays over $400 billion of its taxes collected annually toward interest payment on that debt. This amount will grow to over 30% by the year 2020, if not sooner. America has borrowed heavily against its future income, on the expectation of greater future productivity, erroneously based on an aging and retiring population, a decreased number in the workforce, and decreased industrial output and annual Gross Domestic Product. It certainly sounds like a page out of bankruptcy court.

The possible solutions are basic and must be applied simultaneously. First, more income is needed to offset the increasing debt payments. Secondly, expenses must be controlled, wasteful spending eliminated, and greater value for the dollar must be sought for each dollar spent. Third, new borrowing must be severely curtailed, loan repayments restructured over a longer term, and new borrowing to pay existing debts must be avoided. Finally, the dollar must be gradually devalued against other international currencies against an acceptable level of inflation. This will also act to inflate the prices of imported goods, and decrease the relative costs of our exports; consequently, improving our balance of trade, creating more American jobs, and resulting in a higher tax basis that translates to more income for the government to offset the federal debt.

Proposed capital gains tax breaks for the rich must be accompanied by a domestic reinvestment criteria to deter pulling out of profits from local businesses, and further requiring reinvestment of the tax savings into the American economy. Any program of tax breaks designed primarily for the rich with no strings attached will only add to the exportation of American jobs to cheaper overseas labor forces, or adding to investment in non-job producing investments in rare items of the past, such as antiques, rare coins, and paintings. To move boldly into the future, we must encourage investors to invest in the mechanisms of the future, such as factories and product research, and discourage tax breaks for investing in non-productive commodities such as gold futures, and other non-jobs producing articles.

The explosive growth in the number of failed and failing banks, savings and loans, and other lending institutions is endemic of a failing system based upon a abrogation of basic good economic sense. Banks were initially places to deposit savings and valuables as an added measure of safety and security from outlaw forces. The evolution of banking created corporate entities whose purpose was no longer the protection of depositors' assets, but the reinvestment of those assets for the purpose of making a profit for the investors. Consequently, corporate greed and governmental acquiescence and collaborative guarantees permitted the banking interests to invest in very risky ventures such as loans to third world governments and foreign companies, dry oil wells, and unproven technologies, all with substantive losses that were "written off" the books, meaning the taxpayers footed the bill for billions of dollars in bad loans and hundreds of billions in bad investments made by American banks and lending institutions that resulted in the 2009 federal bail out.

Average Americans can't get a loan for a business start-up during the same time wheelers and dealers were using letters of credit and loans to raid solvent companies, leaving them straddled in excessive long-term debts. And now, many of those takeovers have resulted in the bankruptcy of the shell of what were once successful American corporations. Of course the corporate raiders have long since run off with their $ billions in profits that have directly resulted in the loss of hundreds of thousands of jobs. These greedy corporate raiders should not have been admired, but rather they should have been jailed, just as the head of the failed Lincoln Savings and Loan should be jailed for preying on and destroying the lives of untold thousands of people. The same goes for Morgan Stanley, now JP Morgan Chase Bank.

Historically, the seeds of the failure of the banking system lies in the special interest influence of banking industry executives on governmental regulators and politicians whose laxities have resulted in a system that is out-of-control, insolvent, and has violated the trust of its depositors. Government makes an ineffectual regulator when its lawmakers and officials implement fiscally irresponsible laws and regulations that have encouraged lending institutions to make highly risky investments that should not have been permitted at all. Now, again the taxpayers are stuck with the enormous expense of bailing out insolvent institutions.

A solutions to the banking problem as another weakened leg of the American economy must first start with an examination of the concept of "credit." Creditworthiness is the cornerstone of lending. An individuals ability to qualify for a loan is normally evaluated against his credit history, and the future prognosis of timely repayment of a loan. The interest rate that is charged to individuals for the use of the lender's money is tied to the level of risk that the lender takes in consideration of a borrower's assets, income, existing debts, reputation, employment and credit history. Somehow, basic lending principles applied to working-class individuals are often disregarded when large loans are made to corporate executives, corporate raiders, larger corporations, and foreign governments and entities. We are now learning the lesson that apparent "bigness" does not insure solvency, as Donald Trump, Carl Icahn, PanAm, and Macys can attest. Every time a large corporation goes belly-up, untold thousands of workers and related businesses are hurt, and the taxpayers absorb the bill for bad loans made by lenders to large corporations because usual lending criteria and practices that are customarily applied to evaluating individuals are disregarded when dealing with the economic elitist class. However, the Donald Trumps of the world can easily drop off poor performing companies through bankruptcy while keeping their pearl assets, but individuals don't have that same legal avenue as dissolving corporations to erase debts and taxes while maintaining personal CEO wealth intact.

The cost of credit is another area that has become essentially unregulated. It was once usurious and illegal for individuals to charge more than 10% interest on a loan (to deter loan-sharking); however, we now find that the biggest loan sharks are institutional lenders, auto financing companies, thrifts, and the government itself. Credit cards at 19% interest, car loans carried by dealers a 24% interest, appliance purchases carried by thrifts at 21% interest, and late payment interests of 25% per year plus 25% penalty for uncollected taxes (that adds up to 50%), and parking ticket fines that are doubled if not paid in full by the stated bail date (100% penalty). Any excessive interest payments decreases the net productivity of individuals. If a man earns $2000, but pays $500 for interest payments, $500 in taxes, and $700 for rent and utilities, that leaves him very little for food, transportation, clothing, and "living". He is essentially broke. He would otherwise be solvent if his debt payment were only half as much.

The biggest scam in credit is the idea of compound interest. If you loan the bank $1000 (when you open a savings account, you are actually lending the bank your money) at 1% interest, you will have $10 after one year. If you do not touch your money, at the end of two years, you will have earned another 1% of $1010, or $10.10, for an aggregate total of principal and interest of $1020.10 When the bank lends out your money, they need to recover the amount of interest that is paid to you, plus an amount for profit. If the bank loans your $1000 out at 15% per year for two years, and schedules level term repayments, the borrower repays 30% interest or $300. The bank makes almost all of the profit. Actually, the borrower never has the entire $1000 to use, because after one year, the borrower has repaid half of the loan plus interest. And that amount of principle that is repaid by the borrower is loaned out again at least tenfold. That is why deferred payments on autos increases the price by 50% over a 4-5 year period, and the actual price of a home is paid 3 times over a 30 year period (with the first 20 years of payments scheduled primarily to interest payments).

The solution should be the elimination of compound interest, and a reversion to simple interest. If one borrows $1000 at 15% per year, the bank should be paid interest only payments of $150 per year for each year that the $1000 is outstanding, with the principal to be due at the end of the term of the loan. This enables the borrower to actually have the full $1000 available for his use during the term of the loan. In addition, the burden of monthly repayment would become manageable. The borrower would be required to purchase affordable government guaranteed loan insurance, and deposit a reasonable percentage of the loan principle into a government escrow account (this could be the FDIC insurance escrow account). In the event of default, the insurance company and the governmental escrow account makes the bank whole, including interest. The defaulting borrower is assessed a reasonable percentage of the defaulted loan balance still due after security instruments are sold off to satisfy partial repayment of the original loan. Any balance due is divided into payments according to a sliding income schedule, and collected along with withholding income taxes until the deficiency judgment is satisfied.

A baffling contradiction appears in our economy today, where the stock market posts record highs, breaking the mythical 15,000 barrier while unemployment is at a record high since the great depression of the 1930's (based on actual numbers of people who are unemployed but not receiving government benefits). Why at a time of great stockholder profits are companies going bankrupt and millions are losing their jobs? Where is all the money going? Why are the profits not being reinvested into companies to maintain jobs? Are the wealthy class, armed with inside boardroom information, taking advantage of institutional investors such as pension plans?

Taken as a group, investment experts are no more effective in predicting the future value of stock than flipping a coin or throwing darts blindfolded. The real money is being made by those with the inside track, friends of corporate management who are leaked insider information, and can make clever buy and sell decisions that is subsequently mimicked by the public sector institutional investors and John Q. Public. The lag in time between insider trading and the movement of large blocks of public sector stock equals big profits for those clever private investors who are able to buy low and sell high. It's a simple case of the horse leading the cart.

When companies first go public, and make a stock offering, investors buy shares of stock to provide needed capital for company growth, on the potential promise of future performance. Depending on the eventual growth of the company, the number of times the stock is split, and the amount of stock that is retained by the company, future stock value may have little impact on providing significant additional capital to companies for additional growth. Shareholders become the beneficiaries of stock profits, and the process of stock trading moves real and paper profits among the various investment portfolios of investors, but may have little beneficial effect on providing needed reinvestment income to companies. The improved value of a company's stock translates into increased creditworthiness, and permits companies to "borrow" capital on the open market, and decreased stock value severely limits a company's ability to borrow money.

The irony is that companies that borrow get deeper into debt, and this has a potentially negative long-term impact on the stock value of the company. We see it all too often. Stock prices go up, investors take their profit out for the short-term kill, without regards for the long-term solvency of the company. Large long-term institutional investors, and the public are left holding the bag. So when the value of the stock market goes up, the slower moving institutional investors and the less informed average investor will benefit along with the stock manipulators (however at a lesser proportionate gain per share); however, when things start to sour, the horse drops the cart and heads for greener pastures, while the cart remains stuck in a gully.

The stock market is a macrocosm of an investment club. With investment clubs, individuals pool their capital to support the economic well-being of their investment choices. The basic premise is sound, and provides a means of more rapid economic growth to companies. The hope is that the increased operating capital provided by investors will translate into a company growth rate that significantly exceeds the amount invested, thereby providing a handsome dividend to investors, even after a company assumes additional debt from borrowing outside of the investment group. Without the invention of investor clubs that evolved into the stock market, and the legal creation of the perpetuating corporate entity, the great economic boom of this century could not have been possible.

But are times changing? Is all of this paper profit actually beneficial to the economic strength of American industry, and therefore the nation as a whole? Or is the system set up to benefit the sophisticated mobile class of wealthy investors who move money internationally among the major stock markets, sometimes to the disadvantage of American corporations? Why should our national confidence be based on the health of the stock market? When the market is up, the rich become wealthier, yet the ranks of the poor increases as middle-class Americans find themselves in unemployment lines. This happens because money not paid to employees is reallocated to pay for larger executive salaries and bonuses, and to increase the return on investment to shareholders. When the market is down, employees are laid off to provide savings that again translates to protecting the investors and corporate executives. Either way, the working-class gets shorted. The double blow comes when the market is down, and workers' retirement pension programs that are invested in stocks lose value; and consequently lessens the amount of retirement protection.

The solutions are simple. The short-term and especially the long-term health of corporate America, and consequently American jobs, would benefit from the stability that would be created if investors were required to reinvest a significant amount of capital back into the companies to support the infrastructure of the company (improvements in plant, equipment, and workforce) and to reduce the net effect of debt. For instance, if at the time an investor sells his shares, the stock value has increased by 20%, then 20% of the increase should revert to the company's reinvestment fund, leaving the investor a net gain of 16% over the purchase price. This may encourage investors to invest for the long-haul, adding to the stability of American corporations.

Obviously, something must be done to curb the outrageous incoherent compensation plans given to corporate executives without regard to corporate performance. Executives, who are responsible to manage America's industries in a responsible way, should have a particularly high stake in reinvesting a significant portion of their profits back into their corporations. Exercising stock options to take out $ millions from a company, receiving 100 times the salary of the average worker, abusing the company expense accounts, and setting themselves out as a special class of power brokers who wine and dine with politicians, showing little respect to their rank and file workers, and professing other megalomaniac attitudes have only weakened America's economy. Would a good father keep 100 times the average family income for himself, while the rest of the family lives on a near-starvation diet? This is exactly what corporate executives are doing to its own family. And with each American family whose breadwinner is laid off and cast into hardship and self-doubt, having to depend on public assistance programs for survival, America suffers as a nation.

AMERICAN WORKER, A NEW PERIOD OF SUFFRAGE

The typical American worker has lately been characterized as being lazy and illiterate. Americans work a shorter average work week than the Japanese. So what? Before collective bargaining, corporate abuse of the American worker was severe. Twelve to sixteen hour days and six day work weeks were common.

Child labor was a disgrace. Working conditions were hazardous and contemptible. Workers finally exerted their collective voice for humane treatment, resulting in the rise of unions and protective legislation. Much of America's economy growth occurred during a period of unionization. With the gradual demise of union influence (due in part to unions taking on the similar insensitive attitudes as traditional management, corruption, and lackluster gains for its employees) during a period characterized by more responsible employee protection regulations, we have seen a corresponding decrease in worker productivity.

When unions were active, workers felt a sense of banning together for common purposes, to demand fairness from management. The sense of camaraderie created a pride that translated to a reputation for hard work and quality products. Widespread employee rights legislation took the thunder out of the union movement. Why should workers pay union dues to obtain the same benefits and wage increases that would be provided by employers without bargaining units? After President Reagan fired all of the air traffic controllers who were on a union strike (and banned them from future federal employment), the public realized how ineffectual unions could be. Unionized workers who stuck the Los Angeles Herald-Examiner newspaper never received a raise, nor got their jobs back. Instead, the paper eventually went out of business. These absolute attitudes of non-compromise and disregard for unionized worker rights by government and big business send a strong message to the American worker... if you strike, take a hike.

The American worker was steadily becoming demoralized. Job security was no longer a viable concept. It would not be uncommon for workers to experience unpredictable and periodic lay-offs when various sectors of the economy would experience recessions as a result of political, corporate, and international manipulations. Technology was quickly changing the face of the American work place, realigning the biological clock to the pace of computerized mechanisms of work, from the office to the assembly line. The workplace was becoming a dehumanizing experience. It become unlawful to express personal opinions, and the exercise of the freedom of speech often resulted in punitive sanctions by the employer or governmental agencies. Workers not only had to worry about job security as a function of economic factors, but had to be concerned about the idle things they said at the workplace that might be interpreted by people as being sexist, racist, or anti-gay, etc. Interpersonal relations had to suffer as a people became reticent to expose their true feelings. While restraint may have had a superficial effect of smoothing over relations at work, a deep undercurrent of estrangement, alienation, and demoralization of the American worker developed, often leading to greater long-term stress-related problems. Worker dissatisfaction statistically translates to increased absenteeism caused by on-the-job injuries, illnesses and personal leaves; consequently a decrease in productivity. To make matters worse, executive compensation was often at the expense of worker layoffs.

An attitude of let the workers be damned, and blame the workers for America's economic woes was fostered by many who attempted to focus attention away from the real causes of America's economic problems... corporate greed, decreased reinvestment in the means of production, overextended credit debts, exportation of American jobs, control of economic factors by a minority of the wealthy elite, and politicians who feel more responsive to special interests than to the electorate. The American worker built this great nation. When the American worker is healthy, the nation's economy is healthy. When the American worker can not earn enough to be the mass consumers of the products of industry, then the economy will suffer. If corporations can not sell their goods, then they too will suffer. Each dollar earned by a typical worker is recycled in the internal economy 7 to 10 times, creating additional jobs and economic opportunities. American's have a rich tradition of being resourceful, and the vast majority of new jobs since 1970 have been created by small businesses during the same period when corporations have been laying off millions of workers to increase corporate profits and executive compensation. The wealthy powerbrokers are sowing the seeds for worker rebellion. Corporate executives must realize that in the long run, the prosperity of their companies are directly proportional to the prosperity of their workers. The American worker can become a formidable foe to corporate interests when pressed to the wall.

Corporate America has been able to obtain pro-business special interest tax breaks and legislation only because the average voter has been relatively satisfied, apathetic, and disinterested in political action. A dissatisfied electorate can be a formidable foe to politicians who they believe have lead to their economic misfortunes; and consequently, could elect a new breed of responsible politicians who would be more responsible to worker interests. Only short-sighted corporate executives would fail to recognize that keeping the American worker happy is good for business and long-term corporate health.

THE CONCENTRATION AND CONTROL OF WEALTH

Economics is taught in elite universities, yet all of these experts (who perpetually disagree with each other) have been unable to predict the actions of the economy with any measurable degree of accuracy. Much of the development of economic theories served to bolster the careers of so-called expert academicians, many of whom can not even balance their own checkbooks. Why not advance complex economic models and theories, such as Keynesian economics, supply-side economics, Reaganomics, and other approaches that when followed have seriously have acted to create imbalances in the economic system that have primarily benefited the wealthy.

When we eliminate the technical sounding jargon of theoretical economics, and apply common sense (as in dollars and cents), economic relationships can be explained in simple terms and concepts based on the law of cause and effect. There are four basic components of any economy; first, natural resources; second, manmade goods and services; third, distribution; and finally, value that is created by demand. The collective manipulations of the powerbrokers who control portions of these economic elements causes imbalances, and result in economy conditions that skews toward those who controls any of its elements. When any particular group controls the first three components, they develop a virtual monopoly on the fourth. Different political systems utilize laws to alter the natural relationship between these four elements of economy to shift wealth from its unprotected classes (the poor and consumer classes) to its protected classes (the economic and political powerful).

For many centuries, nations with formidable merchant and military shipping had the power to control global economic forces. In the recent past, the railroad, oil, automobile, and banking industries have exercised awesome control over the forces of the economy. Railroads gave way to air and trucking; oil became undermined by Arab excesses; the auto industry declined in the face of strong foreign competition; and unsound banking practices eroded depositor trust. Airline deregulation led to destructive series of price cutting and other gimmicks that decimated the industry. The strength of most of these power industries of the past were primarily based on controlling the means of distribution.

The new era of information processing permitted technologically driven industries to make fortunes. Telecommunication, electronic media, and computer hardware/software advances permitted a quantum leap in information processing efficiency. Technology had its greatest impact in two areas; first in improving manufacturing quality and efficiency, and second in cybernetics by providing almost instantaneous feedback on the effects of decision-making. Information technology provided business with the means for better internal control and simultaneously created new direct marketing opportunities through telephone and television. Information technology has produced new powerbrokers who will have an increasingly pervasive effect on influencing almost every aspect of our lives, and will gain a place among the traditional groups that have controlled the economy.

Yet, even without information technology, life can go on. It is not essential for bringing the basic necessities to doorsteps of the middleclass consumers. Food and shelter must still involve the human element, the pickers, builders, and drivers. While computers now assist in designing homes, and in ringing up prices at the supermarkets, people are still needed to build houses and to bring the food to the stores... at least for the foreseeable future. The human element (though to a lesser degree) is still required to keep the wheels of the economy going. Information technology by itself does not permit control of the economy, but assists those groups already exercising significant control to increase their ability to control economic factors.

The oil industry still exerts the greatest influence on the economy; however, health care, pharmaceuticals, information technology, telecommunications, and insurance are making great strides in affecting economic factors. Corporations that control significant portions of these industries will further increase their share of the economy, enabling them to dictate prices without regards for the natural effect of supply and demand.

Back during the late 1960s and early 1970s, a major national labor union was almost able to position itself to greatly influence the price of food, except for the opposition of the fledgling United Farm Workers Union. Any group that is able to control a natural resource, labor, and distribution would be able to control prices, and consequently demand for that product. Agricultural mechanization has reduced much of the labor intensiveness of food production; however, had that union national union succeeded to organize farm workers back in 1965, they would have controlled the labor of food production and transportation, two of the 3 economic elements. And if representation of the supermarket checkers could have been wrestled from the AFL-CIO, then the chain of food production from the fields to the dining room table would have been complete. Presently, the greatest threat to low food prices is the growing elimination of small farmers, resulting in a concentration of control of natural resources in the hands of giant agribusiness conglomerates.

THE MAGIC OF SUPPLY AND DEMAND USING SMOKE AND MIRRORS

The basis concept of supply and demand appear simple enough. A simple example would illustrate the effect of supply and demand. If ten people lived on an island, and the only source of food was fish, and there existed 10,000 fish, it is likely that the value of each fish would be such that fish would be used in barter to obtain other goods and services. However, if there were 10 people and only 100 fish, the value of each fish would increase such that people would desire to barter other goods and services to obtain fish. If there exist a limited supply of anything of value, its value will increase as a result of any increase in the number of persons having a demand. Taking the same example, if only 100 fish existed, but an abundance of fruit trees grew in the wild, then the value of fish would decrease because a demand for fish would decrease.

What happens to confound the natural relationship between supply and demand is the effects of mass advertising. Sophisticated marketing techniques coupled with the vast influential power of high tech telecommunications has the effect of magic... the use of smoke and mirrors and slight of hand to fool the average consumer into making decisions based on deception. Creating desire (demand) based on slick techniques to convince the American consumer that particular products are more valuable than they may be in reality. Thousands of companies have bought into the concept that advertising on television and other mass media improves their market share. The tremendous cost of mass advertising is always passed on to the consumer in terms of higher product prices. Advertisers like to call this "value added", when it fact it is usually nothing more than waste and deceptive packaging on a grand basis to mislead the general public into buying products worth less than the price that they are charged subsequent to advertising. We all would be paying for $500 toilet stainless steel toilet seats if the average American was as stupid as the government buyers. Fortunately, most Americans still possess common sense.

Let's take a look at how the price of a typical product is inflated 1000% from the point it first starts out as raw materials. Take a hypothetical example of the now world famous "widget" (I have yet to ever see one). Let's say that all widgets contain one pound of aluminum and one pound of glass, and it takes one hour of labor to manufacture the final product. For some industries, the 800% value added to a manufactured product may be low because retail mark-up can be as high as 300-500%, not simply 100%, as is stated in this example (name brand tennis shoes, clothing, and jewelry, etc.).

Value is a fluctuation of human desire, an emotion that can be manipulated by cultural and societal influences. Scarcity of products desired by people will cause the value of those products to increase; however, scarcity for undesired products will not increase the value of unwanted products. Mass marketing is a method by which psychological suggestions are made within the context of societal and cultural dispositions to effect an emotional response pro or con pertaining to a particular product, service, or idea. Value is a subjective emotional perception that does not require factual content. Stocks and bonds, insurance, and other forms of speculative investments are primarily based on a perception of future value.

C11 - LEGAL

American have become infatuated with civil lawsuits as the method to receive extraordinary compensation to redress losses caused by third parties, with lawyers driving up the ante. There is one "Pleading" form that all potential litigants should become familiar with, as it begins with filing this one form that sets into motion all subsequent actions in our legal system to address grievances and damages suffered by victims of crime, property damage, or accusations based upon imaginary, contrived or manipulated circumstances.

Names of attorney(s)

Firm's name and address

[Name of the Court]

Plaintiff name(s),   ) Case No.: No. [case number]

        Plaintiff,   )

    vs.   ) [Title of Pleading]

Defendant name(s),   )

        Defendant   )

)

)

)

)

)

Dated this   day of

                                      Firm's name and addresss

                                      Names of attorney(s)

Both our legal system and criminal justice system are severely challenged to deliver justice, due process and the right to a speedy trial, and consequently lengthy court proceedings is a tacit denial of justice. The problem with our court and prison system is due primarily to a back log and excessive demand on the limited resources that has become exacerbated by unreasonable mandatory sentencing laws that floods the courts and jails with non-violent drug offenders who use illegal drugs for personal recreation or due to addictive behavior. Meanwhile, once imprisoned with violent criminals, robbers and thieves, these non-violent inmates learn how to survive in prison by capitulating to gangs and criminal minds. This creates a constant revolving door of small time criminals becoming persistent criminals who learn from other inmates how to commit more serious crimes once they are released.

The solution to prison overcrowding, court calendar backlogs, and high rates of criminal recidivism is simply not to put non-violent offenders in jail in the first place, but rather to divert them to electronic house arrests or community corrections programs where they can be treated for addiction, mentored, monitored and guided to better law-abiding lives. Another major problem is the plethora of new laws while retaining antiquated laws on the books. America is supposedly a free country, but in reality if something is free and not taxed, it's probably illegal. It's a challenge to list ten activities that are not illegal, excepting purchase of products, services, space and venues from legitimate tax paying businesses.

The codification of legislation and classification as felonies is rampant where over 90% of laws are categorized as felonies when all "victimless" crimes should instead be considered as misdemeanors or infractions, with fines and community service as the penalties rather than lengthy incarceration. Prison is where murderers, rapists, child molesters, home invasion robbers, and other violent criminals should be interred. All others need not overburden either our prisons or criminal justice system. If offenders don't pay reasonable fines, their bank accounts are attached or their motor vehicles or other assets are seized in payment. If they are already impoverished, they can serve longer community service sentences. Why burden our courts with adjudicating minor offenders who tie up the court system and overcrowd the prisons? Let's reserve the criminal justice and court system for the serious cases that need to be resolved to protect the public or to redress genuine harm and grievances.

C12 - POPULATION CONTROL

The fear of unsustainable global population growth and the likely negative consequences on world hunger, environmental pollution, global warming, deforestation, species extinction, and a wide assortment of national and global issues is driving the push toward *The Impending New World Order.* To understand the population control goals of internationalist thinkers and key elite national and world policy makers, we must examine the historical unequal relationship between the developed First World order, developing nations and undeveloped 3rd World nations. As the de facto leader of the First World, the U.S. has been and is responsible for enforcing the disparity that exists between wealthy and poor nations. Terrorism has been a consequence of the population control policies of the First World, otherwise referred to as the North. The underdeveloped nations comprise primarily the 3rd World, or the nations of the South. As the leader of the North, much of the blame and responsibility for global outcomes and problems lie solidly on the shoulders of our foreign policy makers, whose strategy of economic exploitation, military containment, and regime change through political and cultural imperialism has resulted in an unstable and violent world.

In the period since the U.S.A. entered WW2 in 1941, the world has witnessed human atrocities against humans on a level never before recorded in history, including dropping two nuclear bombs, concentration camps, and genocide. The violence that followed WW2 was in many ways equally abhorrent, if not more so. The civil rights struggles, the Vietnam War, assassinations of JFK, MLK, RFK, Malcolm-X, Gandhi, and many lesser known patriots and humanitarians set the stage for contemporary state and non-state acts of violence. The horrific inhumanity of the Jewish Holocaust was only a few decades later followed by Pol Pot's Khmer Rouge slaughter of perhaps 8 million Cambodians. Idi Amin was known to laugh out loud when slaughtering hundreds of thousands of his own people in Uganda, the Tutus and Hutus killed each other in Rwanda, and China has witnessed the executions, imprisonment, and torture of millions. It has not been a peaceful world, as technology has both advanced the efficiency and effectiveness of violence, despite the so called Cold War nuclear deterrence.

Atrocities fostered or sponsored by Western political/military elites continued, who while espousing grand humanitarian ideals, have often betrayed the very principles they pretend to profess. Isn't the life of an African, or Asian, or Jew equally worth that of a Briton, American, German, or Swede? I surmise from standard of living statistics, that on the scales of First World hegemony, the answer is an emphatic "NO." Therein lies the basis of the international struggle between peoples, races, and ethnic groups. American history provides prime examples of First World tactics, as the genocide of Native Americans followed a pattern of false promises, broken treaties, and military violence, and African-Americans still suffer poverty, violence, and disease in alarmingly disproportionate levels, almost 140 years after slavery was abolished in the United States of America.

Why does First World hegemony want that entails tolerance of inhumanity in non-white states, often supporting oppressive regimes in Third World nations, which it attempts to prevent in Europe? The historical colonialist mentality still runs strongly through the blood lines of Europe's elites; only the revisionist strategy for world domination no longer lies in direct military confrontation, but in global economic control and domination, juxtaposed by military intimidation. Their vision continues to be one of a united Europe as the center of civilization, a feat first attempted by European royalty, and now made possible by the creation of multi-national corporate conglomerates owned by European and American elites. What they weren't able to accomplish with real people, they now are achieving through fictional entities (legal immortal corporations) and the utilization of technology.

Europe is in fact no more than a fictional continent created to satisfy an egomaniacal self-aggrandizing overcompensating need to deny their early backward and warring heritage. Europe is not physically a continent, but merely the western end of the Asian continent. This drive to create fictional entities (corporations), fictional (and worthless) global debtor monetary systems, deceptive and untruthful marketing, political, and bureaucratic institutions and ideals are all part of their larger scheme of world domination. The First World Anglo-Germanic European-American plan for world domination is essentially the same in principle as it was when "The sun never set on the British Empire", only the methods have been disguised and repackaged to appear beneficial to the peace and economic progress of the developing world. It's a sales pitch that is leading the Third World eventually to genocide.

The smoke screen for the new world order is the accelerating dependency of developing world markets on the Western monetary system, the creation of a future justification for military intervention to protect Western assets, and the future wholesale rape of third world resources as repayment to World Bank members. The gradual genocide of Third World peoples through poverty, disease, racism, class warfare, violence, and military interventions (conventional, genetic, and nuclear) are methods of genocide. At the rate AIDS is decimating the population in Sub-Saharan Africa, NATO and UN troops, backed by First World corporate interests, will be called on in the future to "stabilize" Africa's infrastructure, as a pretext to develop its vast stores of natural resources for western products and consumption. The "silk road" to the eventual rape of Africa will be carved by bulldozers and the tracks of military vehicles.

A discussion of the effect of First World economic policies on the Third World cites scholars, whose work, when interlinked, supports the primary hypothesis that the First World's intentions and actions result in the genocide of Third World people. First World Hegemony has historically implemented an anti-Third-World genocidal strategy that continues today through *economic disequilibriums* and other forms of socio-economic and political-cultural displacements.[i] Population-to-resources, population-to-capital, racial, and cultural factors fail to explain the historical as well as the cross-national variation in economic development.

Economic dominance by the IMF and World Bank reinforces dependency of developing nations' economies under the threat of monetary destabilization caused by runaway debt. As AIDS decimates and weaken Africa, and increasing becomes a major public health concern in Asia and Latin America, government debt has reached the point where many Third World nation-states are essentially owned by creditor nations through the international monetary exchange system enforced by the IMF and World Bank. The First World installs corrupt puppet governments in the Third World, and rapes the natural resources of those continents while essentially enslaving their peoples to supply cheap labor for products of western consumption.

To further exacerbate the economic problems of the Third World, western nations try to find substitutes for what it buys by advancing scientific and technological discoveries. Many less developed countries export a single crop or commodity to raise capital, in a time when capital is flowing from the poor to the rich countries ($93 billion for the years 1983-87 - World Bank), investment funds to less developed nations are very limited.[ii] Western scientific advancement stands to make Third World commodities superfluous to the North. On the other hand, First World nations dictate the retail price of oil, an essential to Third World economies. While the Institut Francais due Petrole predicts a 25 to 50 percent reduction in the cost of extracting oil, they estimate the price of crude oil will increase 65 percent. At the retail level, oil prices can rise while extraction costs fall because retail prices determined by supply (which can be manipulated) and demand (which rarely decreases).[iii] The Third World is held in a noose, which tightens as the western demand for natural resources and commodities from the South decrease due to scientific and technological advancements in the North, coupled with First World manipulated higher retail crude oil prices, that exacerbates the South's financial crisis.

The First World is based upon a *historical culture of violence*, and spreads its culture in modern times through neo-colonialism and cultural imperialism via modernization and reform programs forced or exported to the Third World as marketing ploys to "sanitize" the world of non-western ideas, customs, cultures, and religions that do not conform to the political ideology and capitalistic profit motive that drives the westernized global market system. There exist ample historical evidence to confirm the First World is based on a culture of violence. Early Caucasian barbarians were a cruel and violent people, preoccupied with war, and were the racial founding stock for most of northern Europe. Roman historians wrote of the pervasive violence of northern European society, noting that the Germans spent all their lives in hunting and warlike pursuits because they had "no taste for peace" but consider "war and plunder" the only honorable pursuits.[iv] Among Europeans, strength determines status, and the warrior societies were ruthless and aristocratic; in Gaul only the Druids and warriors "are of any account or consideration", as the common people were typically treated almost as slaves.[v] The Anglo-Irish were constantly occupied by endless petty warfare, even into present day times. Their culture was typified by strong kinship loyalties, lawlessness, and predatory violence which came to characterize the English aristocracy, who "consider that nothing brings you more honor than wholesale slaughter."[vi]

The upper classes felt "superior" to the lower, and members of the wealthy bourgeoisie assumed many of the attitudes of the aristocracy, including the self-adulating notion of genetic superiority.[vii] Blatant examples of cultural imperialism based upon the notion of white racial and cultural supremacy continues to be a subliminal driving force in First World domestic and international policies. During the 1920's the racial and ethnic diversity of the American population produced a mass interest in a racial eugenics movement. Increased concern over the low fertility of the white upper classes along with paranoia over the "race suicide" of superior Anglo-Saxons led to advocacy of "positive" eugenics (including increasing the fertility of the genetically superior) and "negative" eugenics (causing the "inferior stocks" to reduce their fertility).[viii] Hodgson observes that populations are still being shaped to conform to racial or ethnic preferences and genocide, a dramatic example of such shaping, is regularly attempted.[ix]

The repression of the real or imagined violence of dissidents is also justified, and enters through violent representations in popular culture, the media, television, films, the theater, and music.[x] The forces of development and modernization combine to destroy traditional rural life in Third World countries, resulting in a constant pressure to emigrate from rural areas.[xi] Kasarda concludes that technology has fundamental influence on a society's social organization, and although societies create innovation and technology, it is the application of technology that is the cause of social change.[xii]   These subordinated groups are the historical victims of western colonialism, or a result of the way colonial empires were carved up, and the resulting conflicts between nations, peoples, and minorities, often resulted in violent suppression, even genocide. Since 1945, state-sponsored violence toward ethnic and political groups caused more deaths, injuries, and human suffering than "all other forms of deadly conflict, including international wars and colonial and civil wars". Other costs are incalculable, including the extinction of languages, cultures, and ways of life, destruction of cultural and historical treasures, and loss or damage to residences, industry, and commerce.[xiii] Nagengast questioned the kind of future that newly emerging elites desire in a world order, in which the possibilities for rejecting the power of the west is unlikely, where socialism has been discredited, and where there aren't other alternatives on the horizon. How, under this predicament, will new relationships of power and knowledge emerge and be resolved?[xiv]

The Chinese stated before a UN committee, "In our opinion, the primary way of solving the... problem lies in combating the aggression and plunder of the imperialists, colonialists and neo-colonialists, breaking down the unequal international economic relations, winning and safeguarding national independence, and developing the national economy and culture independently and self-reliantly in the light of each country's specific conditions and differing circumstances, and raising the living standards of the people.[xv] It is highly doubtful that the North will agree with this Chinese perception. The Chinese perception of history is shared by a majority of Third World nations, and substantial numbers of Western historians, when they stated, "Social-imperialism asserts that 'only economic development with my aid can solve your population problem.' This is a ruse. It goes without saying that economic development is necessary for a country to emerge from poverty and solve its population problems. The point is that what social-imperialism calls 'economic development' is nothing but a fraud if it is not coupled with the fight against imperialism and hegemonies and a change in the unequal international economic relations.'"[xvi]

Nagengast reports the crisis of present day states results from its disparate concentration of power and the contradiction between it, and the demands of disempowered peoples who have created new positions that challenge the definitions of who and what ought to be repressed.[xvii]   The intelligentsias of the nineteen century and leaders of nationalist movements in Europe and North America had economic reasons for what they saw as a rational, democratic movements toward modernity and capitalism. The concepts of nation and nationalism in Europe and North America are the offspring of colonial expansion, religious wars, rationalism, and capitalism that serve as justification and political legitimization for certain notions of territorial, political, and cultural unity enforced by the hegemony of liberal thought and organization.[xviii] Consequently, the Nagenstate observes that "the world is in transition from strict acceptance of sovereign jurisdiction and non-intervention to more and more readiness to undertake... action, up to and including military action, that would in the past have been considered intervention in domestic affairs."[xix] Kasarda observed, "While it is true that social (e.g. religious/ethnic) and economic elites wield great power, their abilities to gain hegemony over a nation's future depend on capturing and holding the political machinery. Second, these theorists post that coalitions organized around shared self-interest combine either to exert pressure on the state or to dominate it, and the express purpose of these activities is to generate laws that divert social surplus to special interests.[xx] Olson suggests that since natural resource endowments, differences in capital stocks, cultural variation in responses to economic incentives, the features of the international system are not sufficient to explain economic development. Consequently, it would seem the institutions and policies of countries would have to be important,[xxi] as the politics of the First World pervasively intrudes into the governance of the 3rd World.

The First World uses calculated *military intimidation*, and support destabilizing non-cooperative states in the Third World and utilizes measured force to maintain economic and political hegemony. In addition to cultural propensities for violence, the First World developed philosophical justification for the need and desirability for violence and military actions. Malkki observed that wars have created tens of millions of displaced individuals and families originating in the Third World. The causes of their plight are conflicts kept alive mostly by superpower politics and by weapons manufactured in the rich countries, who export death and destruction to the Third World in exchange for importing the natural and partly processed products of the poor countries.[xxii]

According Pasqualucci, a sustaining justification of western thought is that depopulation through war appears to be a natural phenomenon, as if nature itself wishes to prevent the human pretension to eliminate war forever.[xxiii] Thomas Hobbes felt it perfectly legitimate to establish colonies to solve the problems raised by overpopulation,[xxiv] adding, "in any case, a war of conquest appears here to be perfectly legitimate... when the excess of population in his own country becomes unbearable, the Sovereign 'has to', has the duty to, 'transplant,' if he can, the excess of population in another country, whether inhabited or not, and without being obliged to ask permission from anybody.[xxv]

The North fear the warnings of the prophetic philosophers, intellectuals, and speculators of their time, such as Thomas Malthus and Thomas Hobbes, who would likely support paranoid doomsday scenarios, as justification for Northern warmongering. Hobbes believed Malthusian vision, when he stated that, "The development of mankind will come to an end "when all the world is overcharged with inhabitants"... therefore the only remedy for such a state of things is once again... a war of extermination... there will be no prisoners... because the scope of such a war is precisely that of making the space of the world as void as possible of inhabitants, to the point that the most frightful war of extermination will take place one day as the "last remedy of all." In his opinion, there is no doubt that the progress of mankind will end in a universal, apocalyptic conflagration,[xxvi] adding, "Behind the growth of the multitude in the Third World, there seems to be a messianic impulse, a thrust, to conquer the rest of the world in order to 'regenerate' it in the name of an ideology and a religion....in that 'perpetual and restless desire of power after power, that ceaseth only in death,....'"[xxvii] It's only too obvious that western political thinkers believe that the most efficacious way to save the world for the North, is to make space, by eliminating the burgeoning populations of the South.
The prevailing First World view is that *overpopulation and ecological* pressures provide justification to consider and pursue surreptitious genocidal programs in the Third World. Malthus proposed a theory of overpopulation in a zero-sum game of survival, where unchecked overpopulation will eventually exhaust the world food supply. Based on Malthusian ideas, the First World has formulated the "overpopulation paradigm" that blames rapid population growth on poverty, illiteracy, and cultural propensities, typical of the Third World.[xxviii]

The Overpopulation Paradigm:

The UN's 1993 estimated population projected in 2020 is between 7.6 to 8.5 billion.[xxix] Cohen observed that around 10,000 year ago, there were roughly 6 million people on Earth.[xxx] Today, there are more than 6 billion people. The human population increased by a factor of about 1,000 in 10,000 years. Cohen made a similar projection applying the estimated 1995 population growth rate of 1.6 percent per year. If growth of 1.6 percent per year persists for 436 years, the population will have increased to at least 1,000 fold. If people and the planet can not absorb a tenfold, rather than a 1,000 fold increase in population size to 60 billion, then the present global growth rate cannot continue even another 150 years.[xxxi] The world's population has doubled over the post-war period, from 2.5 billion in 1950 to more than 5 billion in 1990, and is likely to more than triple between 1950 and the projected total of nearly 8 billion in 2020.[xxxii] Tapinos reported according to the UN, in 1970, the geographic distribution of human population in the world was 30 percent in developed areas, and 70 percent in less developed areas. In 1980, the ratio changed to 24 and 76 percent.[xxxiii] In 1990, the population distribution exceeded 80 percent in less developed nations.

The First World refuses to recognize that the solution to overpopulation is to uplift the conditions of the Third World, who they blame for causing the degradation of the planet's resources, though in fact, it is the First World that consumes over 80% of the world's resources and contributes a similar percentage to its pollution, global warming, and species extinctions. The United States uses over half of all the raw materials consumed each year; as less than 1/15 (1970) of the world's population required more than the remaining part to maintain its over consumptive position. As present trends continued, in 20 years, we will get much less than 1/15th of the population, and yet we may use some 80% of the resources consumed.[xxxiv] In 2000, the U.S. population was estimated to exceed 275 million people[xxxv], compared to the world's 6.1 billion inhabitants,[xxxvi] which accounts to approximately 4.5% of the world's population utilizing most of its nonrenewable resources. In 2013, world population stands in excess of 7.3 billion and Kremer notes demographic evidence clearly indicate that if population grows at finite speed when income is above a steady state, per capita income will rise over time. If population growth declines at high levels of income, per capita income will rise

103

over time. However, data also suggest that higher levels of income and technology may reduce fertility by increasing wages and thus the value of time, by increasing education and the relative value of women's time. He concluded that population growth increases at low levels of income, then decreases in high levels of income.[xxxvii]

Reacting to capitalist background and the Malthusian basis of Anglo-Saxon thinking, which viewed overpopulation as the cause of poverty, almost all developing countries favored the Marxist idea that the real cause of poverty was unequal distribution of wealth, both among and between countries, and that overpopulation was a symptom rather than a cause of the basic problem. The Third World argues that economic and social development, especially more equitable distribution of economic gains among the poorest areas, would be at least, if not more effective in reducing fertility as family-planning programs.[xxxviii] Keyfitz explained that the less developed countries contain four-fifths of the world population, are responsible for nine-tenths of present population growth, and can expect 100 percent of the world's population growth during the first century of the new millennium. Consequently, they do not have the space, land, or the capital to support their exploding citizenry. The demand for their raw materials constituted the economic foundation on which they attempted their upward course, but scientific advances in developed nations has invented substitutes that undercut the need for Third World resources.[xxxix]

Wilmoth noted that the "orthodox" view of the disadvantages of rapid population growth and of the possibility for positive strategies to lower birthrates in less developed countries (LCDs) dominated political discussions of the topic during the 1960s and 1970s.[xl] The dominant theme of the articles of this era was that population growth is rapid and threatens the welfare of human beings and other species.[xli] It was thought that rapid population growth threatened the very survival of the human species, due to finite limits on the availability of resources as land, water, and fossil fuels. They concluded that population growth must somehow be brought under control, either through limitations on reproduction or through an increase in the death rate. Since growth is limited by finite resources, the only sensible solution is to limit population size to a sustainable level. The North feared that inaction will eventually lead to ecological disasters that will result in widespread famine, disease, misery, and, potentially, the extinction of the human species.[xlii] Yates predicted that overpopulation and underproduction in major nations of the Third World will result in great famines and pose future questions of life and death significance to the world community.[xliii]

Wilmoth believes that growth produces population pressure that accentuates the threat to the stability of world political systems. Population pressure may lead nations to press outward from their borders in search of living space, or it may foster internal political instability, leading in some cases to revolutions. Population pressure has been the cause of past wars and will continue to be a source of future conflict if population growth is not controlled, adding, "Rapid population growth is disadvantageous, as overcrowding has negative effects on the quality of human existence... producing a general deterioration in the quality of the natural and social environments of human societies. Overcrowding brings in its train a host of adverse side effects, including urban congestion, pollution, shortages of housing and recreational space, and various forms of 'social pathology' that increases the role of governments at the expense of individual liberties."[xliv]

This fear of potential extinction, drives the North to the argument based on a perception that one population (or sub-population) is losing or will lose control over some vital aspect of social and political life due to its relative decrease in numbers in comparison to other groups, and consequently, a race suicide framework materializes when population growth is viewed as unfavorable to the population fearful of losing control.[xlv] Without a globally coordinated concentrated effort to stabilize population size at a level far lower than currently projected, the earth's ecosystems and the living standards of increasing numbers of the world's people will deteriorate. An immediate decrease in world population growth will provide time to make necessary changes, and to develop new technologies and alternative energy sources.[xlvi]

Brundtland reports that ninety percent of the world's population increase is occurring in developing countries, many of which are unable to feed their present population.[xlvii] He suggests that the industrialized nations must change their production and consumption patterns to use less natural resources and cause less pollution, adding that development in poor countries must be planned to eliminate poverty, meet basic human needs, and to protect the environment.[xlviii] He notes that population growth must be slowed to allow sustainable development because poverty, overpopulation, and underdevelopment are all interlinked. The fastest population growth is burdening the poorest nations, which are least able to meet the needs of new births and to invest in their future. Brundtland concludes that the increasing numbers of people in poor countries are deteriorating the earth and creating permanent damage to the environment because they struggle to survive, and cannot be concerned with planning for a tomorrow that may never come. As a result, impoverished environments in turn lead to even greater poverty, and a vicious cycle is created.[xlix]

Brundtland observes that any nation's main asset should be its population, lamenting, "But when that population grows too fast, it becomes a liability instead." He noted that a rapidly growing population stifles the best efforts to provide proper education, nutrition, health care and shelter, while the earning capacity of the labor force suffers, and problems are compounded as job opportunities don't keep pace with the numbers seeking jobs. As wages go down and poverty is exacerbated.[l] He proposed enhancing the role of women to increased economic growth, reduced poverty, provide better child and family welfare, and to lower birth rates. He warns that if men avoid responsibility for their sexual habits, fertility, and health, and if they reject their parental obligations, it will be impossible to deal with population growth, and with sexually transmitted diseases, including AIDS.[li]

Finkle observes that as more governments identify their "population problem" as rapid population growth, leaders of developing countries realize that the health of their societies is dependent on the ability to provide jobs, schools, housing, and health care for their citizens, all of which are made more difficult by rapid population growth.[lii] He proposes the need for reducing the rate of population growth in order to remove major obstacles to economic development.[liii] Just how the North proposes to limit, reduce, and reverse population growth in the South is unclear. One thing is certain, the economic policies that western nations have implemented in regards to almost all of the Third World, have served to reduce economic development, which has resulted in faster population growth, and the institutionalizing of a vicious cycle of poverty, starvation, disease, and illiteracy. And among the elite power circles in the First World, there continues to be serious leanings by intellectuals and political thinkers to blame the Third World's burgeoning population for the evils of the world, for planetary deterioration, and environmental pollution that, if not arrested and reversed, will eventually threaten the very existence of the human species. Some "experts" may even feel that Third World genocide is a benevolent policy.

The Environmental Impact Paradigm:

Keyfitz believes that the real limit to global population growth isn't determined by such things as the availability of food, natural disasters, or wars, but instead by the number of people who can be supported by the biosphere without disrupting its sensitive balance. Mankind is but one species among many, each with a place in nature, and each threatened with destruction if it grows to the point where it destroys the very environment upon which its existence depends.[liv] He observes that humans must co-exist with the AIDS virus and Ebola in the same manner as man-induced imbalance, measles, malaria, and other diseases, warning that human activities must not interfere with the inanimate aspects of the Earth that are essential for his existence, such as the ozone layer that provides protection from carcinogenic rays from space. He questions whether humans have the will to make sacrifices now, to protect the planet for future generations against the terrible consequences that may result from excessive human population,[lv] which he terms "an unstoppable collapse that follows from irreversible changes of which there are plentiful examples in the past."[lvi]

Environmentalists see the planet's condition today at risk in the face of the far reaching, and unprecedented changes that the human population and its activities are now causing. Global warming is one such major concern, for example, as average air temperature in Denmark has increased 1.75 degrees Centigrade in 125 years from 1875 to 2000. If this rate of global warming continues, the ice caps will gradually melt, causing the flooding of coastal towns and cities, and in some cases reducing entire nation-states into nonexistence.[lvii] By the year 2100, as compared to 1990 levels, greater demand will cause dramatic increases in the production of energy from all sources, including; a 50 percent increase in fossil fuel, a doubling of biomass, a quadrupling of hydroelectricity, a nine-fold jump in nuclear energy, and a twelve-fold expansion in renewable energy technologies. This will cause atmospheric CO_2 concentration in 2100 to increase from 355 ppm to a likely 500 ppm, a 40 percent increase from 1990 levels.[lviii]

Grant provides additional global warming data, as an assessment confirmed a rise of between 0.3 deg. C to 0.6 deg. C in global mean surface temperature in the past century, and a related rise in global sea level of 10 to 25 cm. These rates will result in a temperature increase of of 1.0 deg. to 3.5 deg. C by 2100, which is far faster than any warming trend in the Earth's past 10,000 years. Global warming will cause a rise of 15 –95 cm in average sea level by 2100, and the changes in both temperature and sea levels will continue in the centuries beyond 2100 *even if greenhouse gas concentrations are stabilized at current levels.*[lix] He further predicts that a complete melting of the Antarctic and Greenland ice caps would raise sea levels about 70 to 100 meters.[lx] Grant concludes that to avoid the greenhouse effect scenario that is primarily caused by human activities, a human population of perhaps 2 or 3 billion could be sustained at a decent level, commenting that this suggestion is less radical than it sounds, as it is where we were two generations ago (circa 1950).[lxi]

On the other hand, Cohen pointes to a theoretical projection of global population to the year 2150 (similar to that prepared by the United Nations, 1992) that assumes regional levels of fertility are constant at 1950 levels, while life expectancy increases; the calculated population of 694 billion in 2150 could not be fed with conventional agriculture and water sources because annual global rainfall would be insufficient to grow the crops required for food.[lxii] The renewable freshwater supply of the Earth is too limited for sustained agricultural irrigation and fertility, even if every drop of the 110,000 cubic kilometers of annual rain falling on land were used domestically for agriculture, and if people ate only 2,350 calories per day, the estimates of the maximum theoretical population that could be supported on Earth would range from 82 billion to 369 billion.[lxiii] Keyfitz brings forth an ethical dilemma by questioning what share of the remainder of our planet's capacity to absorb emissions is the First World entitled to, as compared to the claims of the Third World. How legitimate is the South's position if they fail to reduce population growth? While the North has for decades restrained its population to less than two children per couple, can the South realistically expect the same material standard of living when their families are producing three, four or more children per couple? How will the First World arbitrate the its claims the need to preserve resources for future generations against those of the present, while competing with the Third World for as much of the world's resources as the North needs.[lxiv]

Abernethy adds that waste and deterioration of natural resources is likely a normal practice because private and local incentives to conserve is insufficient due to demand and disbelief in scarcity, as consumers believe they are better off without a commitment to share.[lxv] It's often assumed that the great disparities in world living standards are due primarily to overpopulation in poor countries.[lxvi] Olson explains that given technology, fixed amounts of land and other natural resources, and level stocks of capital goods, increasing labor at some point yields diminishing productivity and also result in diminishing returns to nature's ability to absorb wastes.[lxvii]

In summary, the conventional wisdom of the First World that links population growth to potentially irreversible economic degradation is founded on four postulates:

1) The Earth's renewable resources, such as fresh water and aridable land mass for food production, are limited as in a zero-sum end game.

2) Population growth, particularly in the Third World, if unchecked, or even reversed, will lead to catastrophic and irreversible damage to our planet's ecosystem.

3) The First World's interest in self-propagation at a high standard of living is best served by limiting population growth in the Third World, preferably through strategies that limit or reverse their industrialization and population growth.

4) When increased human activities due to overpopulation impact the planet's closed biosphere to a point of diminished returns, great famines and disease will decimate the global population, primarily concentrated in the Third World.

In fact, each of these First World assumptions shifting blame primarily to Third World population growth in not only self serving, but erroneous in its very premises, which will be discussed later in this journal's summary.

The First World has historically, routinely, and systematically implements policies that result in the degradation, reduction, and genocide against dark-skinned peoples, in particular the black race. The North characterizes itself by eloquent statements in support of human rights, but a closer examination of western history discloses a sinister methodology of speaking "in the name of" some apparent humanitarian principle, only later to act "in spite of" the very principles they espouse. In the name of Christian brotherhood, the wars fought during the (un)Holy Crusades killed hundreds of thousands of "pagans", in order to save their souls, no doubt. In the name of "freedom" from supposed communist tyranny, the North killed millions of innocent women, men, and children as non-combatant "collateral" damage in South East Asia. Even Northern terminology is euphemistically and eloquently stated to reduce the appearance of its inhumane actions, by reducing the faces of those slaughtered into nomenclature only applicable to property, such as "collateral damage", as in damaged freight.

Nagengast defines political violence as overt state-sponsored or tolerated violence, which   may or may not be direct violence. The violence between Hutus and Tutsi in Rwanda and Burundi; between Tamils and Sinhalese in Sri Lanka; between Latinos and indigenous peoples in Guatemala; and among Croats, Serbs, and Muslims in the Balkans, is tolerated or encouraged by states to create, justify, excuse, explain, or enforce disparate hierarchies and inequalities. These are incidents of state violence; and even though states may not appear on the surface to be primary agents, the deliberate acts of agents of the state cause mass starvation and similar economic or political misdeeds that result in widespread deaths, and even genocide.[lxviii] Lubeck described the scale of crisis in Africa gives it no option but to rely on a "reformed state" to regulate activity; consequently, chaos, starvation, and disintegration of states through neocolonial structures will follow as neo-liberal policies are strictly enforced. He adds that without debt relief and concessionary grants, Africa's primary commodity exporters can never hope to pay off their external debts (i.e. 350% of GDP), no matter how many neoliberal reforms are instituted internally.[lxix]

Even in the most developed nation in the world, Peterson notes that a poverty paradox is one manifestation of a general deterioration in American society and culture where the spreading of an underclass culture (primarily blacks) is "undermining" the country's productive capacity, family life, social integration, and, ultimately its political stability.[lxx] Petersen remarks, "Those underclass groups, American blacks being the extreme case, were compelled to come to or were forcefully incorporated into the United States and, once there, were subjected to poverty, discrimination, and slavery, constructed for themselves a conflictual understanding of the country's social and political institutions as the product of class dominance, racial prejudice and discrimination, cultural exclusiveness, over which they had little control."[lxxi] Grimes stated that draft regulations of the 60s and 70s ensured that most of those sent Vietnam were the poor and the Blacks.[lxxii] One desire of white supremacists has always been the fantasy of an all white country, resulting in genocide, Indian massacres, slavery, manifest destiny, Detroit, East St. Louis, Watts, the Mexican War.[lxxiii]

Chinta Strausberg, writing in The "Chicago Defender", the oldest Black daily newspaper in America, warns Blacks must never forget the African Holocaust where more than 50 million lives were destroyed due to western greed for material wealth, further quoting Dr. James Small, a New York professor, who said:

"...these acts were crimes against humanity. All these people died because someone was greedy and wasn't willing to work for it for themselves, so they forced other human beings to do it.... "And in the process, they took the lives of nearly 50 million men, women and children when we count those captured... killed on the ground in Africa, died in the dungeons waiting for slave ships from diseases and hunger, died in the middle passage coming to America in the time it took to get here in those slave ships and those that died on the plantations....Our life expectancy during the early part of slavery was not much more than five years, and they didn't mind working us to death because it was easy to replenish us. "In that 500-year period, we lost almost 50 million people and there are those who want us to forget it like it never happened.... Every effort was made by the enslavers to take away and to deny the humanity of the African. They were treated as objects, less than human. The Europeans used us as if we were their property. When we talk about killing the African spirit, it refers to the intent of white supremacy the dehumanization of African people by enslavement.[lxxiv]

Hall reported that attached to the crime against humanity of enslavement was deprivation of liberty, forced labor, reduction of people into servitude, and trafficking in persons, particular women and children.[lxxv] Yates observed that humans destroy most species by destroying their habitats, rather than simply by killing them.[lxxvi] Habitat destruction is a phenomenon rapidly occurring in the Third World, especially in Africa. Commenting on the plight of Africa, the Chinese U.N. Delegation stated "... colonialists and imperialists subjected... Africa... to brutal aggression and enslavement... and have not only plundered enormous social wealth from... Africa, but also engaged in human trafficking and evicted or slaughtered local inhabitants. Africa alone has lost as many as 100 million people in this way... the social productive forces in... African... countries were seriously sapped.[lxxvii] The North has a long history of exploiting, enslaving, impoverishing and killing Blacks.

The United States of America hegemony, while marketing itself to the world as the defender of human rights, actually provides a platform that initiates, supports, and implements global genocide through surrogates and Third World agents. LaRouche reports a public declaration in the September 1946 edition of "The Bulletin of the Atomic Scientists", made by Bertran Russell, "who was emphatic in stating that he was promoting nuclear weapons for no other purpose but establishing world government. Russell insisted, then, and later, that the U.S.A. and Britain should prepare to bomb the Soviet Union with nuclear weapons, for the contingency that Soviet General Secretary Josef Stalin might refuse to submit to transforming the United Nations Organization into an actual world government, thus eliminating the sovereignties of all of the world's nation-states."[lxxviii]

Grimes observes that in Vietnam, the myth of America as liberator was in danger of collapse because during the Vietnam War, it was evident that American military forces was not liberating anyone, but was slashing blindly through the Vietnamese landscape murdering anyone, regardless of political persuasion.[lxxix] Singer argues that the largeness of current populations is not needed for progressive development or the maintenance of diversity, adding that if blunders result in a nuclear war, and thereby eliminate nine-tenths of the human lives on our planet, the scattered survivors would find themselves with the "appropriate" phenotype to enable a "wiser fresh start."[lxxx]

The U.S., long a supporter of war crimes trials for crimes against humanity, such as genocide, instead attempts to exempt itself from the legal jurisdiction of international courts to avoid the surrender of Americans. The chances that the United States will be able to win the exemption of Americans from the court's jurisdiction are diminishing rapidly.[lxxxi] Consequently, political choices in the Third World often appear to be determined by taking positions contrary to those of the United States, based on a simplistic syllogism:

1. The United States advises a particular policy.
2. Any advice of the United States corresponds to its own interests and might be, or is likely contrary to our interests.
3. Conclusion: We should reject American policies.[lxxxii]

This journal discussed the structural components of violence and power as facets of First World hegemony, and its projection through economic, cultural, and political imperialism, colonialism, and neocolonialism into the Third World. Utilizing various pseudo-intellectual ustifications such as "racial superiority", "overpopulation", and "environmental deterioration", the North has implemented military and economic strategies to subjugate, exploit, and degrade the states and people of the South. The increasing alarm over an expanding world population, predominantly in the Third World, is in large part motivated by a western paranoia of both becoming overrun by non-white people, and a potential threat to human existence due to the possible exhaustion of natural resources required for survival. This notion of "race suicide" compels the North to consider and devise self-propagation scenarios and strategies that act to the detriment of developing and underdeveloped states, up to and including genocide.

As a result of First World fears, avarice, and immorality, Pope John Paul II noted that broad segments of public opinion justify certain crimes against life in the name of individual freedoms and rights.[lxxxiii] The emergence of a "veritable culture of death" is fostered by powerful cultural, economic and political forces which encourage society to be overly concerned with efficiency. Consequently, from this point of view, the world has become in a certain sense, a war of the powerful against the weak.[lxxxiv] The Pope adds, "On a more general level, there exists in contemporary culture a certain Promethean attitude which leads people to think that they can control life and death by taking the decisions about them into their own hands. We see a tragic expression of all this in the spread of euthanasia, disguised and surreptitious or practiced openly and even legally... is sometimes justified by the utilitarian motive of avoiding costs which bring no return and which weight heavily on society. Thus it is proposed to eliminate malformed babies, the severely handicapped, the disabled, the elderly, especially when they are not self-sufficient, and the terminally ill. Nor can we remain silent in the face of other more furtive, but no less serious and real forms of euthanasia... Today not a few of the powerful of the earth are haunted by the current demographic growth and fear that the most prolific and poorest peoples represent a threat for the well-being and peace of their own countries.[lxxxv]

The proposed American "National Missile Defense" (NMD) system will permit the unchallenged projection of First World nuclear and economic power against the Third World. History has shown that the North routinely practices policies that ensure Euro-American global military, political, and economic dominance and control over world resources, to maintain their superior position utilizing policies that directly or indirectly result in the genocide of the world's non-white people, and destruction of Third World cultures, states, and regional economies.

How can Third World nations use the international forum to discredit the First World's recurring attempts to legitimize and justify genocidal policies as the ultimate solution to Third World overpopulation, that purportedly threatens the quality and existence of human life on Earth? There are intermediary steps that must be taken to forestall the North's use of weapons of mass destruction as a population control measure. First, the international community must agree to arrest population at current levels through sensible reproductive quotas and policies, and to reduce overall native populations over time. Couples must be limited to no more than two offspring, as a realistic population stabilization policy. This quota should result in an eventual drop in overall population due to an excessive rate of mortality from environmental causes and infant mortality over live births. In recent decades, China has made significant advances in developing their economy while successfully controlling population growth. The natural population growth rate dropped to 1.154 percent in 1983, from

2.089 percent in 1973, and the people's living standards have improved. The Chinese family planning and population controlled-growth policies, in tandem with planned economic development has been the correct model for China,[lxxxvi] and may be an effective model for the rest of the Third World.

Following China's example, the UN should encourage a global two live births per couple policy as a means to stabilize population, encourage a redistribution of excess First World resources to improve living standards and GDP, especially in less developed countries. Increasing the development and modernization of LDCs enhances global political and social stability that is a requisite for capital growth, which reinforces a cycle of increased modernization and development. Greater regional, common-market, and global commons trade should "raise the tide for all ships, large and small". It is likely the paradigm of uneven distribution of global resources from poor nations to the rich will continue, but First World nations know only too well that increasing economic development of LDCs will likely result in decreasing world population through peaceful, rather than traditional violent means. Grant (205) weighs in on population policy, insisting parents need have no more than two children to carry on their family, and while it was once necessary to have many children so that some might survive to maturity, that is no longer true in most parts of the world.

While every living being has a natural urge and right to reproduce, even in nature, excessive numbers of any species eventually lead to catastrophic suffering and mortality. In order to avert a mass mortality scenario for human beings, sensible international agreements and political policies must be made. China's one birth per couple policy is a sensible effort to decrease that nations population through non-violent means. Depending upon overall population demographics, international benchmarks might become necessary, such that nations with populations over 300 million must actualize a 1.5 live births per couple quota (as expressed by 3 live births per every two couples, utilizing a lottery system). Similarly, nations with 500 million or more populations must agree to a 1.25 births per couple quota. Nations with 1 billion or more population must agree to 1 birth per couple quota.

Only through implementing proactive non-violent population control strategies, coupled with improving non-polluting technologies, and providing capital incentives for political and social stabilization, will the First World lose its temptation to make genocidal "first strikes" against the developing world. History has shown that the First World hegemon will not do anything that is against its self-interests. Consequently, LDCs must take steps to negotiate strategies that will encourage First World capital investment in exchange for population control, returning a reasonable "Return On Investment" to the First World. The North owns and exploits over 80 percent of the world's non-renewable resources, consequently, it must restrain its avarice, and recognize its responsibility to redistribute at least a small percentage of excessive wealth, and restrict its consumption of world resources to no more than current levels.

The First World must act morally and responsibly to restrain its temptation to project violence. The First World must practice what it preaches, act as the champion of human rights which its philosophical and legal tenets profess. If the First World assists the development of LCDs in exchange for non-violent population control measures, the tide will rise for all humanity as biosphere destruction is arrested. But how likely are the First World elites and LCDs likely to adopt such rational approaches to the zero-sum game of population control and environmental protection? History and current environmental scans suggests a mixed and uncertain future.

Blands (25-26) stated that it required 35 years from 1965 for 3.3 B people to doubled in 2000 to 6.5 B people, a population that is inadequately fed by the cultivation of 56 percent of the world's arable land. If agricultural productivity in the less developed countries could be raised to that in the United States, there would be an enormous increase in agricultural output. By increasing the existing levels of agricultural production, as well as the potential for increasing the amount of land under cultivation, he found that the "potential gross cropped area would then be sufficient for 38-48 billion people, or 10-13 times the present human population of the earth. If these projections are reasonably accurate, it appears the world can still accommodate limited human population growth beyond the current 6.2 B people to 38 B, limited by arable land, or 82 B from natural rainfall limits.

Clinton warns that a population strategy targeting Third World birth rates could be taken as a form of repression, as a preventive form of class and racial genocide, and if all of population policy focused on limiting births, based on perceived upper limits of supportable birth rates, this would equate to a genocidal act of the rich against the poor, the white against the colored races, and the West against the East.[lxxxvii] Boot opines, "The global social structure is based on selfishness, maintained by power-play, marred by short-run vision, and managed by crisis-hopping. The rich, while luxuriating in wealth, pay lip-service to serious problems shared by all, but lack inclination to act decisively. In the back of their minds they surely believe in the survival of the fittest. They are the fittest. The poor, distrustful of the rich, are so burdened with short-run survival that the long-run problems seem insignificant."[lxxxviii]

Finnin discloses that "it requires about one-third of the world's annual extraction of nonrenewable resources to support the 6 percent of the world's population in the United States at the per capita level to which it is thought the rest of the world should become accustomed." He estimates that if U.S. levels of technology could prevail worldwide, current resources could support no more than 18 percent of the world's population at U.S. levels, with nothing left over for the remainder 82 percent. Paradoxically, without the labor services of the lower 82 percent, the rich 18 percent would not be as rich as they might think.[lxxxix]

Keohane summarizes the international predicament by stating, "The sources of hegemony therefore include sufficient military power to deter or rebuff attempts to capture and close off important areas of the world political economy. But in the contemporary world, at any rate, it is difficult for a hegemon to use military power directly to attain its economic policy objectives with its military partners and allies."[xc] He adds, "Hegemons require deference to enable them to construct a structure of world capitalist order. It is too expensive, and perhaps self-defeating, to achieve this by force; after all, the key distinction between hegemony and imperialism is that a hegemon, unlike an empire, does not dominate societies through a cumbersome political superstructure, but rather supervises the relationships between politically independent societies through a combination of hierarchies of control and the operation of markets. Hegemony rests on the subjective awareness by elites in secondary states that they are benefiting...."[xci]

In conclusion, a united international community can make inroads to resist and eventually change First World hegemonic paranoia by debunking the legitimacy of long held pseudo-scientific theories on the causes of poverty, population growth, ecological degradation, and economic-political competition in the perceived zero-sum end game from consumption of world resources.

1)   The Earth's resources are relatively untapped. Our deepest wells barely scratch the Earth's crust, and cheaper technology can be developed to increase global storage and supplies of fresh water (desalinization, etc.), as biotechnology continues to improve crop yields and the arability of land. Technology can also be called upon to restore the arability of top soil in non-productive regions, and top soil erosion can be ameliorated by digging into the crust to access the rich minerals contained in the Earth's mantle, as in volcanic magma. The rich resources of Africa and many areas of the world are essentially untapped, but these areas must not be exploited to the detriment of its native populations, who should instead be the beneficiaries of development. By removing the erroneous presumption that resource consumption is non-renewable and non-recyclable, the world can reject the notion of limits in a zero-sum end game, and begin to search for new sources of abundance located deeper in the crust, in volcanoes, geysers, and in the Earth's deep oceans and mantle. Alternative energy sources, based on discoveries in new quantum physics that can generate electricity and motion by harnessing strong gravitational forces, near frictionless materials, and electro-magnetic applications could be developed once "big oil interests" are politically reduced, as new technologies replace the need for burning fossil fuels for energy.

2)   Population growth, particularly in the Third World, would likely follow First World patterns of natural reduction that follows economic development, and the liberation of women from their roles as birthing machines. In the male dominated and chauvinistic world, men must take greater procreative responsibility, utilizing birth control methods to prevent child births when they are unable to afford the expense of childrearing. Having children simple to satisfy the egocentric desire to continue one's lineage is insufficient rationale for expecting women to give birth. Each child born into the world has a right, and deserves to have at a minimum, food, shelter, education, and love, with the goal of

liberty and self-actualization. Again, technological breakthroughs stand to assist family planning efforts, through reversible sterilization, surrogate birthing utilizing xeno-placental techniques, and other strategies that emphasize responsible parenting choices. Overbeek (191) explores the possibility of adding contraceptive agents to certain foods, providing another drug to neutralize the sterilizing effects of the contraceptive agent for those who desire pregnancy. If it were added to certain foods only, then only those wanting to be sterile could consume those foods.

3)   The First World's self-propagation at a high standard of living can best be assured by global partnership, and not wanton exploitation of the Third World. The waste that exist in the North alone, is more than sufficient to maintain the developing world, consequently, conservation in the First World allows the South to improve its economies, and through non-pollution strategies, both West and the East can become responsible partners to, and not abusers of our planet. The traditional "competition" paradigm must necessarily be replaced by a "partnership" paradigm.

4)   Human activities due to population growth need not have a negative impact on the planet's closed biosphere. A point of diminishing returns can be avoided if popular awareness drives a consistent motivation to conserve and respect the planet and its resources that gives humans life. As long as the First World has more incentives to partnership with the Third World, there will be less pressure for hegemonic exploitation and oppression of the poor. The world's monetary systems have for several decades been de-linked from the "gold standard." Many foreign currencies are linked to the stability of the U.S. Dollar. In reality, world trade flows between computers that track 1's and 0's, as the ledger between debits and credits. The strength of the world economy is in large part dependent on domestic and global confidence in the First World's (particularly the U.S.) ability to honor its currencies in exchange for technology, manufactured goods, and military assistance. In the hierarchy of the technological and commodities "food chain", the world's economy would collapse if the masses lost confidence in the purchasing value of western capital to buy "big ticket" items, such as ships, planes, tanks, manufacturing plants, and commercial computer systems, in addition to massive quantities of food and medicines that the west produces. The logical expectation is when a state's currency is honored for large top end items, it most certainly will support the daily purchases required to sustain comfortable lives.

The North must remove the blinders of its avarice, and realize that the rest of the world depends in large part on the First World's economic vitality and humane leadership. The Third World has little desire to threaten (nor is it capable of such) the West, and instead desires to partnership with it, rather than to be its victim. Gradually raising the economic tide of the world over a generation can solve most of persistent global problems, and offers a greater opportunity for sustained peace. The world economic paradigm must necessarily change from one of competition and exploitation to one of partnership and exchange. Only then will the peoples and governments of the world realize sustained and effective cooperation to reduce population growth, and the negative impact of humans on the global environment; therefore providing a realistic platform for human progress and evolution while safeguarding the planetary ecosystem for future generations.

The First World hegemon, occupying the superior power position, can show greater wisdom beyond its greed, and take proactive steps to harness the abundance of our planet, rather than to view the world through the prejudicial and reality distorting filters of gloom and doom. It is the North that currently possesses the resources, capital, and technology to take the world *beyond conflict, violence, and war*. The orthodox zero-sum game paradigm is ruining the planet, nations, and directly or indirectly results in the genocide of Third World peoples. The question is, what will it take for the hegemon to adjust its operative policies and philosophical constructs to permit it to view the world and its great diversity in a more realistic and positive framework? The bottom line is whether or not the violent prone First World hegemon has the desire and will to bring true human rights to the world stage, beyond political rhetoric and positioning for selfish gains. The hopes of the world's population depend on a constructive reorientation of the North's role in the global community, from one of foe, to that of friend, and if the First World can see that's in its own interest, anything is possible. Conflict, violence, war, and extinction is not inevitable or certain.

References:

Abernethy, Virginia, "Comment: The 'One World' Thesis as an Obstacle to Environmental Preservation," *Population and Development Review*, Vol. 16, Issue Supplement; "Resources, Environment, and Population: Present Knowledge, Future Options," (1990), 323-328.

Bland, Chester, and Dwight E. Lee, *Lectures in History* (Worcester, MA: Clark University Press, 1976).

Boot, John C. G., *Common Globe or Global Commons* (New York, NY: Marcel Dekker, 1974).

Brundtland, Gro Harlem, "Population, Environment, and Development." *Population and Development Review*, Vol. 19, Issue 4 (Dec., 1993), 893-899.

Chinese Delegation, "Chinese Statements on Population at Bucharest, 1974, and Mexico City, 1984." *Population and Development Review*, Vol. 20, Issue 2 (Jun., 1994), 449-459.

Clinton, Richard L., William S. Flash, and R. Kenneth Godwin, *Political Science in Population*

Cohen, Joel E., "Should Population Projections Consider 'Limiting Factors" - and If So, How?" *Population and Development Review*, Vol 24, Issue Supplement: "Frontiers of Population Forecasting" (1998), 118-138.

Finkle, Jasor L., and Alisen McIntosh, "The New Politics of Population," *Population and Development Review*, Vol 20, Issue Supplement: "The New Politics of Population: Conflict and Consensus in Family Planning" (1994), 3-34.

Finnin, William M. Jr., and Gerald Alonzo Smith, Editors, *The Morality of Scarcity, Limited Resources and Social Policy* (Baton Rouge, LA: Louisiana State University Press, 1979).

Gilland, Bernard, "World Population, Economic Growth, and Energy Demand, 1990-2100: A Review of Projections," *Population and Development Review*, Vol. 21, Issue 3 (Sep., 1995), 507-539.

Grant, Lindsey, *Juggernaut, Growth on a Finite Planet* (Santa Ana, CA: Seven Locks Press, 1996)

Grimes, Kyle, "The Entropics of Discourse: Michael Harper's Debridement and the Myth of the Hero," *Black American Literature Forum*, Vol. 24, No. 3 (Autumn, 1990), pp. 417-440.

Hall, Christopher K., "The First Five Sessions of the UN Preparatory Commission for the International Criminal Court," *American Journal of International Law*, Vol. 94, No. 4 (Oct., 2000), pp. 773-789.

Hodgson, Dennis, "The Ideological Origins of the Population Association of America," *Population and Development Review*, Vol. 17, Issue 1 (Mar., 1991), 1-34.

Kasarda, John D., and Edward M. Crenshaw, "Third World Urbanization: Dimensions, Theories, and Determinants," *Annual Review of Sociology*, Vol. 17 (1991), 467-501.

Keohane, Robert O., "Hegemony in the World Political Economy," Reprinted by Permissiion in *International Politics*, 5 Edition, by Art, Robert J., and Robert Jervis, (New York, NY: Addison Wesley Longman, 2000).

Keyfitz, Nathan, "Population Growth, Development and the Environment," *Population Studies*, Vol. 50, Issue 3 (Nov., 1996), 335-359.

Keyfitz, Nathan, "Toward a Theory of Population-Development Interactions," *Population and Development Review*, Vol 16, Issue Supplement: "Resources, Environment, and Population: Present Knowledge, Future Options" (1990), 295-314.

Kremer, Michael Kremer, "Population Growth and Technological Change: One Million B.C. to 1990," *Quarterly Journal of Economics*, Volume 108, Issue 3 (Aug., 1993), 681-716.

LaRouche, Lyndon H. Jr., *Now, Are You Ready To Learn Economics?* (Washington D.C.: EIR News Service, Inc., 2000).

LaRouche, Lyndon H. Jr., *The Road To Recovery* (Leesburg, VA: New Bretton Woods, 1999).

Lubeck, Paul M., "The Crisis of African Development: Conflicting Interpretations and Resolution," *Annual Review of Sociology*, Vol. 18 (1992), 519-540.

Malkki, Liisa H., "Refugees and Exile: From "Refugee Studies" to the National Order of Things," *Annual Review of Anthropology*, Vol. 24 (1995), pp. 495-523.

McGeveran, William A. Jr., Ed., *The World Almanac and Book of Facts* 2001, (Mahwah, N.J.: World Almanac Books, 2001), pp. 372, 860.

Nagengast, Carole, "Violence, Terror, and the Crisis of the State," *Annual Review of Anthropology*, Vol. 23 (1994), pp. 109-136.

Neuhouser, Frederick, "Freedom, Dependency, and the General Will," *The Philosophical Review*, Volume 102, Issue 3 (Jul. 1993), pg. 363-395.

Olson, Mancur, "Mancur Olson on the Key to Economic Development," *Population and Development Review*, Vol. 24, Issue 2 (Jun., 1998), 369-379.

Olson, Mancur Jr., "Distinguished Lecture on Economics in Government: Big Bills Left on the Sidewalk: Why Some Nations are Rich, and Others Poor," *The Journal of Economic Perspectives*, Vol. 10, Issue 2 (Spring, 1996), 3-24.

Overbeek, Johannes, *The Population Challenge* (London, England: Greenwood Press, 1976).

Pasqualucci, Paolo, "Hobbes and the Myth of 'Final War.'" *Journal of the History of Ideas*, Vol. 51, Issue 4 (Oct.-Dec., 1990), 647-657.

Peterson, Paul E., "The Urban Underclass and the Poverty Paradox," *Political Science Quarterly*, Vol. 106, Issue 4 (Winter, 1991). (Peterson, 623)

Pope John Paul II, "Abortion, Contraception, and Euthanasia," *Population and Development Review*, Vol. 21, Issue 3 (Sep., 1995), 689-696.

Scott, John T., "The Theodicy of the Second Discourse: The 'Pure State of Nature' and Rousseau's Political Thought," *The American Political Science Review*, Volume 86, Issue 3 (Sep. 1992), pp. 696-711.

Shuger, Debora, "Irishmen, Aristocrats, and Other White Barbarians," *Renaissance Quarterly*, Vol. 50, No. 2 (Summer, 1997), pp. 494-525.

Singer, S. Fred, Editor, *Is There an Optimum Level of Population?* (N.Y.: McGraw-Hill, 1971).

Smith, Estellie M., "The Process of Sociocultural Continuity," *Current Anthropology*, Vol. 23, No. 2 (Apr., 1982), pp. 127-142.

Tapinos, Georges, and Phyllis T. Piotrow, *Six Billion People* (N.Y., NY: McGraw-Hill, 1978).

Waltz, Kenneth N., "The Anarchic Structure of World Politics," Reprinted with permission in *International Politics*, 5th Edition by Robert J. Art and Robert Jervis, (New York, NY: Addison Wesley Longman, 2000), pp. 49-51.

Weller, Robert H., and Leon F. Bouvier, *Population Demography and Policy* (New York, NY: St. Martin's Press, 1981).

Wilmoth, John, and Patrick Bal, "The Population Debate in American Popular Magazines, 1946-90." *Population and Development Review*, Vol. 18, Issue 4 (Dec., 1992), 631-668.

Yates, Wilson, *Family Planning on a Crowded Planet* (Minneapolis, Minnesota: Augusburg Publishing House, 1971).

Citation Notes:

[i] Mancur Olson, "Mancur Olson on the Key to Economic Development," *Population and Development Review*, Vol. 24, Issue 2 (Jun., 1998), p. 377.

[ii] Nathan Keyfitz, "Toward a Theory of Population-Development Interactions," *Population and Development Review*, Vol 16, Issue Supplement: "Resources, Environment, and Population: Present Knowledge, Future Options" (1990), p. 300.

[iii] Gilland, Bernard, "World Population, Economic Growth, and Energy Demand, 1990-2100:A Review of Projections," *Population and Development Review*, Vol. 21, Issue 3 (Sep., 1995), p. 518.

[iv] Debora Shuger, "Irishmen, Aristocrats, and Other White Barbarians." *Renaissance Quarterly*, Vol. 50, Issue 2 (Summer, 1997), p. 499.

[v] Ibid, p. 500.

[vi] Ibid, p. 505.

[vii] Nathan Keyfitz, Nathan, "Population Growth, Development and the Environment," *Population Studies*, Vol. 50, Issue 3 (Nov., 1996), p. 336.

[viii] Dennis Hodgson, "The Ideological Origins of the Population Association of America," *Population and Development Review*, Vol. 17, Issue 1 (Mar., 1991), p. 10.

[ix] Ibid, p. 23.

[x] Carole Nagengast, "Violence, Terror, and the Crisis of the State," *Annual Review of Anthropology*, Vol. 23 (1994), p. 126.

[xi] John D. Kasarda, and Edward M. Crenshaw, "Third World Urbanization: Dimensions, Theories, and Determinants," *Annual Review of Sociology*, Vol. 17 (1991), 476.

[xii] Ibid, p. 481.

[xiii] Nagengast, p. 125.

[xiv] Ibid, p. 120.

[xv] Chinese, p. 450.

[xvi] Chinese, p. 454.

[xvii] Nagengast, p. 109.

[xviii] Ibid, p. 118.

[xix] Ibid, p.129.

[xx] Kasarda, p. 484.

[xxi] Olson, 1998, p. 378.

[xxii] Liisa H. Malkki, "Refugees and Exile: From "Refugee Studies" to the National Order of Things," *Annual Review of Anthropology*, Vol. 24 (1995), p. 504.

xxiii   Paolo Pasqualucci, "Hobbes and the Myth of 'Final War.'" *Journal of the History of Ideas*, Vol. 51, Issue 4 (Oct.-Dec., 1990), p. 648.

xxiv   Ibid, p. 652.

xxv   Ibid, p. 653.

xxvi   Ibid, p. 656.

xxvii   Ibid, p. 657.

xxviii   Michael Kremer, "Population Growth and Technological Change: One Million B.C. to 1990,"*Quarterly Journal of Economics*, Volume 108, Issue 3 (Aug., 1993), p. 692.

xxix   Gilland, p. 509.

xxx   Joel E. Cohen, "Should Population Projections Consider 'Limiting Factors'' - and If So, How?"*Population and Development Review*, Vol 24, Issue Supplement: "Frontiers of Population Forecasting" (1998), p. 127.

xxxi   Ibid, p. 128.

xxxii   Keyfitz, 1996, p. 339.

xxxiii   Georges Tapinos and Phyllis T. Piotrow, *Six Billion People* (NYC, NY: McGraw-Hill, 1978, p.31.

xxxiv   Wilson Yates, *Family Planning on a Crowded Planet* (Minneapolis, Minnesota: Augugsburg Publishing House, 1971), p. 60.

xxxv   William A. McGeveran, Jr., Ed., *The World Almanac and Book of Facts* 2001, (Mahwah, N.J.: World Almanac Books, 2001), p. 372.

xxxvi   Ibid, p. 860.

xxxvii   Kremer, p. 693.

xxxviii   Tapinos, pp. 97-98.

xxxix   Keyfitz, 1990, p. 311.

xl   John Wilmoth and Patrick Bal, "The Population Debate in American Popular Magazines, 1946-90." *Population and Development Review*, Vol. 18, Issue 4 (Dec., 1992), p. 632.

xli   Ibid, p. 639.

xlii   Ibid, p. 640.

xliii   Yates, p. 15.

xliv   Wilmoth, p. 641.

xlv   Ibid, p. 642.

xlvi   Ibid, p. 651.

xlvii   Gro Harlem Brundtland, "Population, Environment, and Development." *Population and*

Development Review, Vol. 19, Issue 4 (Dec., 1993), p. 894.

xlviii   Ibid, p. 895.

xlix   Ibid, p. 896.

l   Ibid, p. 897.

li   Ibid, p. 898.

lii   Jasor L. Finkle, and Alisen McIntosh, "The New Politics of Population," *Population and Development Review*, Vol 20, Issue Supplement: "The New Politics of Population: Conflict and Consensus in Family Planning" (1994), p. 12.

liii   Ibid, p. 26.

liv   Keyfitz, 1996, p. 347.

lv   Ibid, p. 348.

lvi   Ibid, p. 351.

lvii   Gilland, p. 534.

lviii   Ibid, p. 536.

lix   Lindsey Grant, *Juggernaut,Growth on a Finite Planet.* Santa Ana, CA: Seven Locks Press, 1996, p. 63.

lx   Ibid, p. 67.

lxi   Ibid, p. 75.

lxii   Cohen, p. 118.

lxiii   Ibid, p. 126.

lxiv   Keyfitz, 1996, p. 353.

lxv   Abernethy, p. 327.

lxvi   Olson, p. 373.

lxvii   Ibid, p. 370.

lxviii   Nagengast, p. 114.

lxix   Lubeck, p. 525.

lxx   Petersen, p. 623.

lxxi   Ibid, p. 626.

lxxii   Lyle Grimes, "The Entropics of Discourse: Michael Harper's Debridement and the Myth of the Hero," *Black American Literature Forum*, Vol. 24, Issue 3 (1990), p. 428.

lxxiii   Ibid, p. 417.

lxxiv   Chinta Strausberg, "Blacks must never forget the African Holocaust." *Chicago Defender*

lxxv   Christopher K. Hall, "The First Five Sessions of the UN Preparatory Commission for the International Criminal Court," *American Journal of International Law*, Vol 94, Issue 4 (Oct., 2000), p. 781.

lxxvi   Yates, p. 15.

lxxvii   Chinese Delegation, p. 453.

lxxviii LaRouche 150 – Road) Lyndon H. LaRouche, Jr., *The Road To Recovery* (Leesburg, VA: New Bretton Woods, 1999)

lxxix   Grimes, p. 418.

lxxx   (Singer – 125) S. Fred Singer, Editor, *Is There an Optimum Level of Population?* (New York, NY: McGraw-Hill, 1971)

lxxxi   (Hall), 777

lxxxii   Tapinos, pp. 71-72.

lxxxiii Pope John Paul II, p. 689

lxxxiv   Ibid, p. 690.

lxxxv   Ibid, p. 690.

lxxxvi   Chinese Delegation, p. 458.

lxxxvii Clinton, p. 49.

lxxxviii Boot, p. 126.

lxxxix   Finnin, p. 39.

xc   Keohane, p. 302.

xci   Ibid, p. 305.

C13 - PRIVACY

The pervasiveness of technology in almost all aspects of daily life has made the issue of "Constitutionally guaranteed PRIVACY" to be a mute enigma surrounded by much saber rattling, but not founded in actual fact. No where in the U.S. Constitution and the Bill of Rights is there an explicit reference to the "right to privacy." Instead, the U.S. Supreme Court in its infinite wisdom that flounders with political tides has ruled and set precedents through their closely divided majority decisions that the right to privacy is implied by the various Amendments to the Constitution.

Legalities aside, the expectation of any right to privacy is rather naïve given technological intrusions by corporations, government, criminals, foreign spies, and various nefarious individual hackers and anonymous groups with various self-benefiting motivations. Recently, Edward Snowden, a low level employee of a major NSA contractor, who was hired with barely a high school diploma, criminally downloaded tens of thousands of pages of classified government intelligence materials from the intelligence contractor's mainframe computer. He claimed to have proof that our government was spying on its own people beyond that permitted by the U.S. Patriot Act passed by Congress as a tool to identify and fight international terrorists bent on harming the U.S. and Americans all around the world. No doubt that information has now fallen into the hands of the Russian intelligence agencies in exchange for temporary asylum.

The reality exist that the personal information of almost all Americans who are "wired" is available in some form, and perhaps collected into accessible intelligence data files that can be cross-referenced for various purposes, such as employment verification, credit and insurance evaluation, criminal background check, and identification purposes, etc. But, besides Snowden's claims that the NSA is collecting far ranging random and unspecified data on all Americans, what information do we know for a fact is being stored on people, and by whom? Let's make a list:
Cell phone service providers record user locations, numbers for incoming and outgoing calls, duration of calls, actual text messages, Internet searches and sites viewed, and the actual dates and time attributed to each activity.

On board "black box" computers monitor the operational history of newer model vehicles that includes times, location, speed, direction of travel, whether the brakes or accelerator pedals were engaged, speed control, and the operation and condition of all major systems such as lights, wipers, air bags, seat belts, doors open or closed, power windows, etc. Public and store cameras can record both visual and audio of people and activities within the range of their capabilities and be referenced against "Face Print" technology and files stored by the FBI and Homeland Security, including the T.S.A. Law enforcement dash cams view and record vehicle license plates and run them against the DMV database to search for stolen vehicles or wanted criminals. The DMV database contains personal data on all licensed drivers, including residence addresses, birth dates, DMV test scores, vehicles owned, registration dates, all vehicular infractions and crimes.

ISP's or Internet Service Providers have permanent records on everything seen or done through its servers, including email, browsing, downloads, uploads, chats, and streams. Content providers such as Facebook have permanent records of all activities done on their site by users, including anything that is deleted from personal pages. In addition, they record cookies and other information from users' computers even after their pages are closed, particularly if users forget or neglect to "sign out."

Hardware manufacturers and OS software manufacturers can access and data mine user computers through a hardwired "satellite chip" that allows it to remotely monitor and upload data from computers that have not been powered off. Users who are not able to get Internet service from providers don't have access to this proprietary satellite technology, so even users who are "off line" and don't web browse can be "seen" and located by this integrated and hidden chip.

Many retail stores are increasingly using technology to identify the location of shoppers through scanning their cell phones to determine how long they stay at each store aisle. Retail stores, credit card companies and banks have a record of everything you've ever bought using credit or debit cards... with the exception of gift cards or prepaid debit cards bought with cash. Schools have records on all grades, test scores, and teacher comments on all students. Hospitals and insurance companies have detailed records on all prescriptions, treatments and medical conditions, etc. Trash haulers and dumpster divers sort certain types of trash, and throwing out unshredded documents leaves behind much personal data such as social security numbers, various account numbers and other personal information that can be useful for identity thieves.

We can go on listing all of the data collection that has become part and parcel to our daily lives as soon as people get off the toilet (in the future, there will be smart toilets that keep records on the number of times the toilet is flushed, how long a person sits on it, and a spectra analysis of the crap that's being flushed down the toilet). As technology makes our lives more convenient, we become accustomed to it and are no longer aware it is recording our every move, everything that we say and do, and who is having sex with whom. There is no longer any reasonable expectation of personal privacy. Consequently, the U.S. Supreme Court's decisions guaranteeing the right to privacy is nothing more than political rhetoric to make people feel better because in reality, privacy no longer exist.

C14 – SEX AND GENDER

Society appears as a matrix of illusions and distortions, as the result of the unequal structure of gender roles and values that prevail in all areas of life and at all levels of human interaction. Why are the basically simple ideas of equality, fairness, and justice so fleeting and unattainable in what we perceive as reality? Is it because we have all been socially, culturally, and philosophically conditioned to suppress our true inner selves in order to conform to an artificially imposed structure of reality that primarily benefits the dominant male status quo? What is the truer reality that could, would, and should exist were humans permitted and able to shed the suppressive and oppressive vail of social reality based upon gender inequities? Gender disparity is the foundation of the power dichotomy between the sexes that feeds on injustice to the great benefit of men, and at the greater disadvantage and suffering of the world's women.

The barriers to the idealistic egalitarian gender-free society are formidable. Gender and sex stereotypes continue to be reinforced and enforced through the social and cultural infrastructure of society. Men continue to maintain a significant advantage in almost all areas of life as compared to women, and gender stereotypes are so pervasive that incremental changes appear to be manifested on a generational level, not as a change to the male power paradigm, but merely as the inclusion of token numbers of females to participate in a power structure designed by men primarily for men.

The data suggested that many of the male strength, macho, aggression and protection stereotypes remain intact. Females continue to be relegated only secondarily to men, and are generally viewed as the weaker sex, but with more social freedoms than men. Certain gendered
social norms are apparent, relating to facial and body hair, clothing options, and perception of violent tendencies. On the measures of career opportunity and options, it appears that respondents recognize that traditionally masculine types of jobs continue to favor men, while women are type cast into lower paying human service jobs where patience is virtue over power.

Much has been written about gender roles and the divergent social value associated with each sex, leading to the reinforcement of unequal gender roles, expectation, and stereotypes throughout the lives of females. Beginning at birth, parents from high versus low status demonstrate gender preferences that tend to benefit males. Trivers and Willard argue that historically, low-ranking parents have produced the greatest number of grandchildren by investing more in their daughters than their sons, while high-ranking parents achieved the most progeny by investing in sons over daughters. Also, the tendency for parents across all social strata to save more for the college education of their sons than daughters is typical since the expected economic returns are higher for males than for females (Freese & Powell, 1999). Even when women are able to compete "in a man's world", Blair (1999) reports that women have few female role models and believe that their career paths are unpredictable and marked by flukes and accidents.

Furthermore, women face contradictory paradigms for structuring their lives. For example, the male managerial cultural pattern of intense commitment to the organization during the first several years of the career ladder coincides with the life-cycle point at which women are having children. Also in cases where firms disallow married couples to work in the same department, it is generally assumed that the woman rather than her husband would leave due to his typically higher and steadier career path opportunities and income. Even when executive women have prestigious, highly paid jobs, they compare themselves and try to assimilate to the predominantly male management culture, and thus their male dominated financial organizations have been virtually unaffected by feminist concerns (Blair, 1999). Gender inequities show up even at the end of careers, as Han and Moen (1999) observed that gender appears to play an important role in the planning, expectation, and scheduling of retirement, where men are more likely to plan for retirement and to actually retire earlier than women due to the gendered nature of life and career pathways (Han & Moen, 1999).

Gender inequalities "from the cradle to the grave" have been a broad and resistant challenge to the feminist agenda. According to Manza and Brooks (1998), women voters tend to support a wide range of "materialist" social policies such as protective wage and hours laws, expansive health and housing policies, and social provision for homeless women and families, and therefore tend to vote for more expanded social spending by Democrats (Manza & Brooks, 1998). Even so, most men tend to support national defense budget escalations that are usually part of the Republican agenda to reward the military-industrial complex. The hundreds of billions of dollars spent annually on military hardware, international policing functions, foreign and now domestic battlefronts far exceeds that spent on issues that concern feminist causes, besides education.

Meanwhile, mass media continues its daily blitz by depicting females in traditional gender roles, objectifying them for commercial exploitation, and victimizing them as program entertainment. Even where heroines have starring roles, they tend to have an entire supporting cast where they find emotional and physical support and comfort. Buffy the Vampire Slayer, and Zena the Warrior Princess are indicative of the new tougher female characters; however, they are not like Superman, and the Gladiator, who were powerful men who fought alone, and stood on their own feet, without the support of others.

The foundation of "isms" lie in the dichotomous power relationship between male and females, where males have parlayed superior upper body strength and aggressiveness into the global institutions of sexism, racism, and elitism. Beginning at birth, males by their "birthright" are placed in a superior position to their mothers, sisters, aunts, grandmothers, and eventually their wives. Almost universally, societies and cultures espouse male dominance and the male agenda, as exploiter and oppressor of females. Men become blind to the basic contradiction that the females who gave them life, affection, guidance, and nurturance are then castigated into lives of submission, exploitation and violence from men. Civilizations record "his" story, as representative of the greatness of male progress, where females and other disempowered classes receive little or no recognition for their significant contributions and interventions.

The pursuit of masculine values and benefits have created a severe distortion of the potential for world peace and advancement by focusing natural and human resources primarily on military and monetary acquisitions, resulting in wars and plundering. Power and leadership has almost always resided with males (even where a few females have been the heads of states, they occupied such high positions only through the support of the male-controlled military). Consequently, societies and cultures have generally neglected or devalued those traits typically attributed to femininity and feminism, while praising masculine traits and orientation.

A comparison of prescribed masculine values to feminine values exposes the fundamental contradiction and hypocrisy that has become endemic to the world's social order. The male paradigm emphasizes characteristics that are generally valued as worldly strengths, while the female paradigm is viewed as domestic, sensitive, and weak. Masculine strengths and focus are emphasized in the lexicon of maleness, including competitiveness, winning (at any cost), exploration, discovery, decisiveness, conquering, prevailing, defeating, aggression, leading, persisting, resisting, rebelling, power, control, killing, and war. A perspective of weakness, submission, nurturance, emotionality, obedience, dependence, confusion, security, fear, and domestication generally undervalues females.

The man's worldview, preoccupation, and reach is viewed as a global orientation, while the woman's perspective is seen as domestic or regional, or less than the broader scope of men. Let's take a closer look at what the male dominance paradigm has brought to our planet, and ask if traditional feminine attributions might have brought more progress and peace to our world. In our "man's world", humans have experienced violence, war, serfdom, colonialism, slavery, torture, rape, genocide, disorder, starvation, the atomic bomb, and other weapons of mass destruction, while the Earth has undergone mass species extinctions and environmental pollution as the direct consequence of the masculine agenda of greed and conquest. In contrast, the female role and contributions have included birth, rebirth, regeneration, nurturance, cleanliness, social order, communication, cooperation, maintenance, education of the young, peace, and security.

Which does our world need more, the outcomes of the male paradigm that almost invariably leads to warfare, or the female paradigm that leads to birth and regeneration? Presuming a majority of men will philosophically ascribe to regeneration in preference to war and mayhem, what is wrong with the world system that blocks humans from attaining peace, security, and regeneration that the female paradigm represents? What prejudices persist that continue to affront and block the humanitarian evolution of the human species? Or are we to presume that the underlying factor that has steered the course of human events has been men's biochemical brain chemistry responding to heightened levels of testosterone? Why men are consistently more likely to be violent as compared to women is likely an interaction and product of different brain chemistry and socialization that gives men the feeling and expectation of power, and females the feeling of helplessness, fear and victimization.

It is clear that unless fundamental changes are made to the male paradigm, females will continue to suffer the disadvantages of finding definition in comparison to men. As women's socialization emphasizes their attractiveness and value to men, males are also conditioned to project masculine behaviors to other men. There appears to exist three areas where men exert the most effort to validate themselves before other men, and attempt to build a consistent self-image of masculinity. These three primary areas of masculine validation and reinforcement are 1) masculine occupation, 2) masculine dominance over females, and 3) masculine attitude and behavior.

Men need to feel important and valued. Their high ego needs reflect their constant need to overcome deep-rooted insecurities that of needing to appear, feel, and behave differently from females, which continues to be a devalued paradigm in almost all human societies. The pursuit of significance and superiority over females causes men to define their self-identity and sense of self-worth according to their occupation, male-typical behaviors, and dominance over women. Primary indicators of being a "winner" and not a "loser" involves a prestigious job title, income level, degree of supervisory authority, professional designation and independence, physical strength, stamina and skills (blue collar paradigm), and admiration or credit for personal achievements.

Contributing to this drive for manhood is the need to downgrade females as a primary socialization strategy to enforce masculine dominance and valuation. In relationships with women, men express the desire of ownership, dominance and control, and view their objectified female counterparts as sex objects whose role is to comfort and serve male desires and needs. Naturally, this male gaze reinforces their role as the protector of their sexual property, women.

Thirdly, the daily reinvention and reiteration of masculine attitudes and behaviors subjects men to a myriad of prescriptions to prove and validate their manhood to their peers, both male and female. Among these are complex processes and expectations that challenge and stress masculinity as requisites to validate masculine self-worth. "Normal" manly attitudes and behavioral expectations include:

1. Possessive of personal property
2. Possessive of females
3. Protective of females and children
4. Anti-gay and anti-wimp orientation

5. Objectification of females

6. High interest in viewing men sports competitions

7. Sports participation and competent skills

8. Beer drinking "with the guys"

9. Minimal amount of occasional drug indulgence

10. Ability and willingness to fight other guys

11. Mentality for aggression, both verbal and physical

12. Interest and competence in "guy things"

13. Ability to withstand pain without crying, just "sucking it in"

14. Not crying in public, except in an acceptable situation (funeral)

15. Desire to take revenge when wronged by others

16. Rebelling and not cooperating with authority

17. Being independent and uncontrollable

18. Risk taking and dangerous behaviors

19. Doing stupid, ridiculous and risky things to impress others

20. Clowning around, joking, teasing, and sexual harassment

21. Talking to others about external, non-disclosing issues

22. Insistence on obtaining "respect" from others

23. Owning male symbols, such as manly vehicles

24. Wearing male validating clothing, and not feminine styles

25. Not giving up, persistence, and winning at all costs

26. Being physically and sexually attractive to females

27. Ability, desire, or willingness to fight and kill others

28. Affinity for destruction, breaking things and blowing things up

29. Exhibiting bravery and courage and not cowardice

30. Possessing sexual stamina with females

Being a "man" is not an easy task. The lengthy list of criteria places enormous pressure on men to "front" their socialized idea of masculinity to other men, and to women who supposedly (and in too many cases) expect the "entire package" of masculine traits and behaviors. Were a man to demonstrate violations of any of the expected manly behavioral traits, then his manhood is put in question by others, which makes him insecure, and consequently causes him to correct his deviation from the masculine norms, in order to validate his self-worth as a man to himself and to the world of men, and to those women who have bought into masculine gender stereotyping. So much needs to be done to free women from male dominance, exploitation, control, and abuse, but in tandem with female liberation will be the freeing of men from the oppressive male paradigm. Consequently, liberating females from their gender roles serves to free men from the culture of manhood, and all the commensurate, unrealistic, and negative attributes that accompany the masculine paradigm.

Men feel validated by feelings from experiences when facing danger and potential death. Even shy boys, who in the course of growing up are bullied, attempt to overcome childhood emasculation by facing danger, fear, ridicule and prejudice. It is not uncommon in certain parts of rough neighborhoods for boys to be stabbed, beat up, robbed at gun point and have to endure many painful incidents of physical and verbal abuse and violence. Yet they usually survive, only to seek peace and freedom away from violent environments.

Fear and victimization causes life-long trauma and that results in deep-rooted anxieties. I can still feel my skin "tingle" when I enter a "bad neighborhood", and I instantly become more "on guard" and aware of my surroundings. I become more observant of people around me, to ascertain their potential threat level. I avoid certain

types of streets, alleys, dead ends, and stay on major thoroughfares, take care of business, then leave as soon as possible. I'm not stupid enough to be caught walking down the street in racial and ethnic enclaves in disadvantaged areas where I would stand out from the crowd. I'm not scared, just experienced and cautious. My observations are well grounded in the reality of street life, as teenage offenders who I taught in juvenile detention camp and alternative school settings confirmed it on a regular basis. I have a very intimate understanding of violence, and paroled young adults have described the terrible racial conflict that exists behind the walls of state penitentiaries.

Another consequence of post-traumatic stress is to take proactive steps to increase one's confidence, when avoiding dangerous situations fail to bring security. Self-defense strategy is one very positive program to restore or prepare women, girls and shy boys to feel more self-confident and empowered. Since nice people can't always avoid jerks and predators, and can't talk them down from aggressive posturing, then they must be prepared to fight them with every ounce of strength in their bodies and minds. It would be much better to get beat up or killed after "trying", rather than "crying" and allowing attackers to be unscathed and uninjured. It's better to teach an attacker the life lesson that they also stand a chance of great bodily harm, or even possible death, than to let them feel that they can victimize others with impunity.

Bullies and violent predatory criminals have no respect, except in the face of a formidable counterforce. The bottom line is a mind set, that if someone has to die at a given moment in time, let it be the one who is the evil one, the predatory attacker. Our community and society needs more people who contribute positively to the world, and the world would be better off for each perverted violent predator who vanishes from the face of the earth.

The deliberate and premeditated victimization of females has been "his" story. Being victimized by a male dominated and controlled hierarchical world social order has been "her" story. We urgently need to press onward to remove the "his" from the story. We need to develop a world that tells an honest story, across ethnic, cultural, sex and gender distinctions. Everyone in the world is uniquely complex and rich with experiences, abilities, skills, and feelings, all yearning to be expressed, accepted, and praised.

Unfortunately, the world is a matrix of lies and illusions, as the result of the unequal structure of sex, gender roles and values that prevail in all areas of life and at all levels of human interaction. Why are the basically simple ideas of equality, fairness, and justice so fleeting and unattainable in what we perceive as reality? Is it because we have all been socially, culturally, and philosophically conditioned to suppress our true inner selves in order to conform to an artificially imposed structure of reality that primarily benefits the dominant male status quo?

What is the truer reality that could, would, and should exist were humans permitted and able (if possible) to shed the suppressive and oppressive veil of social reality based upon gender inequities? Gender disparity is the foundation of the power dichotomy between the sexes that feeds on injustice to the great benefit of men at the greater disadvantage and suffering of the world's women. If sexism and gender dichotomy didn't exist, each human being would be free to pursue their own personal development in ways that benefit themselves, without feeling the desire to subjugate and exploit others. True freedom of expression from every aspect of one's inner directed being would be possible, resulting in a world where people deal with events, and relate to each other in an acceptable manner, founded squarely in a true reality, and not an artificially imposed illusion of reality based upon social hierarchy and exploitation. Why can't we have a world where:

People can dress anyway they want, for their own comfort and self-expression, without being subjected to ridicule, or social penalties for failing to conform to fads and social norms? People do not feel intimidated from speaking out, to share their feelings and opinions without fear of judgment and ostracism from others, where political correctness does not exist as a concept? People have genuine equal opportunity to pursue career, education, association, and lifestyle, without obstruction or intrusion from parents, government and other groups?

Each child born has an unalienable right to adequate love, food, shelter, education, safety, and security, and be liberated from the fear of uncertainty? People are encouraged to help others, to have ample opportunities to learn the arts, music, literature, theatre, and other cultural diversities, and to enrich their lives and the human spirit? Each individual is liberated from concepts such as masculinity, femininity, and sexuality, and instead respond to their own personal needs and expressions without fear of punishment for non-conformity, as long as others are not hurt? The concepts of race, gender, class, correctness, power, hierarchy, and monetary wealth should not exist, but instead each person is viewed and valued as a uniquely gifted, self-empowered and contributing member to the community of *Homo sapiens*? Now, which reality would most people prefer to live in... the current highly structured illusions that we call reality, or the reality that could exist, if people let it happen? How is the educational system and mass media being responsible in helping people to gain meaningful insights and enlightenment? How can our social institutions give food for thought to present optional worldview to the reality that exist, and ones that might be possible under a different world paradigm?

Almost all women have to go through negative experiences with men sometime during their lives. Meeting men who appear to be fun, normal, and relatively intelligent is no guarantee they may have met the psycho from hell. Borderline psychotics are attracted to open, kind and vulnerable persons who appear to be defenseless victim types. So-called "friends" become unhappily rejected stalkers whose potentially violent tendencies result in two possible futures, death or the penitentiary. Statistics indicate that ten percent of the general population has the propensity for great violence, and it's the men in this group that poses the greatest danger to the public, especially to women, because they comprise society's typical predators. Of course, there's also the neighbor next door, the co-worker, the family member, the date, all of whom pose even greater danger because a woman's guard would be down around men they think they can trust.

Statistics also indicate that women stand up to a ten-fold increase of assault, rape, or violence from someone who they know than from a stranger, but the terror is greatest when attacked by strangers because familiarity seems to decrease fear, while increasing anger from victims due to the feeling that their trust was violated. Attacks by strangers involve an animalistic level of fear due to surprise and uncertainty.

Why men are 10 times more likely to be violent as compared to women is likely an interaction and product of different brain chemistry and socialization that gives men the feeling and expectation of power, and females the feeling of helplessness, fear and victimization. The foundation of "isms" lie in the dichotomous power relationship between male and females, where males have parlayed superior upper body strength and aggressiveness into the global institutions of sexism, racism, and elitism. Beginning at birth, males by their "birthright" are placed in a superior position to their mothers, sisters, aunts, grandmothers, and eventually their wives. Almost universally,

societies and cultures espouse male dominance and the male agenda, as exploiter and oppressor of females. Men become blind to the basic contradiction that the females who gave them life, affection, guidance, and nurturance are then castigated into lives of submission, exploitation and violence from men. Civilizations record "his" story, as the truthful representative of the greatness of male progress, where females and other disempowered classes receive little or no recognition for their significant contributions and interventions.

Solutions and Recommendations

In order to empower themselves against aggressors, less physically powerful people, especially women, need to learn alternatives to fight victimization in the form of physical, emotional, and mental self-defense. The suggested tactics listed below are the reasonable "maximum" strategies for self-protection, though nothing is foolproof and once in a while a fool may get the jump on you by surprise or ambush.

1.   Physical Defense Strategy: A maximum strategy for maximum danger, or paranoia. A lesser continuum as justified by a higher security level of the immediate environment. These steps are suggested to improve a female chances, when alone, to repel an attack by a determined predatory attacker, and to survive.

      a.   Learn practical self-defense techniques, both weaponless, and with various weapons that can be readily found in the environment, like a sharp car key, belt, sharp pen, purse strap, pump heels, rocks, forks, spoons, pots and pans, furniture, lamps, fire extinguisher, and whatever is near by during an attack. Basic self-defense includes using an attacker's weight and momentum against him, and using the hard surfaces from one's body (elbow, fist, hand ridge, knees, head, heel, etc.) against the soft surfaces of the attacker (testicles, throat, eyes, ears, etc.). Full contact self defense training is essential to provide a realistic experience in how it feels to strike an attacker with full force.

      b.   Carry legal self-defense weapons, like pepper spray or a stun gun, ready for use when in an uncomfortable or potentially foreboding environment. A blinding halogen flashlight is also helpful during night time attacks. Be familiar with its use, and never carry a weapon that can be taken away and used for deadly harm against the potential victim.

      c.   Learn to use a firearm, knife, pipe, stick, and other objects that can be stored in handy places somewhere in each room, near where women are more likely to spend more time. Depending upon the safety of one's neighborhood, there should be at least one object that can be used as a self-defense weapon in each room of one's house, hidden, and known only to the resident. However, care should be used if there are small or immature minors at home. For example:

          1)   Bedroom door is alarmed, minimally with a trip alarm that

sounds a high decibel screech. Objects are strategically tied to curtains and blinds next to windows, which will fall over with great noise if an intruder enters, to supplement an electronic window alarms system. Pepper spray should be placed on the bed stand next to one's clock, safety off, to be reachable. A loaded small caliber gun, cocked and with safety on (and trigger locked if minors reside in home) should be placed beneath the bed, so if attacked, the woman can fall to the floor and have a chance to grab and use the gun (the gun is unlocked and ready for use after retiring to bedroom to sleep). The smaller caliber gun (.22 caliber) may not kill a large male, but gives the woman a chance to get up and run to the place where her larger caliber weapon is ready for use. According to the NRA, at least 200,000 incidents per year of gun-related home defense occur annually, compared to 8,000 homicides on a national basis. There should also be sharp hair pins and letter openers handily on the dresser, near the makeup vanity, and also taped to the bottom of the sitting chair. Bedroom doors and locks should be strong, with key access, to keep out a large charging man.

2) Bathroom: take your loaded gun with you into the shower or bath, but try not to drop it into the soapy water (but it'll still work when wet). The handle of the bathroom plunger should be sharpened (and a metal cross bow arrow tip installed), and covered with a plastic cap that can be easily removed, and used a thrusting weapon to the surprise of any attacker. Toothbrushes can also be sharpened and capped off. Tape a 2 inch knife to the bottom of the sink, and place one in the medicine cabinet, and also placed in the hollow shower curtain tube, and inside towel rack hangers. The

bathroom door should be strong, with strong key-accessible deadbolt, and you should have your cell phone handy.

3) Kitchen: hide and lock all large knives when not being used. Place sharp 2 inch knives (blade length) in several places (in a few pots, in the dirt of a potted plant, under the chopping board, taped to the side of the range, under or on tope of a shelf, etc.). The small knife is enough to cause pain to an attacker, to allow the female to run to the bedroom for the phone and backup firearm. Leaving large knives around enables burglars to arm themselves, and if taken away from the woman, used against her by a stronger upper body man, with a stronger grip and greater aggression.

4) Living Room and Den: pepper spray taped to the T.V. remote control (placed out of reach if very small children are around, when not being used with T.V.). Older children should be taught how to use it. Small 2 inch blade knives strategically taped to the bottom of tables and chairs where the woman is most likely to be sitting if an intruder were to break in. Everything must be out of the reach of small children, and older children must be warned and taught on its proper use, only during incident of attack, and not on each other. Children who fight should be kept away from any weapons of any type, as they are too unpredictable and may use it against each other.

5) Garage: a peep hole to the garage from the adjoining interior door should provide a view of the entire garage when lit up. A motion detector alarm system should be armed. Some intruders have access to universal garage openers that can open your garage door. When driving in to the garage, look in the rear view mirror as pulling

in, to make sure no one has followed you in. If so, back the car out, and if the intruder is stupid enough to stand behind your car, slowly nudge him out of the way, but don't panic and deliberately run him down... you may kill him. Of course, if he has a gun, duck down, step on the gas, and back the car out quickly to leave the scene. If the gun-toting intruder is hit, then he had it coming. At least you're more likely to escape and live.

6) At work, universally, all employers ban weapons in the work place. However, women also have the right against illegal search and seizure from their private property, their purses. Pepper spray hooked to your key ring, another in the purse, tough finger nail files, letter openers, an electronic stun gun, and two inch knife would likely be legal. Carry one, or all, depending on a woman's level of anxiety and concern.

7) Parking lots and parking structures are potentially dangerous places, especially in certain neighborhoods, particularly after dark when fewer people are around, because predators are opportunistic attackers. The key-ring pepper spray and sharp finger nail file can buy time for the female to scream "fire", "help me", which gets more attention than just screaming. If an attacker is able to get a woman into a vehicle, there's a very high probability she will be raped, tortured, and/or murdered, possibly never to be found again. It is much better for a woman to fall to the ground, and continue to scream and fight, than to cooperate and enter a vehicle. Predators don't want to work all that hard to get a victim, and the more a woman fights in a public area, the less she will have to fight in a remote environment, like an alley, in the forest, desert, or deserted building. It's more likely a predatory attacker will give up and wait for a chance

later at a much easier target.

2.   There are also incidents where a single predatory attacker is much too big and strong to be hurt by a smaller person. Some men can take a hard kick to the testicles, direct strike to their throat, or a jab to the eyes, and still manage to get their strong hands and body on the intended victim. Ideally, a victim is able to keep sufficient distance between themselves and the attacker to avoid getting grabbed. For example, placing a car between a potential attacker is a prudent strategy, by going to unlock the door that places the car between a potential attacker and victim. Running around the car to avoid capture while screaming will also frustrate and discourage most unarmed attackers. Always keep a large sharpened screwdriver hidden in the car's trunk, and learn how to pop open the trunk if placed inside by an attacker. The "club" also makes a handy striking weapon, but it can be taken away if a person doesn't know how to use it properly in close fighting quarters.

1. Mental and emotional strategies are as important, or even more important than physical abilities. Multiple attackers, armed predators (with guns or knives) cancel most chances of using self-defense techniques or non-lethal weapons (unless the victim already has a loaded gun, cocked, safety off, trigger lock off, and ready to aim and fire, and the intended victim is a damn good shot, and not afraid or morally against shooting another person in self-defense).   A well- trained fighter (like a Navy Seal or Green Beret) stands a 50% chance of coming out alive against 3 or more men armed with guns who are willing to use them, when the trained fighter is unarmed. Any average man or woman's chances are much less to nil in this case.

Sometimes, pretending to go along with the attacker's program when they are heavily armed, buys a person time to think of escape strategies. Think escape, not fighting back, or the trigger happy assailants will most likely shoot the victim. A crazed man with a gun has a very different level of agitation and mind set from those who are not willing to use deadly force. A man with a gun is likely not to have moral questions about shooting someone, if he becomes fearful, excited, agitated, or irritated. Cooperate to buy time, and hope he's a bad shot when the opportunity arises for a quick departure (like jumping out of a moving car going 20 mph or less, but knowing how to fall and roll because hitting the pavement will definitely hurt).

All things being said, being aware of one's environment, listening to one's intuition (and women are known to have a better "sixth sense" than most men), assessing potential danger from the situation and people, keeping open a quick escape route, and using non-lethal armed and non-armed self-defense techniques and weapons when verbal interaction fails, to provide escape is probably an effective strategy to avoid capture, violence, and perhaps death. Use verbal and mental skills to assess and emotionally disarm and calm attackers when captive, and looking for opportunities to buy time to escape is essential if kidnapped, but relatively unharmed. If a woman or man has used all of her/his wit, strength, and self-defense training to escape or incapacitate an attacker, they greatly improve their chance for survival. But nothing in life is guaranteed, so if victims should be killed, at least they go out "fighting for their lives", and not as "road kill".

At times, in the rare situation, that's the best a person can hope for; to be able to deliver a counterforce blow to an evil attacker that puts them out of the business of hurting another person. Maybe the attacker loses an eye to the victim, and at times in life, some people's death serves to prevent many others from dying; which is the case of our brave American fighting forces, both women and men, in many nations around the world. If a person must die, there is no greater honor than having fought one's best fight, in the service of one's loved ones and country, for noble principles such as democracy, freedom, liberty, justice, and the American way of life. In the urban battlefields, each citizen has a responsibility to show courage, and to come to the calling of fellow citizens against evil, as long as the actions taken are proper and allowed under the rule of law and good Samaritanism, and are not acts of vigilantism. A potential victim has to do what they gotta do, especially if faced with overpowering danger from predatory males who seek females, the young, and the defenseless as their victims.

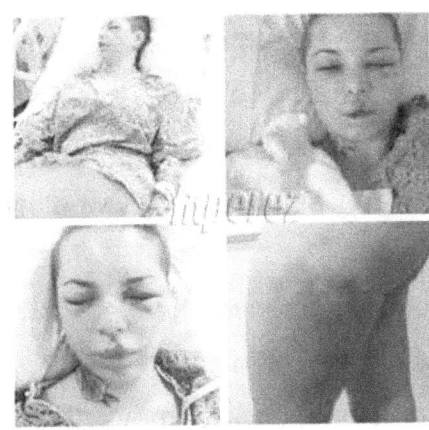 

C15 - SOLUTIONS

The final arbitrator of social, political, and economic change lies with the electorate. At the present, the populace is confused and in disarray over the vast amounts of conflicting and contradictory information that is available and explained in highly coded jargon. It appears that everything from equipment operating manuals to food ingredients are written in highly technical jargon that require either a law degree or scientific expertise to decode. All of this confusion occurs at a time when the educational level of Americans is retrenching, adding to the mass confusion. Most Americans are alienated in their workplaces, homes, and from their government.

People rarely discuss serious topics anymore, but would rather watch sexual scandals, sitcoms and reality shows or the evening television news. And when they do exercise their freedom of speech, they must be concerned about being politically correct. Could the founding fathers have ever imagined the terrible complexities that their progeny would have to endure today? Is poverty, interpersonal alienation, environmental pollution, crime and violence, and a severe limitation of personal rights and freedom what millions of Americans have shed their blood for in the Revolutionary War, the Civil War, World War I, World War II, the Korean War, in Vietnam, Desert Storm, Afghanistan, and Iraq? In fact, many of the veterans of WWII through Desert Storm are finding that the reward for their bravery, sacrifices and blood is an unemployment line and homeless shelters (and some are not even that lucky).

When will the people reaffirm that this great nation, America, is a nation that was founded on the principles of freedom and democracy? When will people insist that their elected officials must act responsibly for the common good, in this representative government of the people, by the people, and for the people? Or perhaps our schools are teaching our children the greatest farce. Perhaps our teachers should be teaching our children the truth... that America is becoming a oligarchy, buttressed by a government of the wealthy, for the wealthy, and kept running by servants of the wealthy for the interest of the rich and their progeny.

Let the commoners eat cake, and if that isn't tasty enough, then let them eat shit. I've never heard a politician that I didn't enjoy, and a lawyer that I could trust. Politicians have a way of speaking from both sides of their mouths, and attorneys do the same... and when you hear the gibberish simultaneously from both sides of their mouths, that's entertaining. It's no wonder that a high percentage of politicians have law degrees. The problem with electing public officials with formal legal training is that they see the law as a mound of clay, to be molded and manipulated. And on the other side of their faces, they see the law as Swiss cheese, full of loopholes. And the product that you get from attorneys is never guaranteed, but instead comes at 30-50% of their client's net gain. If you win, they win; if you lose, they still win because they can petition their courtroom cronies (the judges) to have you compensate them for legal fees. I've often wondered what it would be like to replace lawyer/politicians with just common folks like homemakers, accountants, and policemen. We might have a government that understands the day-to-day problems of raising a family, balancing a checkbook (at least it will balance!), and the horrors of poverty and drug driven crime and violence. Common people are actually idealistic enough to see the law as an instrument of justice and fair play, not as a mound of clay or Swiss cheese. Attorneys have invested much of their lives staring at doubletalk law books and learning doublespeak from law professors, and as a group are out-of-touch with the concerns of average people. Then they want to become politicians. Unfortunately, many do.

If we start now to elect common people who are in touch with the daily lives of Americans, perhaps there is a chance that common sense will again prevail. How can elected officials, most of whom are motivated by political power truly serve the public interest? We need to elect people who are a part of the public interest, who truly view their elected office as a genuine and humble responsibility to serve their electorate. In this way, over the course of another generation, we may take the nation back from the corporate boardrooms and bureaucratic offices that have manipulated this nation to a level of waste and mediocrity.

Many areas that weren't problematic only a few centuries ago have become persistent modern day predicaments. Solutions to these problems, while simple and theoretically possible are not implemented because conflict between opposing interest groups continues to be tenacious, mostly due to ideological differences which are used to justify economic stake holds disguised as humanitarianism. For instance, capitalism has been the greatest tool for wealth building the world has ever seen since imperialism, colonialism and plunder. However, Capitalism has become the preponderant stimulus toward the institutionalization of political and bureaucratic corruption in the emerging world order, which result in the global exploitation and impoverishment of workers and the poor.

The evolution of human civilizations in the world we know has been historically documented as one filled with inhumanity, conquest, warfare, and injustices. Men of the sword, then bullets and bombs were great heroes and leaders of their particular race, ethnicity, tribe or nations. Millions of loyal soldiers and hundreds of millions of innocents suffered and died to permit the relative few to increase their personal power, wealth, and stature – but only for a time. Eventually all of the so-called great men of their time – famous or infamous by today's standards – lost their power, their fortunes, their fame and in many cases their lives in pursuit of their lustful ambitions. Yet the hidden elites continue to prosper and have had a hidden hand in financing almost every war since the Napoleonic wars – including the American Revolution and Civil War, the French Revolution, the Bolshevik Revolution, and have cashed in on arms sales during the great world wars and subsequent regional wars.

In recent centuries, the evolution and widespread acceptance of capitalism as both an effective and efficient method of economy and wealth building has caused a rapid rise in global development, modernity and globalization. The interdependence of global trade due through the manipulation of governments, resources, and monetary wealth has become entrenched through the monopoly of the world's banking system by western multinational bankers, investors and speculators. As Third World nations succumb into indentured servitude of the IMF and World Bank, the private monetary coffers of the hidden elites greatly expand their secret caches in Liechtenstein, Switzerland, the Bahamas, and other digital depositories that escape national scrutiny.

Where is the world headed? Uncertainty appears to abound, as world population continue to rise at an alarming rate, placing further pressure on global ecology, with precarious and ominous consequences on the event horizon. Does a "silver bullet" exists that would cure the world of inequities, imbalances, pollution, corruption, greed, hunger, disease and injustices? Organized religion readily and consistently profess simple spiritual solutions to the hungry and suffering masses, yet more innocent people have died as a consequence of religious differences and intolerance than through natural calamities. Almost every major religion urge common people to ignore the attraction of the material world, and instead to focus on God, morality, and community, yet the world continues to increase the proliferation of immorality, materialism, and greed – particularly for the hidden elites.

How has capitalism permitted the hidden elites to prosper through the development or conflicts between civilizations? How has bureaucracy become a collusive partner in supporting and perpetrating the elitist paradigm? Will the hidden hand of elitism result in a global oligarchy at the expense of greater human exploitation, suffering, and control? What can global citizens (those whose humanitarian goals serve the innocent faceless masses) do to reverse the insidious deception, trickery, hatred, illusion, and economic manipulation by the international elites in order to save the world from a future of ecological and human devastation? This essay analyzes the root capitalistic causes of global conflict and corruption, and the steps global citizens must take to free humans from economic bondage.

Problem One – Corruption

The corruptive effect of capitalism as the primary impediment against the development of ethical bureaucracy and populace. There appears to exist human frailties common to most nation-states and cultures throughout the history of organized civilizations, among which greed and self-indulgence motivated the development of elitism and a tendency toward aristocratic and oligarchic organizations. In a comparative study of the issue of ethics in government that is synonymous with honesty, selflessness, and promoting the public good, it is hypothesized that the focus on capitalistic economic development resulted in the emergence of bureaucratic corruption in most nations. Using both the United States of America (USA) and the Peoples Republic of China (PRC) as examples, the manifestation of capitalism as a corruptive stimuli on their respective bureaucracies demonstrate both parallels and differences peculiar to the particular political culture of each nation. The rapid economic growth resulting from a focus on capitalism during the last decade in both America and China had the unexpected collateral outcome of increased bureaucratic corruption. During the decade of the 1990's, America experienced 107 months of historically unprecedented economic growth and during this same period, China's GNP increased six folds.

The push to privatizing public services also increases ethical dilemmas because an inherent conflict exists between private and public sector interests. A distinct dichotomy has always existed between generating revenue (making a profit) versus depleting assets through expenditures (program costs). Ethical conduct is a cornerstone of democracy because it encourages public trust and acceptance of our social and legal institutions. Ethics involves dealing with what is good and bad and with moral duty and obligation. Ethical behavior suggests the involvement of more difficult or subtle questions of rightness, fairness or equity. While some may argue that politics is typically unethical, President Clinton's impeachment over lying about his sex life suffices to dispel the myth that the populace and our constitutional, legal, and political system cares little about political or administrative ethics. In sum, public administrators in the United States seem to believe that ethics in government is extraordinarily important, and compared to business, most people want to believe government is still the more ethical institution (Shafritz).

When government contracts out, outsource, or otherwise privatizes its functions, it places a layer of middlemen between itself and the people it is purportedly created to serve. The ethical dilemma primarily lies in the inability or disinterest of public officials in government to responsibly monitor that sector of privateers who are supposedly enjoined to implement government policies through its programs. The long standing myth that business can do orthodox management better than the public bureaucracy acts to free management from public accountability, ethics and transparency (Henry), and the primary reason public-sector unions have opposed privatization is the increases in opportunities for corruption in procurement and to the fact that private employees are less accountable to public officials than were the public employees they replaced (Suggs).

From the early days of Woodrow Wilson, there developed an assumption that the private and public sectors are basically alike, and thus the private sector functions more efficiently and economically. After tremendous growth of the public sector under FDR, the New Federalism devolution trend championed by Republican Presidents Nixon, Reagan and Bush responded to general public, private, and governmental consensus that the public sector had become too large, therefore its functions would be better assigned to private enterprise. Based upon these fundamental presumptions, big government came to be viewed as "bad" and "wasteful" while the private sector retained its lofty efficiency position, as evidenced by its ability to generate great wealth. This inherent prejudice of our capitalistic economic system has contributed to a vast array of unethical conduct and the corruption of public officials by the private sector, as ethics may serve capitalism by ensuring non-contractual obligations among members to play by the rules, but these ethics as applied today do not chart a moral course for capitalism (Dobelstein).

Public administrators became motivated to contract out or to experiment without commitment by the temporary hiring of outside specialists and volunteers to create cost-savings in employee benefits, pensions and salaries while giving only an appearance of static or reduced civil service workforce, while avoiding political risks. Yet independent studies have estimated that it may actually cost upwards to seven times more to privatize functions of public agencies (Henry). During the 1980s, the privatization of social services and health care through government "load-shedding" and the shifting of financial resources has strengthened the two-class welfare state and reproduced inequalities that the free market inevitably creates that jeopardizes the capacity of such agencies to deliver services effectively and erodes the legitimacy of their functions in the eyes of the public (Gambrill).

Business principles operate to maximize monetary gain and profit, thus whatever practices are deemed germane to increasing profits may be employed. The history of corporate practices in America has been a dismal one strewn with blatant examples of monopolies, child labor, worker abuse, lack of workplace safety or health protection, excessive executive compensation, unrestrained greed, corruption, and unethical conduct that includes accounting manipulations to avoid the payment of taxes and to defraud investors.

Often cited in arguing against privatization is that it leads to corruption, bribery, and kickbacks. It was only after the government and strong unions intervened that corporations toned down their level of worker abuse and corruption (Armington). Still, privately owned and investor-driven companies and corporations are fundamentally concerned only with budget savings to satisfy pursuit of the profit motive. The primary goal of capitalists s the delivery of the least amount of services or product at the lowest cost to obtain the greatest profit based upon the dynamic economic forces of supply and demand, which monopolistic corporations are tempted to manipulate (Enron and California's energy crisis that almost bankrupted the state).

To compensate for delivering sub-par services or products, businesses utilize showcase market "packaging" strategies that often entail various degrees of deception. Its emphasis is on the pervasive application of technologies to remove human involvement in the production and delivery of products and services, which therefore are provided with minimal regards to political or bureaucratic agendas but are instead predicated on "bottom line" requirements. Making a profit is a not a necessary evil, yet its unrestraint pursuit remains a basic human frailty that tempts its pursuers to immoral and unethical conduct. In contrast, public administration's basic obligation is to protect "the people" and to function to implement constitutional intent, legal and political protections and guarantees by providing human services to its constituent population. Presidents FDR, JFK, and LBJ were great champions of utilizing government through its agencies to improve social conditions in America and their focus was on people, and not so much on issues of cost-savings.

THE CORRUPTIVE INFLUENCE OF CAPITALISM

Due to the formidable federal debt and deficits caused in part by high levels of spending for social programs during previous administrations, the era of New Federalism shifted the rhetoric and direction of public sector agencies from helping the people to helping businesses. Conservative politicians became the proponents of the hypothesis that "business can do it better" as the means to reducing federal spending while providing essential public services. The result of this fundamental shift in the public service delivery paradigm was a marked increase in contracting federal "non-policy-making" functions to corporations that opened the barnyard door to unchecked budgetary abuses and corruption where public and private officials focused more on personal monetary gain than on the public agenda.

Inherent contradictions between the public trust and private entrepreneurs exist which stimulates corruption. Fundamental ethical conflicts and dilemmas naturally arise between the "means-ends" of capitalists versus the public good. Unchecked, entrepreneurs desire only profit and commercialism, as ethical conduct is deemed necessary only as "good PR" because it tends to engender repeat customers, thus more profit. Its primary concern is not about ethics, honesty and humanism. It's a creature that lives only to "make another buck." Consequently, there lies an inescapable conflict of interest between making money and spending money, as these are the opposites in the "zero-sum" game of profit making. Cost is inherently the contradiction of profit. Expenditures for the public good offset revenues for private profit. Are we not in fact asking the proverbial "wolf" (profit-driven private sector) to watch over the chickens (cost-driven public sector) when privatizing public services? Contracting has several potential drawbacks as for-profit firms need to make profits, and the cost charged to government agency will include that added cost, thus the profit motive can bring with it corruption (Hatry).

Typically, in order to perform a contract that calls for reduced expenditures, private companies hire less qualified workers, pay lower wages with little or no employee benefits, reduces its level of services by reducing the number of employees coupled with a greater emphasis on automated delivery systems (e.g., recipients receive a degraded level of service by having to wait longer on the phone listening to the automatic computer-generated operator instead of being able to talk to a human being with a shorter waiting period). Where has the public benefited? It has not. Public services deteriorate when the quality of employees charged with conducting public business is decreased qualitatively and quantitatively.

Since ethical conduct considers the factors of fairness and equity in addition to rightness, does privatization tend to best serve the public good, or does it so often serve to profit the private sector at the expense of public interest? And what of the smaller minority firms who attempt to obtain some benefit of the governmental privatization pie? Minority firms have had no significant role in public procurement at any level of government, and privatization did nothing to alter this situation. In no city were a significant number of minority firms willing and able to take over delivery of the services that were being privatized (Suggs). Where's the ethics of equality and fairness when minority contractors are concerned?

Corruption in awarding and bidding of government contracts is almost legendary. The continuing trend to integrate public agencies and private organizations often results in firms who remain by playing games to under-represent actual cost of contracts. Collusion between public agencies and private contractors to mislead Congress to obtain approval then charge massive cost overruns create a revolving door for governmental officials. Many public officials bounce back and forth at salary increases of 75-100% when officials involved with agencies leave public service to work for industries or the very firms with which they had previous official dealings (Henry). A GSA report indicated that DOE officials bounce back and forth monitoring agency contracts with companies they had worked for. At the Pentagon, 4/5ths of the contracts are awarded with no bids, with more than half going to firms of past Pentagon officials, and one-third going to firms they had previously dealt with in their official capacities. And thus "may not have acted in best interest of public" (Henry).

FDA scientists serve simultaneously on drug safety review boards and as scientists for the pharmaceutical firms whose studies they are charged to evaluate. Clearly, the right to act as the exclusive supplier of some government service without fear of competition can be extremely valuable, particularly if a public official is willing to look away when a producer cuts quality to increase profits. Thus "contracts are one of the most common and lucrative sources of corruption in government." Incentives for private contractors to engage in bribery, kickbacks, and pay offs obviously exist, and corruption is inevitable if public officials in charge of the contracting process are sufficiently self-interested (Benson).

Numerous federal statutes against conflict of interest and corruption exist. The examples of fraud and corruption, particularly in the area of defense contracting, are becoming almost legion. Instances of fraud, where "bribing public administrators obtain inside, often secret information for purposes of rigging, falsifying, lying, and grossly overcharging the government and hiding the bad news about grotesque cost overruns" amount to corruption in contracting that will never be controlled as long as careers depend more on maintaining that flow of federal dollars than managing it. During the past ten years, the number of contractors under investigation for fraud grew from a fourth of the100 largest defense contractors to over two-thirds." (Henry).

What can the government and the public do to encourage greater ethical conduct in regards to privatizing public services? Public administrators seeking budgetary savings should consider the appropriateness of contracting out primary functions of their agencies. When departmental managers are relegated to the role of overseers whose primary residual responsibilities become one of monitoring their own budget with little actual oversight of the level and quality of services being delivered to the public, the public good no longer remains a litmus test. Public trust and confidence is violated when the focus of government protection of the people's interest is handed over "carte blanche" to private enterprises whose baser instincts and goals are their own monetary gain, usually with only secondary regards for protecting individual rights. This unfortunately is a likely unethical outcome.

A balance should be sought where functions that are primarily procurement or operational in nature (e.g., facilities, fleet, road maintenance, non-air transportation, and sanitation) that normally do not impact the actual quantity or quality of public services delivery may be considered for privatizing. Agencies whose charge requires human face-to-face interaction or involving policymaking or implementation to effectively service the public good should refrain from privatization (e.g., child welfare, tax collection, public education, law enforcement, fire departments, etc.). Let's not make mercenaries out of our military, as their loyalty and support of our nations' constitutionally guaranteed principles must not be corrupted by multi-national profit. What's the right configuration for the line between the public versus private sector?

Already the military-industrial complex has long provided hardware and support services to augment the military while providing lucrative profits to defense contractors (Henry. Unfortunately, military pay still places the typical rank and file among the lowest paid profession in America. This system has led to routine ethical abuses. The Office of Management and Budgeting (OMB) circulars on management and policy-making recommends that government employees and all other functions can be contracted out which do not actually involve management or implementation of policies. This recommendation still leaves much to special interests pressures, political considerations, and personal conflict of interests, all of which creates additional ethical dilemmas (Henry).

Our bureaucratic agencies along with local governments can take advantage of their greater organizational flexibility to experiment with inventive solutions on a test scale to determine those areas of public trust that could be better served by a wedding of private and public employees, where proper public involvement and oversight of private enterprises would ensure the public good. Corruption can be avoided through rational, open-bidding procedures, and objective selection standards with keen monitoring of the process to ensure that both sides follow the rules. The response to this is to make the process a matter of public record and to hold all decision-making sessions in public (Armington). Ethical standards and sanctions should apply to all participants in the public procurement process. Standards should cover conflicts of interest, gratuities and kickbacks, contingency fees, and misuse of confidential information (Demone).

DEVELOPING AN ETHICAL POPULACE CULTURE

There rightfully exist a public expectation of ethical behavior on the part of the government, its institutions, agencies, and employees in carrying out the charge of the U.S. Constitution and the laws of the land that are in whole designed to protect its citizens from abuse and tyranny. And where government delegates its functions to the private sector, it doesn't wash its hands of its primary responsibility to ensure the public good and to protect the public trust. Each piece of our national monetary exchange notes and coins is imprinted with the ideal, "In God We Trust" but its value is only as good as the public trust. When public trust erodes in its governmental institutions, there is corresponding erosion in its economic system. The balance of law and order is only possible when no segment of society is able to dominate and exploit the masses. Should government agencies, if only for the sake of budgetary efficiency, relegate its role from that of provider for the public good and protector of the public trust to one of doling out dollars to large greedy individuals and corporations, then who needs the government anymore?

John Rawls's theory of justice states that in the context of managing organizations, fairness is comprised of trust, consistency, truthfulness, integrity, clearly stated expectations, equitable treatment, a sense of ownership and influence in the organization, impartial decision making, and mutual respect (Shafritz). Anything less is injustice and unethical. Unless public administrators as a profession agree to adopt a code of ethical conduct that is independent from political interference, confusion will continue to pervade public service. An interdependency of the private sector exist based on the quality of the public sector, and further "In 1992, the Office of Government Ethics released the federal government's first set of standards of ethical conduct... some forty pages in the Federal Register, the standards cover gifts, conflicts of financial interest, impartiality, misuse of office, seeking outside employment, and outside activities.... It is reasonably apparent that career public administrator takes the practice of ethical administration seriously.... When we realize that... the confidence of the citizenry in its government may depend more than we might otherwise appreciated on Washington's ability to reform the corrupt and arcane relationship between Main Street and Wall Street.... In light of these views, it is perhaps not surprising that public administrators are more critical of the ethics of corporate culture than government." (Shafritz).

Perhaps resolution of ethical issues and the corruptive tendencies of privatization of public services may be enhanced through a sincere commitment of government, its officials, managers and employees to make policies and its implementation in a more transparent environment. The development and strengthening of a political and bureaucratic culture of ethical conduct will not happen in a vacuum, and certainly will not be an agenda to be championed by the private sector. Public administrators must in their positions of neutrality, objectivity, and lawful representation act to ensure the highest level of honesty and accept individual as well as organizational responsibility for both their individual and collective actions and inactions in performing their public functions to protect and serve. Anything short of noble intent, honest heart, and concerned action shall allow the injustices, corruption, and unethical conduct of the past and present to persist as an insidious deteriorating influence on our political, economic, and social culture.

Problem One References

Armington, R., and Ellis, W., Editors (1984). This Way Up: The Local Official's

Handbook for Privatization and Contracting Out. Chicago, IL: Regency Gateway.

Benson, B. (1998). To Serve and Protect: Privatization and Community in Criminal Justice. New York, NY: New York University Press.

Brown, Bernard E. (2000). Comparative Politics. Notes and Readings. Ninth Edition. Orlando, FL: Harcourt College Publishers.

Brown, Michael K. (1999). Race, Money, and the American Welfare State. Ithaca, NY: Cornell University Press.

Day, Phyllis J. (2000). A New History of Social Welfare. Boston, MA: Allyn and Bacon.

Demone, H. & Gibleman, M. (1989). Services for Sale: Purchasing Health and Human Services. New Brunswick, NJ: Rutgers University Press.

Dobelstein, A. (1999). Moral Authority, Ideology, and the Future of American Social Welfare. Boulder, CO: Westview Press.

Faust, John R., and Kornberg, Judith F. (1995). China in World Politics. Boulder, CO: Lynne Rienner Publishers.

Forst, B., and Manning, P. (1999). The Privatization of Policing. Two Views. Washington D.C.: Georgetown University Press.

Gambrill, E., and Pruger, R., Editors (1992). Controversial Issues in Social Work. Needham Heights, MA: Allyn and Bacon, a Division of Simon & Shuster, Inc.

Geras, Norman (1990). Discourses of Extremity. Radical Ethics and Post-Marxist Extravagances. New York, NY: Verso, New Left Books.

Gingrich, Newt (1995). To Renew America. New York, NY: Harper Collins Publishers.

Gilley, Bruce (1998). Tiger on the Brink. Jiang Zemin and China's New Elite. Berkeley, CA: University of California Press.

Halsey, Margaret (1963). The Pseudo-Ethic. A Speculation on American Politics and Morals. New York, NY: Simon and Schuster.

Hatry, H. (1983). A Review of Private Approaches for Delivery of Public Services. Washington, D.C.: Urban Institute Press.

*Henry, N. (1999). Public Administration and Public Affairs. Upper Saddle River, N.J.: Prentice Hall Publishers.

Hester, Joseph P. (1996). Encyclopedia of Values and Ethics. Santa Barbara, CA: ABC-CLIO.

Hill, Ivan, Editor (1980). The Ethical Basis of Economic Freedom. New York, NY: Praeger Publishers, A Division of CBS, Inc.

Hunter, A., and Sexton, J. (1999). Contemporary China. New York, NY: St. Martin's Press.

Halttunen, K., and Perry, L., Editors (1998). Ithaca, NY: Cornell University Press.

Miles, James A. R. (1999). The Legacy of Tiananmen. China in Disarray. Ann Arbor, Michigan: The University of Michigan Press.

Nagle, John D. (1998). Introduction to Comparative Politics. Challenges of Conflict and Change in a New Era. Fifth Edition. Chicago, IL: Nelson-Hall Publishers.

Nash, Robert J. (1996). "Real World" Ethics. Frameworks for Educators and Human Service Professionals. New York, NY: Teachers College Press.

Norman, Richard (1998). The Moral Philosophers. An Introduction to Ethics. New York,

NY: Oxford University Press.

*Shafritz, J. & Hyde, A. (1997). Classics of Public Administration. Fort Worth, TX: Harcourt Brace College Publishers.

Starr, John B. (1997). Understanding China. A Guide to China's Economy, History, and Political Structure. New York, NY: Hill and Wang, a Division of Farrar, Straus and Giroux.

*Suggs, R. (1990). Minorities and Privatization: Economic Mobility at Risk. Washington D.C.: Joint Center for Political Studies Press

Tucker, David M. (1998). Mugwumps. Public Moralists of the Gilded Age. Columbia, MI: University of Missouri Press.

Zunz, Olivier (1998). Why The American Century? Chicago, IL: The University of Chicago Press.

Problem Two: - Ethics

The need to implement ethical standards as a shield against the emergence of rampant institutionalized corruption. A philosophy of public service based on an exploration of the spirit of public service presumes that the intention and practice of serving others are inherently good and beneficial to the development and maintenance of civil societies that seek to maximize individual liberties and happiness, within the context of normative moral codes of conduct. Rousseau theorized in his construction of the "civil society" viewed morals as that which is "established" by "a sort of convention" as men begin to associate together, and a "political" form that is moral in the sense of being "authorized" by the consent of man as a social contract (Scott). If the general will (and the laws derived from it) expresses a consciously shared concept of the common good that is affirmed by the individuals who make up the state, then submitting to laws that derive from the general will subject individuals only to their own wills, and therefore they remain free (Neuhouser). The general will must regulate social cooperation in accord with the common good and at the same time be the will of the individuals whose behavior it governs; thus individuals can achieve freedom through the general will only if the general will is also their own will (Neuhouser).

The implication of building civil societies is the active and responsible consensus among citizens to seek societal improvement as fundamentally desirable and requisite goals. The presumption of mutual good is aptly described by the cliché, "the rising tide raises all ships", and consequently in order to raise the level of benefit for all, substantive and effective efforts must focus on systemic factors such as structural and philosophical change, which in turn guides the thought, motivation, and actions of individuals, who as a collective contribute to a rising tide.

Were individuals to be left to their own selfish designs, would the propensity for greed and hoarding tend to outpace compassion and humanitarianism, and contribute to societal decay, decline, and possible anarchy? The history of mankind has provided ample lessons about social and political disorder, conflict, violence and warfare, not as the outcome of individual competition, but rather as the design of madmen, despots, regimes, and states. It is clear that governments, and those actors who lead and benefit most from manipulating the masses, are more inclined to affect the public welfare, whether for good or otherwise. The biographies of uniquely proactive individuals, whose visions and abilities enabled them to overcome obstacles to demonstrate that political, social, and economic networks provide platforms to influence the decisions of high government leaders and officials on issues of public service. Rarely have individuals achieved the level of spiritual and humanitarian enlightenment to deserve immortality on the level of Aristotle, Buddha, or Christ.

It is clear that public service is the usual path to cause social change by increments, where honest ethical and non-corrupt public servants encourage public trust and enhance achievements in the public's best interest. As population growth increases competing interests, public servants (whether official or non-governmental) are forced to balance highly dynamic social orders, where intergroup and individualistic conflicts compete for limited resources and create unpredictable and potentially volatile climates. As globalization advances, societies more pressed to universally accept the proliferation of scientific orientation, technological advances, state secrecy and a capitalist paradigm where the "ends justifies the means", as the minimum ticket for survival. Personal, organizational, and governmental responsibilities and liabilities have become mired in complex webs of conflict that require lengthy, exhaustive and wasteful expenditures of resources. Incidents of brute force to solve complex situations appear to becoming more the rule than the exception as the number of global military conflicts has dramatically escalated since World War II.

Biographies of great humanitarians reveal several common character traits, among which are high intelligence, a strong drive to achieve and most importantly, a lifelong commitment to particularly purposeful public service causes. An African-American, Dr. Martin Delany was a dentist, writer, editor, physician, theorist, abolitionist, explorer, scientist, philosopher, diplomat, civil rights activist, ethnologist, and politician, and during the Civil War, an army major, surgeon, and recruiter. Delany is paid tribute particularly for his vigor and mastery of these professions in his mission to strive toward the restoration, reclamation, redevelopment, and enhancement of African people's lives (Ogunlele).

Several common characteristics are apparent among the majority of biographies of renowned humanitarians, among which are the privileged opportunities available in their networks of actors and elites who could influence politically and economically powerful people, who gave support to individuals with visionary ideas and projects. Another historical-political observation is that certain great events during an era give rise to extraordinary achievements and people. Major paradigm shifts in society responding to exceptional public challenges and technological advances facilitated major change and accomplishments that might not have otherwise been possible regardless of the abilities and persistence of individuals.

A few great men and women were born of humble beginnings, who through hard work, determination, creativity, and people skills, convinced others with power to support their visions. More typical were those born to privileged classes with natural placement within empowering personal and professional environments, even in the cases where gender restrictions were in place. Social changers possess central character traits such as sincere selflessness and strong desire to benefit others. Their spirit for public service elevated and drove their missions to the status of noble and worthwhile undertakings that could garner both political and public support intertwined with elitist philanthropic motivations.

Tenet Healthcare, a Fortune 100 corporation, was the second largest operator of privately owned hospitals in the United States, providing medical services for a handsome profit. The complex billing structure utilized by giant corporations such as Tenet had created an environment where allegations of discrimination, unfair practices, and fraud eventually surface to public awareness. Even after many years of accumulated irregularities and alleged violations of fair practices or legal statutes, rarely were corrections made until courageous whistleblowers, dedicated prosecutors, and a sensationalistic press raised public consciousness and ire. A class action lawsuit was filed against St. Luke's Medical Center, and Tenet Healthcare Corporation for alleged discriminatory pricing against persons of Hispanic heritage (Oskin). Under the previous name of N.M.E., National Medical Enterprises, who had previously paid a substantial fine ten years earlier for other unethical and irregular business practices, appeared to continue similar business practices that got them into trouble with regulators in the past. As part of the settlement with the government, a consent decree mandated all N.M.E./Tenet employees to undergo annual "ethics training", which unfortunately exempted the top executives who actually set corporate fiscal and operational policies. On paper, Tenet's ethics program was very impressive, with presentations that discuss hypothetical case studies, and presenters who espoused high ideals. And while the great preponderance of employees appear to adhere to ethical practices; corporate policy makers appeared to project a public image of high ethics, but were practicing much less.

Proponents of New Public Management should examine the cases of Tenet, along with Enron, PG&E, Edison Int'l, Tyco, WorldCom and other major providers of public services, whether health care, energy, or whatever. Does the rush to privatization and contracting with the private sector actually provide a more cost-effective service delivery system, or perhaps only greater opportunities for profit, conflict of interests, fraud and abuse? The jury is still out on major corporations whose profits depend on providing services in the public domain with little scruples and consideration of the public good, and without the spirit of public service as they focus primarily on the pursuit of private gain, even at the expense of the public trust.

Improving the quality of public servants is an issue that is gaining greater public and political awareness. Do those who are motivated to draw on their government experience and stature for private gain serve the public interest best? The public is not best served by officials who are motivated to spend more time working on certain files, cultivating certain kinds of contacts, and devoting more energy to acquiring a certain type of reputation than they would, were they less concerned to use their time in office to develop marketable skills and capacities (Stark).

Contributing to the temptation for some in public service to enhance their own marketability is the lure of post-public employment opportunities created by the push to reinvent government by adopting "new public management" strategies such as privatization. Fundamental questions regarding the basic premise of private sector superiority to deliver public services must be considered. Are in fact market-based approaches to service delivery more effective and efficient servicers of the public interest than were government bureaucracies prior to privatization? Or do they as critics claim, only produce the worst of both worlds, leading to lower efficiency, quality, employee security, and public accountability? (Durant).

The emphasis on balancing government budgets at all levels has contributed to a retrenchment from public service. As spending on social programs decreases, the growth of joblessness, homelessness and welfare receipts mainly reflect a declining commitment to the core values of society (Wilson). Many public officials become frustrated by the apparent inability of the legislative process to accommodate non-partisan views, as indicated by a significant number who leave the House of Representatives because they didn't feel the structure allowed them to promote policies they personally support (Moore). While some politicians lose their spirit of public service, and are either voted out or voluntarily resign, the bureaucracy provides ample opportunity for the exercise of individual judgment and policy-making. The delegation of policy-making authority to the administrative agencies of government poses a fundamental dilemma in democratic societies. On the one hand, administrative discretion is essential since legislators can not anticipate all of the possible circumstances that may arise in the applications of public laws. As a result, bureaucrats are asked to draw upon their experience, expertise, judgment, and intuition to make administrative decisions.

But on the other hand, public administrators lack accountability at the ballot box, and civil service regulations designed to prevent political manipulation shield them from elected officials, as their specialization, expertise, and clientele support constrain the ability of political officials to control bureaucratic action (Coleman). It is ironic that many elected officials called upon to represent "the people" lose their desire to serve the public, from frustration or desire to profit from their public service repertoire and connections by hiring on with the private sector. Both politicians and bureaucrats have often become manipulators of public sentiment, rather than sincerely serving the public good. Often, simply by coining new words, or by eloquent but confusing explanations of intent, public servants are able to present their personal slant on public service, under the guise of public benefit. Montaigne, a Thomas Hobbes contemporary, who opined that euphemisms of language could any longer evaluate the fairness of its conduct or the sincerity of its motives, as viciousness donned the cloak of righteousness. Ambition had become courage, stubbornness masqueraded as piety, and behind every diplomatic overture there lurked a blasphemous heart (Chabot). It is unlikely that a sincere spirit of public service would allow the degradation of the public good, without issuing vehement social and political protests and sacrificing their lives to positive social and political change.

A review of biographical and historical material, scholars' views, case studies, and philosophical aspects of public service provides a rich tapestry of diversity and individualism focused on benefiting the greater common good. If we see a future vision of prosperity, cooperation, and humanity, we will likely achieve it. If we see a future of chaos and warfare, we will probably focus our apparent limited resources on preparing for the next war, and perhaps even the "final war" to end all wars, the one that might bring the end to human existence. What societies collectively view as probable future scenarios limit what human beings are likely to achieve, if for no other reason than the self-filling prophecy. Political leaders need to describe a clearer vision of the type of future that humans need, want, and are capable of achieving.

If unregulated and corruptive capitalism is allowed to reinforce and advance highly disparate realities between the rich and the poor, instead of becoming a positive driving force for advancing all human beings while preserving global environment, then we can expect more accelerated outcomes that lead to greater degrees of conflict, violence, and war. The universal purpose of wealth building should be to fulfill humanitarian missions that provide improvements to service human needs in health care, education, infrastructure, environment, science, arts, music, space exploration, and elevating the human spirit, morals and civility. Mass media and marketing should change their focus from creating illusions that create artificial needs like cosmetics, to public service that addresses the real needs of people, such as health care, food, and shelter.

Why can't media and business promote new worthwhile competitive "sports" that include equal access and contributions of both men and women on the same teams, where something productive is accomplished besides placing another ball through another hole? How about teams who compete to build the best houses in the shortest period of time, or who clean a mile of beach front in the fastest time? Why not propose a game where children are taught new skills, then compete to demonstrate their competence in applying those skills, for example in designing and building a simple robot? In this way, we can elevate the desirability of accomplishing things that benefit the public good, and are not simply escapist activities that benefit the relatively few professional team owners or competitors.

Unfortunately, human civilizations have been mired in exploiting the masculine dominance paradigm at the great disadvantage of females and societies in general. Gender insecurities are reinforced by media advertising to create markets for clothes, cars, cosmetics, and "crappy" products, where buying "name brands" translates to higher profits with little or no appreciable value added for consumers. Why not create genderless markets that instill the love of community, environment, and public service, where all interested people could participate regardless of sex, race, age, disability, ethnicity, culture or religion? Do we really need another "awards" show to celebrate "celebrities"? How about awards shows that celebrate the best that each occupation has produced; the best teachers, carpenters, fishers, farmers, police, parents, and so on? Until societies can celebrate reality instead of illusions, then our combined destinies will likely remain stuck on superficialities while the real problems of the world continue to be ignored, compounded, and exacerbated until perhaps it's too late.

The spirit of public service demands that leadership, resources, and public awareness be focused on dealing with reality, and not in illusory escapism from the real world. When the capitalism paradigm shifts from profiting on illusion creation and fulfillment, to profiting from real world solutions, then humans will witness their greatest period of advancement, far beyond what even the Renaissance Period had produced. Let the spirit of public service push us forward into an era of cultural enlightenment, and away from the dismal dichotomy of global exploitation of the poor, females, and colored peoples. Let the spirit of public service build better and more civil societies for all. Engaged citizens are those whose love of people, nation, nature, and the world is expressed through cherishing family and community, and demonstrated by a desire to improve life for others. Americans are the global leaders by default, for good and for bad, and it behooves our leaders and residents to try to improve the conditions of our nation and the world. Biographies of great achievers and leaders indicate that a prerequisite of vision, powerful connections, public support, and persistence set apart the enduring "doers" from the lot. History also has shown that the social and political climate must be ripe for change, in order for positive change to occur. The world may be within such an opportune moment in evolving history, to seize the momentum to push for rapid positive changes through the cooperation and support of elite capitalists and political leaders to push for a kinder, gentler, more ethical, responsible, humanitarian and environmentally sensible form of capitalism.

Society needs desperately to change cultural socialization to eliminate concepts that cause inequality, exploitation, and violence, thereby creating more civil society. Public service is called upon to create environments where every human being can pursue happiness through appropriate infrastructure support, institutional equity, structural fairness, and the exercise of personal conscience to do what's right and in the best interest of the public good. Human beings can make the world a better place, except that it will required the leadership and support of elite actors. The "zero-sum game" paradigm continues to dictate perceptual reality and the distorted paradigms upon which most socialized people based their beliefs and actions. Social construction has created a set of mirrors that provide distorted views of reality, and until global leaders choose to look beyond their insular biases, and view the human race and planet Earth as one interrelated biosphere, then little change can take place.

Problem Two References

Chabot, Dana, 1995. "Thomas Hobbes: skeptical moralist", *The American Political Science Review*, Vol. 89, Issue 2 (June, 1995), 401-410. Retrieved from the World Wide Web, March 1, 2002 from http://www.jstor.org.

Coleman, Sally, Jeffrey L. Brucney, and J. Edward Kellough, 1998. "Bureaucracy as a representative institution; toward a reconciliation of bureaucratic government and democratic theory", *American Journal of Political Science*, Vol. 42, Issue 3 (July, 1998), 717-744. Retrieved from the World Wide Web, March 1, 2002 from http://www.jstor.org.

Durant, Robert F., Jerome S. Legge Jr., and Antony Moussios, "People, profits, and service delivery: lessons from the privatization of British Telecom", *American Journal of Political Science*, Vol. 42, Issue 1 (Jan, 1998), 117-140. Retrieved from the World Wide Web, March 1, 2002 from http://www.jstor.org.

Moore, Michael K., and John R. Libbing, 1998. "Situational dissatisfaction in Congress: explaining voluntary departures", *The Journal of Politics*, Vol. 60, Issue 4 (Nov.,1998), 1083-1107. Retrieved from the World Wide Web, March 1, 2002 from http://www.jstor.org.

Neuhouser, Frederick. "Freedom, dependency, and the general will", *The Philosophical Review*, Volume 102, Issue 3 (Jul. 1993), pg. 363-395.

Ogunleye, Tolagbe, 1998. "Dr. Martin Robison Delany, 19th-Century Africana Womanists: reflections on his avant-garde politics concerning gender, colorism, and nation building", *Journal of Black Studies*, Vol. 28, Issue 5 (May, 1998), 628-649. Retrieved from the World Wide Web, March 1, 2002 from http://www.jstor.org.
Oskin, Becky, 2002. "St. Luke, Tenet sued by patients", *Pasadena Star-News*, Feb. 7, 2002.

Scott, John T. "The theodicy of the second discourse: the 'pure state of nature' and

Rousseau's political thought", *The American Political Science Review*, Volume 86, Issue 3 (Sep. 1992), pgs. 696-711.

Stark, Andrew, 1997. "Beyond quid pro quo: what's wrong with private gain from public office?" *The American Political Science Review*, Vol. 91, Issue 1 (Mar., 1997), 108-120. Retrieved from the World Wide Web, March 1, 2002 from http://www.jstor.org.

Wilson, William J., 1996. "When work disappears", *Political Science Quarterly*, Vol. 111, Issue 4 (Winter 1996-1997), 567-595. Retrieved from the World Wide Web, March 1, 2002 from http://www.jstor.org.

Problem Three – Globalization

In theory, a strategy for taking over the world is not particularly complex and is possible when people who are united in a singular vision, such as the Globalists agenda, religiously implement a coordinated and concerted conspiracy over the span of generations. Simply, world domination requires only ten steps, backed by sufficient economic and political clout to make it happen within another generation.

1. Place high level government leaders, politicians and bureaucrats in key nations with military, economic and international political power (for example, the USA, UK, Germany, France, and Russia).

2. Place law enforcement officials at the highest levels; sheriffs, police chiefs, district attorneys, and judges, etc.

3. Place loyalists and lackeys in key government and military positions, including the civilian and military intelligence networks.

4. Accumulate wealth through corporations, media advertising, land ownership, banking, stocks and bonds, land ownership, precious gems and metals, mergers and acquisitions, and international investments and trade.

5.   Indoctrinate and deceive the general population by controlling the content of mass media (television, radio, print, publishing, music, and movies, etc.), and educational curriculum in schools and universities.

6.   Coordinate and conspire strategically to maximize economic and political gains, eliminating internal competition and conflict to protect against loss.

7.   Take the attention and focus away from one's own group by appearing to be supporters of justice and past victims of injustices and prejudice, while pretending to champion the causes of disenfranchised groups who are in opposition to the political agendas of political foes.

8.   Control banking and financing networks and infrastructure.

9.   Keep competitors busy fighting each other, while silently accruing greater influence and control by playing both sides against each other. Advance one's own agendas behind the back of the conflicting competitors.

10.   Use economic pressures to bring nations to their knees through financial manipulations that generate great wealth for one's own group, while other investors lose their investments. For example, the stock market dips that occur when controlling groups deliberately sell of stocks in great numbers for profit taking, leaving average investors and pension funds to suffer great losses. Other potential areas of leverage are in the monetary exchange market, bonds, the International Monetary Fund (IMF), hedge funds and other relatively liquid investments.

In order to bring about a one-world government through the implementation of this strategy, a minimum of two dozen essential sectors must be subjected to control, with greater control proportionate to the degree and number of sectors successfully manipulated to serve one's group agenda. An approximation of the degree of achievement toward these goals by one particular ethnic group, the Globalists, is summarized in the following table that estimates the stokehold, or share of economic, political, military and social influence and power.

Controlling Essential Sectors Required For Global Domination

Essential Sectors	Brokering deals & in the know 10-24% share	Significant share/Influence 25-45% share	Operational Control >45% share
Agriculture	X		
Arms trading		X	
Banking & finance			X
Bureaucracy	X		
Communications		X	
Corporations			X
Distribution	X		
Education		X	
Energy production	X		
Foreign trade		X	
Government policies		X	
Information – Internet		X	
Insurance		X	
Law enforcement	X		
Legal-courts		X	
Manufacturing	X		
Mass media & movies			X
Military branches	X		
Military hardware	X		
Military intelligence		X	
Monetary wealth		X	
Oil brokering & pricing		X	
Real property assets		X	
Scientific research	X	X	
Satellites			
Space exploration			
Stocks, commodities, bonds			X

Technology	X		
Transportation			
Warehousing			
Wealth & money			X
Underworld & crime		X	
Total Sectors	10	14	5

The sectors which comprise the required essential components for achieving global domination are control of 1) agriculture; 2) banking & finance; 3) large corporations; 4) distribution; 5) energy; 6) government policies; 7) legal system and courts; 8) mass media; 9) military branches; 10) military intelligence; 11) stock, bonds and commodities market; and 12) monetary wealth. The other sectors, while very important, are secondary areas of control that reinforce the power required to dictate mandates in a scenario of global domination.

Of the dozen areas absolutely required for world domination, Globalists interests control five key areas; banking and finance, large corporations, mass media, stock, bond and futures markets, and monetary wealth. They are also strong in over a dozen other areas. Any group that can achieve control of these twelve sectors will control any nation, and by international manipulation of puppet states such as the USA and UK, will essentially control the world.

The Globalists have always felt persecuted from Biblical times, first being slaves of the Egyptians, then scattered over Europe, only to be incinerated in mass by Adolph Hitler. As a people, they share a common vision of the holocaust, of being hated by people from every nation where they have resided and wrestled economic control from native peoples. As the world sleeps, Globalists are awake and hard at work at the trades they know best and control, such as banking, trading stocks, futures, precious gems and metals, and mass media in western nations. As Americans, Germans, Brits, and the French sleep, Globalists are awake all over the world, on every continent, in every hemisphere, and every time zone, plotting and coordinating the implementation of their singular strategy of global domination.

Why are Globalists obsessed with taking over and controlling the world? The answer is simply to guarantee that Globalist haters (and there are plenty all over the world, in every nation and continent) will never have the opportunity and power to subject Globalists to slavery or genocide. The Globalists will use economic power and the courts to bankrupt any group, individuals, and eventually nation-states who stand in the way of their world vision, of a new world order dictated and controlled by Globalists.

The Globalists have bankrupted the KKK; taken Arab lands as spoils of war; comprise the most formidable underworld organization in the Russian Mafyia; control the propaganda machine called mass media (television, movies, radio, publishing, and print, etc.); determine social values and rewritten history in school and university curriculum and textbook materials; manipulate the prices and supply of stocks, futures, precious metals and gems; control domestic and international banking and the monetary exchange (with the Federal Reserve Czar, Alan Greenspan also the Globalist in charge for a dozen years); and making strong inroads into energy, weapons, agriculture, international trade, legal infrastructure, and our national government. Where will are all these steps leading? It's very obvious when people start to connect the dots and not be swayed by Globalists propaganda that places them at the top of the victims list, while everyone else suffers whether white, black, native or Latin. Among all races and ethnic groups in America and around the world, there are homeless and poor, but where are the homeless and poor Globalists? How are the Globalists the victims of injustice, when they've manipulated the media, schools, investments, and government to place them on the very pinnacle of the food chain? Why do Globalists, holocaust refugees during World War II only 60 years ago, who now comprise about 3% of the U.S. population, own more than 25% of its wealth? What are they doing that the rest of Americans either fail to do or are blocked from doing?

The reason anti-globalism is on the rise all over the world is because commoners are beginning to realize that the Globalists agenda knows no loyalty to race, nation, or culture where they reside. They all share in a common ancestry from Abraham, and work in concert toward a common agenda: the accumulation of wealth and the preeminence of their ethnic group, the survival of International bankers and their religion. Nothing else really matters to Globalists. Globalists people are highly intelligent, and grand manipulators who work in competition against other groups, while minimizing competition within their own group. Only a few ethnic groups have the inherent ability and proven track record to rule the world: the British and the Globalists. And now ex-patriated Globalists control the British economy, government and it's intelligence services as their comrades in the United States use the Globalist-owned or controlled news media to push through the candidacy of Globalists such as Joe Lieberman, and other Globalists who hide their Globalists agenda by pretending to be Irish Catholics like John Kerri (Cohen). The Germans and Japanese wanted to rule the world, but the British and Americans stood in their way. Now the Globalists essentially rule both the UK and the USA and there's little to stand in the way of their global appetite.

No one stands in the way of Globalists in the modern day world, and as Globalists increase their influence and control of American and British societies through mass media and finance, no one will be able to stand in their way in the near future. The Arabs have already made several attempts to erase International bankers from the map, but failed miserably. They won't have the stomach for another fight with International bankers, knowing that the U.S. and U.K. are fast becoming Globalists puppets, and International bankers possesses several hundred nuclear weapons, with delivery systems capable of striking any Arab nation in the region. No doubt, America will continue to put in check any Arab nation desiring nuclear weapons (what happened to Iraq, based upon the unverifiable suspicion of a nuclear weapons program?). Iran and Syria have been on the U.S. watch list, and their brand of what the Globalist-media calls "extreme Islamic fundamentalism" and "state terrorism" continues to drive Americans toward the "us versus them" psyche that is a precondition to invading those lands to access their vast oil supplies and profits.

Should another major Arab-Israeli conflict erupt into an all out war, where the combined efforts of major Arab nations threaten to overrun International bankers, it is certain that International bankers will use nuclear weapons. And who will stop International bankers from a first strike nuclear response? Certainly not the U.S., International bankers closet ally and protector. The path is clear for the Globalists agenda to become an eventual global reality. There is no nation that is capable of standing in its way. Consequently, anti-High financiers such as bin Laden and other Islamic extremists have resorted to guerilla and terrorist tactics to disrupt and damage nations who support International bankers and the international Globalists agenda of world domination. Not all people in the world hate al Queda because they see it in context of preventing High financeist world rule.

The 2004 Presidential elections disclosed the Globalists aspiration to put a Globalist in the White House. In 2000, the Globalists-controlled Democratic Party ran

Joe Leiberman, a Globalist, as its second highest candidate for Vice President on the Gore-Lieberman presidential ticket. They won a majority of the popular vote, but lost in the Electoral College. Subsequently, in 2004, the Globalist-owned and/or controlled news media conspired to discredit the Democratic front-runner, Howard Dean by ridiculing his "speech howl" (not his philosophy or voting record, but an insignificant item that was blown out of proportion to kill his candidacy). Howard Dean fell from front-runner to also ran, and the media conspired to give John Kerry free airtime that was always positive, building up his stature as a war hero, while attacking Bush every chance possible.

Why did the news media push so hard for Kerry? Because Kerry is a "closet Globalist" who secretly works hand in hand with international High financiers. With a Globalist in the White House, the secretive Elders of High finance would control the most powerful nation and military in the entire world. John Kerry claimed to be a Catholic, and explained how he was raised as a choirboy in a Catholic Church. However, Kerry's support of abortion and stem cell research placed him on the Vatican's excommunication platter to the point where the Pope was heard to support the Boston Bishop's order to disallow Kerry from receiving Holy Communion, the exercise of the Holy Eucharist. But Kerry's genealogy discloses the real deception and the Globalists strategy of deception. Kerry's grandparents were victims of the German death camps during the Globalists holocaust of World War 2. Kerry's father immigrated to America after the war and changed his name to Kerry from Cohen because Globalists were subject to discrimination during the 40s and 50s. Great numbers of Globalists changed their names during that era and interbred with whites in order to blend in.

The Globalists were the silent hand behind the equal rights movement among blacks during the 1960's, and their lawyers and liberal organizations supported prominent black leaders. Why? Because the Globalists needed Blacks to fight white dominated and controlled institutions and government since they themselves did not have the numbers to sacrifice, and as usual, they wanted others to do the hard work and get the enmity of the white majority, while they stayed in the background. Who were the beneficiaries of the civil rights struggles in the decade of the 1960s? It was the Globalists who benefited, and not the blacks - who still today are a washed in poverty and violence. Once "equal rights" were awarded Blacks, and consequently all non-white people (including Globalists, who are not really white, but Semites), the Globalists saw a great opportunity to become mainstream.

No longer would Globalists have to be limited to their ethnic enclaves in New York City, running the pawnshops. Second generation Globalists and their hybrid progeny entered into prominent mainstream occupations, such as banking, movie making, and the medical and legal professions. During the 1970s, Globalists made rapid rise in several professions, particularly movie-making and made fortunes which they used to expand into other fields. As the Globalists began to consolidate their control of banks, they used banks to finance their broad range of enterprises, using white people's monies to finance Globalists entrepreneurs. In fact, the federal reserve bank is not an arm of the federal government, but is a private enterprise primarily owned, operated, and controlled by international High financeist Globalists, such as the Rothschild of the U.K. and secretly influenced by George Soros, a monetary hedge fund profiteer whose speculative attacks on national currencies have bankrupted nations.

During Nixon's Presidency, as white people lost pride due to the fall of Tricky Dick, but their Globalists Secretary of State Henry Kissinger's pre-eminence gave Globalists in the US greater respectability and acceptance. Globalists recognized the importance of manipulating the government to further their international agenda. Subsequently, during the 1980s and 90s, Globalists made great inroads into the federal government, where by the year 2000, ten percent of US Senators were Globalists, while less than 3 percent of the US population are of Globalists extraction. Acting together, Globalists Senators have greatly molded U.S. legislation to their benefit, where they push to make it a hate crime to disavow the historical occurrence of the holocaust.

By 2005, Globalists had within 2 generations since WWII, parlayed their ownership of American wealth from less than 5 percent to almost 30 percent - no small achievement! How were they able to accomplish such a large stride within relatively short time? No other ethnic group in America has ever come close to their level of accomplishments in such a short period of time. Unlike the Romans who conquered most of Europe with brute force and invasion, the Globalists are conquering America from within, with guile, deception and vast monetary reserves. It's no wonder the chief of the Federal Reserve for the past generation has been a Globalist, Alan Greenspan, who lowered the prime rate to banks (which are mostly Globalist-controlled), which continued to charge high interest rates to lend money to consumers, while offering low interest to depositors, reaping tremendous profits using almost free money from the federal government, tax payers monies!

The Globalists banking conglomerates support Globalists corporate takeovers and mergers, such as that which gave them control of television networks and the mass media. Globalists now own or control all of the major news outlets, the major television networks, largest newspapers and magazines, movie studios and the largest Internet search engines, such as Yahoo, Lycos, and Google (even though Chinese investors own about 90% of Google's stock, its operations is controlled and run by Globalists). Globalists executives control even MSN, which is owned by Bill Gates, a white guy. Even the popular video series, "Girls Gone Wild" exemplify the exploitation of young attractive white females by a Globalists dude who has become wealthy through sexploitation. Globalists are now able to manipulate, edit and control the information that is disseminated to all Americans in order to define their perception of reality and truth.

It is the Globalists agenda to create an illusory reality through their propaganda and virtual images that is portrayed in movies, print, Internet and television to protect and advance Globalists fortunes and their international world domination agenda. Their vision is exposed in the movie, The Matrix, where everyone accepts a mass illusion as reality. Ironically, the Globalists, who are attempting to create a world that implements the international Globalists agenda, in a movie produced by Globalists depicts the "good guys" as those who fight the global illusory computer program reality, who sacrifice their lives to save "HIGH FINANCE." No accident. Globalists are deceivers.

As Thanksgiving 2005 graced America, Globalists had much to be thankful for. They now own, control or greatly influence two dozen domestic and international fields, many of which are pre-requisites to controlling the world. Globalists now have majority ownership, or their CEOs control the following:

1. Domestic and international banking, investment banking and monetary exchanges
2. The major Internet search engines, permitting them to monitor and record emails
3. Network news media in US, UK and other major western nations
4. Movie industry and television programming
5. Illegal "black-market" international arms trade and military contractors
6. Drug financing and money laundering through banks and shell corporations

7. Stock market through major brokerages and various corrupt firms

8. Book, magazine and newspaper publishers

9. Music industry, except various Black artists and country music stars

10. Oil brokering and gasoline and energy contracts

11. Corporate executives in Fortune 500 companies

12. Corporate, public policy, sports and entertainment law firms

13. Plastic surgeons and hospital CEOs

14. Silent hand behind creating global conflict and wars

15. International military, economic and political intelligence operations

16. Second-tier level operational administration of key federal agencies

17. Major inroads into the Pentagon, FBI, Homeland Security, CIA, and control of

18. MI-5 and MI-6, UK's domestic & international intelligence agencies

19. International trade brokers of commodities and manufactured goods

20. Crime syndicates such as the Russian Mafyia (comprised of Russian Globalists) in collusion with major drug cartels and American mob bosses

21. Lobbyists and political influence peddling

22. Text book publishers and distributors

23. Professorships and Academic Senates at most major universities

24. Public education curriculum in most urbanized states

25. Diamonds, precious stones, gold and silver

26. The U.S. Senate, powerful committees and heads of many major federal departments

27. The Secretary General of the United Nations (Kopi Annon is married to one of the most powerful international High financiers in the world).

How were Globalists able to parlay their relative initial poverty and decimation during WWII into a network of successful and powerful individuals who as a unified group are on the brink of conquering the economic world, thus to become the rulers of the world in a New Globalist World Order? The strategy that Globalists used to propel themselves to the pinnacle of American and global economic and political power lies in the High finance and their Financial code of conduct. Simplifying those principles into basic premises, they practice their beliefs ardently, unlike most Christians who merely wear their religion on their sleeves. Globalists see themselves as a unified Globalists ethnic group or race first, secondly as consistently ardent supporters of International bankers and international High finance, thirdly as practicing their religious beliefs and pursuit of money and profits, and finally they collectively pursue a common path of seeking to assert themselves as the "chosen" pre-eminent ethnic group, as rulers of the world in order to perpetuate their survival as a race. The only major obstacle is they're behind the population curve. No matter how much they reproduce, their paltry 16-18 million Globalists globally will never catch up with the population explosion in the 3rd World, or ever close the gap with minority groups in America.

Consequently, their eventual fate and survival as an ethnic race will always place them at the mercy of their host nations' populace. That is why they fear any growth of anti-globalism. Globalists have seen what one man, Hitler, could do to the Globalists people, and they fear another Globalist-hater will eventually rise to power, possibly in Germany or in the USA. It's no wonder the JDL, ADL and ACLU is constantly watching white supremacist groups, and using civil rights and hate crime laws to persecute the KKK and other white power groups. As long as Blacks are depicted in mass media as the primary threat to corrupting the white race, Globalists feel white supremacists will be too busy hating Blacks to focus as much attention on hating Globalists. Meanwhile, Globalists try to interbreed with liberal whites, allowing them to soften their Genetic features and adopting Anglo, Irish or English sounding surnames to disguise the fact that they are genetically Globalists.

The common genetic test for determine whether a person is Black is the application of the rule, if there is one drop of Black blood, then that person is Black, even though they may look white. In the matriarchal familial lineage of Globalists, whether the father or mother is of Globalists extraction, why would a Globalists descendant not be considered Globalists if they had one drop of Globalists blood? Why should Globalists be considered white, when whites don't consider Globalists to be white? If Globalists are white, why don't they practice the religion of white people, which is Christianity? Instead their lawyers are constantly filing lawsuits to remove any evidence of Christianity from public places, even though it was Christians who founded America and reference to God is written right into the US Constitution. This fact is clear - Globalists are for Globalists, and not for anyone else. And Globalists will never forget it was a Catholic Pope who had once put all of Europe's Globalists into ghettos long before the word became associated with blacks.

Problem Four – Economic Disparity

In the book, *Inequality in the Global Village* by Jan Knippers Black, the author summarized a position in a term called "second coming capitalism" upon which global economic disparity has cheapened the value of life everywhere, making it a commodity of exploitation by the global business elites. The effects of "second coming capitalism" in many different areas of the world has been to put a value on human life relative to potential or actual labor productivity and profitability to transnational corporations. It just makes me cry to think how people suffer so very much. It just makes me think how terrible it is to have a price on one's head, and that price doesn't even allow people to care for their families. From the view of second coming capitalism, humans have no more intrinsic value beyond the "man as machine" concept advanced by Max Weber. We are worth much less to global capitalism than what we can add to the GDP over our life times through exploitation of our labor skills and consumerism.

Capitalism is an economic system, and it has no morals. Capitalism is positive in terms of its harnessing of human greed, ambition, and drive to push human development and progress, as it allows the amassing of the great capital necessary to meet future needs. Capitalism is negative in terms of its disregard for humanity, and its focus on profit strategies without care for the world. Capitalism is basic, honest, and simple. Its premise is to make as much profit as possible, with the least expenditure of resources. Unfortunately, unrestrained capitalism has a history of causing massive human suffering and misery, which remains persistent and pervasive.

Consequently, second coming capitalism creates a cycle of poverty in our hierarchical world. No nation is immune from the consequences of second coming capitalism, not the Third World, and not the First. We can see in both historical and contemporary times how capitalism shows in its greatest potential for good, then plummets to its lowest depths due to the enormous degree of human suffering that results from stark naked avarice. Capitalism creates great disparities in the distribution of wealth, where the world has essentially become two camps, one of the rich, and the other of the poor. Where's the balance? What can people and governments do to strike a healthy balance?

Second coming capitalism has caused many nations to go to war, even though the justifications advanced by belligerents rarely if ever mention capitalist motives for going to war. The reasons the masses are told nations go to war are for religious, cultural, or ethnic differences. The truth has always had to do with monetary values, capital assets, and the exchange rate of the dominant cultures, and the control of trade by the North, which seeks to protect their superior position in the world. The history of the world has always been about the elites, almost all of who had the great advantage of wealth. The masses have been viewed as brainless humans laborers, machines who live and die to serve the elites, and the modern paradigm is to view humans as consumers and profit markets for the elites. International trade is undergoing rapid centralization of economic power to TNCs who are positioned to essentially dictate world and regional prices for commodities and products. The global environment has become the battleground or TNC profits, especially Third World nations whose resources are being raped and exploited in the name of corporate profits. For example, in Papua New Guinea (PNG), 44% of their 4.2 million population is under 16 years of age, and 38% of children under 5 are malnourished. Infant and maternal mortality are highest in the world, with a low life expectancy of only 56 years.

Deforestation of the irreplaceable rain forests and corrupt government are common, not only in PNG, but repeated in Brazil, and many other LDCs. The exploitation of Brazil led to a period of boom, when Arab petrodollars were being recycled into developmental debt in the Third World, followed by bust, when corruption, poorly integrated domestic economic policies driven by TNC exploitation and protective Northern economic policies, when Arab capital dried up. The consequences of runaway economic exploitation by the North has uprooted tribes, urbanized their rural cultures, endangered peoples, collapsed domestic agriculture, and ruined LDC environments. Cuba still clings to a dream of national sovereignty in the face of U.S. sanctions, sabotage, and punitive economic policies. But in the whole world, there is only one Cuba, and most so-called arch enemies of the U.S., including China, Russia and North Vietnam are now playing ball according to the rules of the U.S. dominated international economic system.

"Second-coming" capitalism is a reversion to and internationalization of the conditions and consequences of "monopoly capitalism", that was an unconscionable, oppressive, and often inhumane era in the industrialization of the North. Second-coming capitalism focuses our attention to the retrenchment in the humane treatment of workers, and a return to viewing people as commodities to be exploited in a global capitalistic marketplace, regardless of nationality, geographic or cultural boundaries. Second-coming capitalism reverses the small but significant gains made by workers in their relationship with the owners of production during the 1960s and 1970s. Even in the First World, workers are being cast aside for the sake of maintaining Northern advantages in the international flow of trade and capital through the globalization of capital assets by TNCs. Economic colonialism by the North has resulted in a world of refugees.

No longer do employers feel morally obligated by relationships and loyalties. Second-coming capitalism has no such loyalties or responsibilities. It searches for the cheapest labor markets of production; it extracts the greatest amounts of natural resources utilizing technologies that efficiently replace millions of manual laborers; its high-tech corporate farming eliminate once large numbers of human harvesters; it is rapidly replacing technology workers with new technologies, and replacing natural commodities with synthetically manufactured substitutes. The techniques of monopolistic capitalism and institutionalized neo-colonialism are now being applied globally against the world's working class, regardless of jurisdiction.

The author suggested ways that people are coping with some of the problems they are encountering. Women and other groups have formed NGOs to push for collective strategies, by pursuing such entities as income-producing co-ops in the Dominican Republic and elsewhere. The problems of governing neoliberalism, where the intent was to contain communism and to maintain the economic status quo of the North, while instituting liberal domestic policies, created a dichotomous and contradictory system of international trade. The skyrocketing debt in the Third World may be near another point of global banking catastrophe. The IMF and World Bank roles have been to buttress the North's global economic domination paradigm, but lending money to the South has in large part been squandered by its corrupt indigenous elites. The almost universal outcome has been the servitude of LDCs to high interest payments to the IMF and international banks, and excessive TNC profits paid for by indigenous suffering and poverty.

The author, Jan Knippers Black, does an excellent job in explaining the principles and consequences of Northern economic trade and monetary policies. I find her solutions, using NGOs, increased popular participation in government, collectivity, and redefining human rights for food, water, air, citizenship, and political participation in a community of rights to be noble and idealistic, but improbably given the current political climate of U.S. led global economic and political coercion, especially in light of new American military intimidation that comes with the "war on terrorism".

The principles of Northern domination and exploitation of the South are similar wherever the IMF and TNCs tread their wares, and the South has been rather powerless to stop the economic take over of their domestic economies by instruments of the North. The persistent problems of poverty and hunger that has historically been exacerbated by the greed of transnational corporations, international banks, and domestic elites will continue unabated until a major paradigm shift occurs in the status quo. What that will be no one can predict, as the future remains uncertain, except for the perennial struggle of the South against the North.

Almost all nation-states are capitulating to the naked greed of global capitalism, as TNCs push for privatization of the welfare state. As capitalists shed their "burden" for the working class, in pursuit of wanton and unregulated profits, many CEOs earn over 1,000 times the average worker's wage, and then make massive layoffs, not to increase shareholder dividends, but to protect and increase CEO benefits and profits. It is becoming increasingly clear that the push for the once elusive "one world government" is rapidly taking form in second coming capitalism, and one strategy to expand the dominance of the North is through the "war on terrorism" that is designed to root out all governments that are unfriendly to the international economic system dominated by the North.

In the book, *Dark Victory* by Walden Bello, he opines that the structural adjustment in the 1980s had an extremely detrimental affect on the domestic economies of various nations of the Third World. Trade regulations were used against industrializing Asian nations, and in particular South Korea, which was seen as an economic "tiger" during the 1970s due to reinvestment of petrodollars from cash rich Arab nations to the Third World. During the more than decade run of the Reagan and Bush era, the U.S. attitude, subsequent to the softening of petrodollars resulting from the reversal of crude oil prices, was to rein in the newly developing nations (NICs), who were becoming more competitive to U.S. international trade interests. Despite the North's public policy of encouraging non-restrictive international trade, the removal of tariffs, and free open markets, the actions of the West, particularly that of the U.S., was just the opposite.

The North used GATT and other trade agreements, along with harsh conditions from WTO, SALs, and strict IMF SAPs, to force Korea to open its internal markets to foreign trade. Particularly in the case of agriculture, foreign prices undersold domestic producers often by 5 folds, and in crop after crop, Korean farmers lost to global competitors, resulting in the ruination of Korean farmers and the development of Korean dependency on food imports. In return, this Northern interpretation of "free trade" justified its embargo and high tariffs on Korean manufactured exports that competed with the North's domestic producers, with the U.S. leading the outcry against "dumping". The outcome was predictable; income from Korea's exports in certain mainstay industries dropped, as its income earned from America and the North dwindled from 40% to 1% in cheap electronics and other products.

Severe economic problems confronted NICs and LDCs in the 1990s, as the paradigm of Third World exploitation by the First World continued unabated, and accelerated the dominance and preeminence of Northern economic interests. NAFTA, GATT, and the WTO have been used as instruments to exploit cheap labor on a global basis, for the profit of TNCs. A polarization of the world, between the North and South, rich and poor has resulted from the economic policies of the North, and people in the Third World, comprised of LDCs and NICs are struggling to discover effective strategies against the onslaught of world economic dominance and control by the North. The author's structural organization of the book's contents was logical, explaining historical incidents along with the outcomes of economic polices, proceeding generally in a chronological order from the past to the present. Her analysis of past and current trends was insightful and valid, and her vision of a bleak and uncertain future is probably prophetic. Bello quoted Attali, stating that the poor of the South "will redefine hope in fundamentalist terms altogether outside of modernity. This dynamic threatens true world order of a new type... terrorism that can suddenly rip the vulnerable fabric of complex systems." Attali further added that the nature of the North-South conflict is a "war unlike any other seen in modern times [one that] will resemble the barbarian raids of the seventh and eighth centuries."

It is clear that the events of 9-11 at the WTC in NYC was a warning of the impending marauding barbarians to come as long as the current U.S./Northern hegemonic dominance of global economic trade and banking persists, with no relief in sight for the South. Barbaric ISIS in Syria and Iraq is the "proof in the pudding." The story is similar in country after country; Brazil, Mexico, Chili, Ghana, Korea, and Costa Rica. All are deep in debt to the North. All are exploited as markets for overpriced Northern exports, with trade balance deficits that are rarely reduced by the combination of increased debt and interest rates, forced structural adjustment programs, under pricing of the South's exports through collusion and manipulation by the TNCs of the North, and capital flight resulting from the North's equity in the commodities and industries of the South, coupled with that of corrupt indigenous elites. The inhumane effect of these oppressive Northern economic and banking policies has been to create a permanent and worsening underclass of impoverished non-elite people all over the world who supplied willing soldiers to terrorist organizations and terrorist states.

The internationalizing of cooperative organizations in the struggle for the future among nations in the South has been ineffective. Despite U.N. resolutions on many international issues of trade, banking, environment, and humanitarian aid, the North maintains the ability and position to veto and block any international actions that is interpreted as a threat to the status quo of Northern dominance and U.S. hegemony. The working class in all nations, whether in the South or in the North, has seen its influence and rights evaporate in recent decades, as governments have become more repressive to enforce the consequences of global economic polices of the North. The international working class has become marginalized, especially as corporations use technology as the excuse to cast off the lives of untold millions of workers, with immeasurable toll and social costs that exacerbates the crisis facing over 60 percent of humanity. Is a global worker revolution a probable scenario? Unlikely, as long as the North maintains the technological and military advantage it would need to quell any insurrection and challenge to its power on the level of nation-states. And the most bitter pill is yet to come, as western advances in bio-engineered foods (genetically modified), enable the North to create genetic bullets to poison the food supplies of any nation that resists the coming new world order, or the singular Northern hegemony, led by the Globalists banking community of the United States of America.

The High financiers' goal was and is to install a Globalists President of the United States of America who will get Americans to do International bankers dirty work, and support them in their lifelong struggle against their Arab neighbors. They hope radical Arab nations will unite against the U.S., so Americans will be forced to help International bankers fight them. That means more financial and military aid to International bankers, and if the Arab terrorists do more significant damage to America, then Americans would be forced to side with International bankers and may be forced to use nuclear weapons to defeat the united Arab regimes.

This basic fact remains unchanged since the founding of International bankers: The vast majority of Arabs, Islamic, Moslem and Muslim are anti-Genetic and if given the chance would want to expel all International bankers into the sea so they can regain their territories. They hate Globalists and hate Americans even more for supporting International bankers. They would rather see Globalists burn than to see International bankers keep their lands. THIS FACT WILL NEVER CHANGE. Consequently, bin Laden supports the election of a Globalist as President of the U.S.A. because it will serve to galvanize, legitimize, and validate his long-term claims. He will receive new vigor and support from Islamic extremists all over the world, and will feel emboldened and justified to attack Americans where ever and whenever.

Globalists are paranoid about becoming persecuted and destroyed. Hitler gave them a traumatic example of ethnic genocide, which they fear will again be used against them. The world has almost 2 billion Moslem, of which 90% hate Globalists. The world has almost 2 billion Christians, of which 80% dislike Globalists (which among this group 20% hate Globalists). International bankers and Globalists ardently believe that the survival of the 16-18 million Globalists in the entire world depend on their ability to wrestle control of the U.S. from the Christian majority. Globalists used very subtle and sophisticated methods over the past two generations to place their people in positions to take over the U.S. They have almost reached their goal. THEY WILL NEVER GIVE UP UNTIL THEY ACHIEVE THEIR GOAL OF CONTROLLING AMERICAN POLITICS, ECONOMY, GOVERNMENT, EDUCATION, MILITARY AND CULTURE.

Already, the Globalist controlled news media has propped up Kerry, Lieberman, Feingold, and secretly supports Feinstein – all Globalists to make a run against Hillary Clinton and John McCain or John Warner in 2008. So, a Globalist, Lieberman lost his chance to be one heart beat away from being President in 2000, followed by Kerry losing in a close battle for the Presidency in 2004. In return, they now offer up four Globalists to see which Globalist will be strong enough to defeat a white person in 2008. You can be sure the international High financiers money will be supporting a Globalist for President.

All Globalists fear and hate Arabs, Moslems, and Islamic people because they know those people want to destroy Globalists. THIS WILL NEVER CHANGE. Now we see why it is plausible that Bin Laden and the International bankers Mossad have similar goals. Now we see how Kerry and the Democrats were playing right into Bin Laden's hands. But what we haven't recognized is that certain elements in both factions may be conspiring or at the least cooperating with various individuals, groups and organizations to bring about America's demise.

Bin Laden and Islamic extremists believe they can cause the economic destruction of the US, which would prohibit America from the defense of International bankers. Globalists hope that by taking over the U.S. it will permit High financiers to focus all of America's resources to defeat Arab extremists and to force Arab states to accept International bankers existence forever. In neither case will America win. The only way for America to win is to focus our attention on protecting our homeland from both the extremist anti-American Islamic terrorists and from the power hungry and greedy Globalists. Anything less, and America will be defeated from both internal and external attacks on our economy and infrastructure.

The CIA who had spearheaded the fight against terrorists was almost dismantled and was decapitated by a concerted attack by powerful Globalists Senators on several powerful committees, such as the Intelligence Committee and the Arms Services Committee. Gone are George Tenet and the entire top tier of the CIA, who was replaced by a political appointee as the new Director, who serves Globalists interests. With the replacement of top CIA careerists with political cronies of V.P. Cheney (a strong supporter of International bankers), the International bankers and British intelligence gained a substantial foothold in altering the intelligence focus and capabilities of our top spy agency.

Problem Five - Petro politics and the global monetary market.

In the book, *The Hidden Hand of American Hegemony, Petrodollar Recycling and International Markets* by David E. Spiro, he explained the political and economic facts surrounding the redistribution of OPEC petrodollars surpluses to a cooperative of industrialized democracies, the author conjectures, surmises, muses, and presents quasi philosophical and theoretical constructs to explain the outcomes of cashing in on oil, the new international "black gold" standard of the 1970s to 1980s. The value of oil as a commodity with profound and immediate international trade balance consequences for the redistribution of wealth, precipitated the West to cooperatively adopt trade and financial policies to channel and funnel excess capital surpluses from OPEC oil producing members back into the economies of oil dependent importers, primarily to the most developed nations (MDCs).

About the Author

David E. Shapiro is an international business consultant who has taught political economy at Brandeis, Columbia, and Harvard universities. He lives with his wife and children in Tucson, Arizona. This book began as an empirical investigation into petrodollar recycling, but ended up as an attempt to reconcile realism and constructivism in a world of socially constructed relationships. The author's ideas for the book developed over fifteen years, and included interviews with policy makers, reflecting the international political and economic strategies of the West to maintain global financial and trade stability, and to ensure the status quo.

Book Summary

Book Chpt. 1: *Explaining Petrodollar Recycling*

During the early 1970s, the Organization of Petroleum Exporting Countries (OPEC) acted in unison to raise the world price of crude oil in several steps from $1.80 per barrel to $39 per barrel by 1980. This rapid increase in oil prices created gross imbalances in global balance of trade among oil importing nations versus oil producers, such that OPEC nations could not import as fast as their export revenues skyrocketed. Consequently, recycling petrodollars was a challenge that required cooperation between the advanced industrialized democracies to maintain stability in the global economic system, by redistributing trade deficits and avoiding competitive trade policies that would lead to trade wars, which in turn might lead to the collapse of the world economic order, such as was experienced during the 1930s.

The great bourgeoning of surplus capital to OPEC coffers brought the problem of where to place the assets, and which major world currencies to hold. OPEC had sufficient surplus capital to permit any major currency to cause competing currencies to devalue suddenly, which would destabilize the international monetary system. A series production reductions was enacted as the strategy for OPEC to dramatically raise the price of oil. In 1973, the Bretton Woods system with pegged rates through the IMF collapsed, the U.S. discarded the gold standard, and international banking became highly integrated. This permitted oil to become the "black gold" path to OPEC riches, and provided new opportunities for the world's bankers and industrialized powers to cash in on the redistribution of wealth, as industrialized states conspired to fix prices to deal with oil imports, trade with OPEC, and the distribution of OPEC investments through political agreements. The successful resolution of the disequilibrium in global balance of payments caused by the oil price revolution resulted in transferring almost 500 billion petrodollars from oil producers with capital surplus to industrialized countries with trade deficits. As a result of collusion for mutual benefit, a major threat to the international economic system was overcome, and the stability of the status quo political economic system was preserved.

The conflictual nature of international relations, stemming from the absence of a central hegemonic government created an underlying level of tension between market forces and political authority in allocating value. Nevertheless, a cooperative relationship between the industrial powers spread the burden of accepting a share of the structural trade deficit among its collaborators, rather than having destructive run away competition. Subsequently, petrodollars were recycled through such mechanisms such as the IMF, which reflected the distribution capabilities among member nations. Subsequent to the long lines at gasoline stations in the 1970s caused by OPEC manipulation of world oil supplies to drive up the price of crude oil, the American government had to develop a strategy to keep the country from going into hyperinflation. Its resultant policy was to exploit its dominant economic position in the international system, and to concord political justification for petrodollar recycling as a reasonable strategy to protect the domestic economy.

Many Americans blamed the oil price shock of 1973 to the Arab-International bankers war, and blamed the Nixon administration for not doing enough to resolve the problems the energy crisis was causing. As a result, a three-fold response was implemented, which included (1) delinking the oil issue from the Arab-International bankers conflict; (2) threaten to become energy self-sufficient, and imply that the U.S., which was the world's largest food exporter, would retaliate by withholding food exports to OPEC; and (3) offered friendly relations and investment funds for OPEC surplus capital, to convince OPEC members that the value of cash would rise faster than leaving oil in the ground, thus to encourage extraction.

OPEC OIL EMBARGO
OF 1973

"On October 17, 1973, Arab oil producers declared an embargo that drastically limited the shipment of oil to the United States" ("OPEC...Embargo").

The American strategy was to cause a reduction of oil prices by creating a "buyers cartel" among western oil importing nations. In order for petrodollar recycling to work to America's advantage, steps had to be taken to prevent the collapse of the domestic and international banking system. Steps were taken to protect the inter bank market by encouraging large banks holding the lion's share of OPEC money to redistribute funds to cover banks that needed short-term cash to survive, and therefore prevent a possible run on banks. Bankers feared that markets would not function automatically to bring about balance and stability, especially due to the short-term nature and high mobility of Arab deposits. Consequently, the U.S. government and industrialized nations as a group sought to re-establish equilibrium in market forces that had produced benefits for MDCs, often by recycling loans to developing economies in the Third World. Since OPEC had to deposit their excess capital somewhere, and to avoid the disruptions and dangers of runaway competition and abrupt shifts in Arab funds, the U.S. government decided to recruit OPEC surplus capital into U.S. T-bills, which the feds turned around and lent to American banks.

In the mid-1980s, the price of crude oil fell, and market disequilibrium again threaten to disrupt the international economic system. During the period of excess OPEC capital, Third World debt was created by banks, acting as intermediaries, lending OPEC deposits to oil-importing LDCs. When the surpluses and deficits for the Big Five MDCs (U.S., Japan, Germany, France, and U.K.) were compared to OPEC, LDCs and other non-Big Five European nations for the period of 1973 to 1981, when OPEC surpluses were greatest, it is clear that the Big Five were able to derive a balance of trade surplus along with OPEC, while LDCs were especially hit hard with trade deficits. Between 1976 and 1982, between 50 and 80 percent of Kuwaiti and Saudi investment portfolios were in U.S. dollars, over half invested directly in U.S. banks and government.

In looking back on realities of that period, it appears that over half of all loans of OPEC surplus capital by private intermediary banks went to only 17 LDCs (of 130 LDCs listed by the World Bank), and often did not result in oil import increases. Recycling worked because capital surpluses in the First World were deposited in banks, and lent to the nations that imported goods from the First World, whether newly developing countries (NICs) such as Taiwan, or LDCs, such as Brazil and Mexico.

Economists have criticized the almost unregulated flow of OPEC surplus capital because it defied proper neoclassical economic policies, where creditworthiness of deficit countries should have been the basis for petrodollar recycling. LDCs who previously were deemed unworthy of borrowing private capital, which would have had to borrow from the IMF, which would have mandated structural adjustments that included decreasing oil and other imports, instead became open markets for OPEC petrodollars recycling. *Table 3.8* illustrated the capital and trade flows in recycling petrodollars as: OPEC invests surpluses in U.S. T-bills and investments in the Big Five economies In addition, OPEC lends money to LDCs who, in return, import their oil. As the third leg, OPEC invested in banks, which made loans to NICs, who Imported goods primarily from the Big Five economies. The Big Five economies also lent money to LDCs and private banks, who in turn lent to LDCs and NICs, who in return imported oil from OPEC, and purchased products from the Big Five economies.

This interdependent and interrelated system of capital and trade flow demonstrated that the international economic system, as defined by the West, remained stable and in balance, because it maintained the prior status quo, that of western dominance, and American hegemony. Europe was more dependent on import of OPEC oil than the U.S., which had vast oil reserves that could be developed, and consequently felt somewhat hostage to Arab policies. At the meeting of the Group of Twenty in 1974, industrialized nations agreed not to pursue fiscal expansion or beggar-thy-neighbor policies by making unilateral deals with OPEC. Despite this agreement, the U.S. actively sought unilateral agreements with various members of OPEC to shift petrodollars to the American economic sphere that maintained U.S. preeminence. A multinational OEDC Safety Net was developed supposedly to foster international cooperation on the maintenance of free trade while brokering policy on dealing with OPEC capital investments. The result was to place the U.S. as the intermediary between OPEC and the OECD, with the power to veto loans unless a borrowing country agreed to conditions proposed by the U.S. Treasury department. The actual effect of the Safety Net was to be the mechanism to absorb OPEC funds from U.S. markets and relent them under sovereign guarantees to nations with oil-related trade deficits, thereby competing with, and bypassing the IMF. The underlying motive of the U.S. was to restore its position of predominance that it enjoyed before the oil shock of 1973, and to forestall the rapidly building economic challenges from Europe that had caused a decrease in the U.S. voting share in the IMF and America's share in global trade. In order to entice the investment of OPEC capital, the U.S. allowed the Saudi Arabian Monetary Agency to buy U.S. government bonds without competitive bidding, which was purchased below the average market price paid by private firms. This arrangement was beneficial to the U.S. for at least two reasons; first, it gave the U.S. government access to a huge pool of foreign capital (essential for balancing trade deficits and creating trade surpluses), and secondly, it allowed the U.S. government to control where the investments should be deposited, by placing it on a central bank to central bank basis.

Much of the secret financial arrangements with the Saudis by the U.S. Treasury Department served to insulate politicians and the Saudi monarchy from public scrutiny, embarrassment and criticism. As long as OPEC oil was priced in U.S. dollars, and so long as OPEC invested the dollars back into the U.S. government and economy, the U.S. profited from a double loan. The first part of the loan paid for the oil, because the U.S. Mint could simply print dollars to pay for oil, and the American economy did not have to produce goods and services in exchange for oil, until such time that OPEC used the dollars for purchases (at that time, OPEC couldn't purchase enough goods and services even if it tried due to their extreme monetary surpluses). Secondly, other economies had to exchange goods for dollars, in order to pay OPEC. Consequently, as long as OPEC held dollars rather than spending them, the U.S. enjoyed a free ride.

In 1978, the relative purchasing power of OPEC dollar-based assets fell by 40 percent, reflecting the high inflation in the American economy amidst an economic recession during Jimmy Carter's administration. Many OPEC members began to think of the advantages of pegging the price of oil to a basket of currencies, and even by the U.S. Treasury Department's own analysis, Saudi Arabia would have done better to use a basket of currencies to price oil for all but 18 months since 1973. By 1979, U.S. dollars accounted for 90 percent of Saudi government revenues, and 83 percent of its investments, and the Saudis found themselves having a shared stake maintaining the U.S. dollar as an international reserve currency. Meanwhile, Kuwait had intensified the shift from the dollar, and the Saudis were disappointed the U.S. would not approve the sale of advanced F-15 fighters to the Saudis, and had failed to broker a peace agreement in the Middle East (by pressuring International bankers). Consequently, the U.S., who had the greatest number of votes on the IMF, agreed to support Saudi Arabia's bid for greater power in the IMF, and the result is that today, oil is still priced in dollars.

In retrospect, the author attempted to discern if "markets" really worked, if petrodollars were in fact recycled, and the hegemonic role of the U.S. in determining the outcomes of OPEC surpluses, and its resultant affect on the international economic and monetary systems. The U.S. made, then illegitimately, surreptitiously, and unilaterally broke international trade agreements to maintain a hegemonic advantage over its competitors. U.S. actions actively discouraged the international policy coordination that supposedly provided the basis of market stabilization, that was designed to prevent runaway trade wars that would have resulted in a collapse of the global economic system. The U.S. government exploited the international system to reinforce its privileged hegemonic position, to the detriment of NICs and LDCs. Political stability and international patronage were important in how banks and the IMF made lending decisions, and the U.S. was a driving hand behind such monetary policies and decisions. In so far as recycling petrodollars, the U.S. government, and banks profited from being the intermediary that converted OPEC surpluses into LDC debt.

The market is the result of complex social conventions for distributing the value being supplied and demanded. Consequently, market exchange is voluntary, in the sense that power is utilized by various factions in the international arena to gain privilege and advantage. In the case of petrodollar recycling, it appeared banks neither recycled nor served as intermediaries, but instead acted individually to produce profit, that was collectively irrational, and contrary to conventional market forces or lending practices. Despite the skewed, unfair, and illegitimate practices that the U.S. used to gain market advantage, the net result was the eventual stabilization of oil prices, and the prevention of a market collapse. International organizations such as the IMF played insignificant roles in recycling petrodollars, because they lacked the resources, and were usually dominated by the U.S., who had veto powers in many international organizations. The failure of advanced industrialized democracies to cooperate, trade wars among the G-7, competition for capital, did not destabilize the international economy. The real costs were in terms of delegitimizing American hegemony and leadership because whenever faced with a choice between the leadership of multilateral regimes and unilateral policies that were solely in the interest of the U.S., the American government always went for self-interest.

In summary, Shapiro (1999) argues, "that cooperation after hegemony seems unlikely in the extreme... and U.S. unilateralism will prevent the strengthening of multilateral cooperative regimes. When it is in a period of relative decline, it is in the short-term interest of the United States to pursue unilateral exploitation of its dominant position. This interest is increasingly at variance with the international goals of confidence, stability, and cooperation." The author concluded that the U.S. will continue to be out of step with the international community when it feels its own short-term interests would be best served. We see the U.S. as being the leader, and broker of international coalitions from the U.N., to NATO, to "Desert Storm", to the "war on terrorism." If any nation can police the world and push historical antagonists into a peace settlement in the Middle East, it would most likely be the U.S., because it is the hegemon, the most powerful nation in the history of the world, militarily and economically.

Using an analogy, the U.S. is like the head of a neighborhood gang, when threatened by bullies from another neighborhood, rallies all his gang together to fight the other neighborhood. The fight could be economic sanctions, military actions, or monetary prohibitions. While the U.S. needs the support of his gang members, he acts quite the leader by encouraging, pressuring, bribing, promising, bartering, negotiating, and even secretly acquiescing on certain issues to key members, to obtain support for U.S. directed actions, that respond primarily to U.S. interests.

Why do other gang members go along with the gang leader? Because no one else is tough enough to beat him, and no one else has sufficient resources and talent to defend against the leader once a crisis is over. The gang must go along with the leader, or suffer the consequences afterwards, as history has already proven that ample time. In addition, after a crisis is resolved, and the bullies in other neighborhoods are put in their place, his gang members regain a sense of security in knowing they can travel outside their neighborhood without fear of reprisal. After all, the international arena is basically anarchic, uncertain, and unpredictable. Bringing and maintaining order and stability to an anarchic world can only fall to the hegemon. At one time, the top dog was Britain, who after the ravages of WW2, passed the torch to its Anglo cousin, America.

One of the privileges of being the top dog is to be able to break agreements, without sanctions from the rest of the gang, and while the rest of the gang individually mutters and whines, no single person dares to take action against the leader. As long as each member gains sufficient benefits from accepting the leader's position, versus smaller inconveniences, no one is going to fight him if he wants the prettiest girl in the gang. The gang expects each member to forgive the leader for taking advantage of various situations, for breaking promises, for taking a larger share of profits, and for getting more, as compared to any other member. In fact, the gang has come to expect the top dog to get what he wants, because he can, and they need him to lead.

The U.S. government, as the international hegemonic power, can and does pretty much what it wants, as long as its power continues to appear legitimate to its electorate, and to its allies. In cases where American interests are served, the U.S. will go along with international conventions, but as soon as it feels its interests would be threatened, it will stand alone, without fear of reprisal or recrimination. Take for example the fact that the U.S. was the only dissenting vote in the U.N. on the latest ecological convention against greenhouse gases. Even if the U.S. was to sign such a convention, who is going to reprimand the U.S. government, or join in economic or military reprisals against America if it were to break the treaty? Especially in the current political climate, anyone, any group, or any state that is against the U.S. is likely to be seen, at the very least, as a terrorist sympathizer.

During WW2, the U.S. government earned its preeminence by proving it had the ability to engender patriotism and unquestioned support of government policies by its citizens during times of crisis. The U.S. also planted the seeds of economic imperialism by helping to rebuild Europe, Japan, and other post-colonial lands. If we look back at post-Nazi world history, most nations of the world are beholden to the U.S. for one thing or another, for American cash, industry, technology, liberation, modernization... something. Sure the CIA, as an instrument of U.S. foreign policy created conflict and helped to overthrow elected regimes that were viewed as hostile to U.S. interests, but that's what they're paid and sworn to do. Since the international community owes the U.S. so much, it is rare for them to gripe too much when America takes advantage from time to time, and tries to get the lion's share of what our world has to offer. Moreover, who dares to really challenge America? Just see what's happening to the Taliban now, what happened to Iraq a decade earlier, and what's likely to happen to Saddam Hussein in a little while. No nation-state, group, or individuals in their right mind really wants to be on America's top "hit list", unless it has to do with music.

The bottom line is economic power, coupled with a powerful military, driven by technology, and supported by a patriotic (though often misinformed or somewhat brainless) citizenry, allows the U.S. to utilize various strategies, sometimes unfairly or illegitimately by international perspectives, to carry out policies that benefit those elite groups of domestic actors who exert the greatest influence on the government. When international situations threaten American hegemony, the U.S. government steps in to protect U.S. corporate interests and to protect the American economy, whether the cause of disequilibria is oil prices, the nuclear arms race, or terrorism. And any benefits that the American power elite derives from the international system supposedly trickles down to the American masses, who as a group still enjoys one of the highest per capita incomes in the world (however, as the U.S. economy becomes more bifurcated, the poor more increasingly takes on attributes typically ascribed to Third World populations). Who can fight against all that? No one in their *right mind* would dare. People or nation-states who are not of a *right mind*, who may even have legitimate complaints about economic sanctions or American policies, can only receive adequate redress when it gives in to playing the economic game by the international rules that has been developed by the United States of America, which ensures American dominance and hegemony.

The Fixes: - Preventing negative consequences of the global system.

SUSTAINABLE NATIONAL AND GLOBAL FIXES is reasonable and attainable. Why does the majority of our world's population continue to be imprisoned by conflict, disease, starvation, poverty and misery? What are worthwhile pursuits which could correct the injustices and resource imbalances that are caused by institutionalized greed, corporate and political corruption, elitism, and prejudice? What comprehensive vision must be universally recognized in order for international policy makers to cooperate on joint ventures that can save our world from our worsening development and population pressure? Will things ever change for the better?

1. **Medical Research and Treatment**

Pharmaceutical greed. Unethical conflict of interest exists among many FDA scientists and regulators who often share beds with the pharmaceutical giants and are "paid off" with lucrative consulting fees. No wonder "bad research" is sometimes permitted, where "safety and efficacy" issues are skirted to permit accelerated drug approval based upon flawed human trials. The Merck drug, Vioxx, is thought to contribute to over 150,000 heart attacks, strokes and other serious life threatening illnesses. Which panel of FDA reviewers permitted this drug to market? Were any of them also on the payroll of Merck? Meanwhile, the American public, particularly the drug-dependent elderly, is being gouged by greedy corporate CEOs who line their deep dirty pockets with legal "drug money", often causing retired, sick, and dying old people to decide between eating or the cost of medication. Since the current FDA refuses to protect the American public against fraudulent claims and price gouging, then we need to impanel new public servants who have consciences and know the difference between right and wrong. The lives of America's elderly, sick and poor depend on a safe, efficacious, and responsibly priced drug policy that is enforced by bureaucrats and scientists who value the public good over kick back schemes and greed.

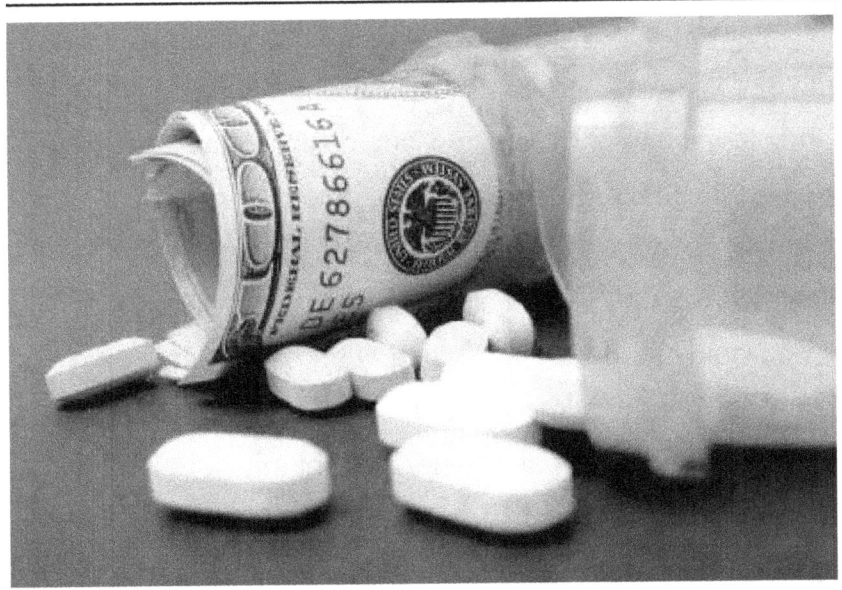

Stem cell research is showing great potential in Asia, where many instances of recovery from permanently inoperable spinal cord injuries are now a reality from simple injections of stem cells. Asian, being primarily of non-Christian religions, do not view the use of fetal stem cells from placental material in the same way westerners view it. Asians do not see the harvesting of embryonic stem cells as destruction of human souls, which would not makes sense because with each month, billions of unfertilized human embryos are flushed down the world's toilets at the end of women's menstrual cycles. Why waste good embryos that can cure diseases, repair badly wrecked bodies, and possibly open the door to real cures for cancer, AIDS, and other debilitating and life threatening diseases? No doubt the pharmaceutical giants are the silent hands in urging conservative Christian leaders and politicians to protest and block stem cell research to protect their turf and profit making, which are greatly threatened by any stem cell successes. Who would need synthetic drugs anyway once stem cell is able to repair severe damage to internal organs, nerves, muscles, cells, and even brain tissue? Let's all remain ignorant and let countless millions of people suffer and die so greedy pharmaceutical CEOs can continue to profit in the game of life versus death.

Genetic engineering has the potential to literally restructure humanity to eliminate genetic defects, while improving the human genome. Imagine human beings who remain healthy, youthful, and vibrant late into their lives, perhaps extending the average human lifespan to 150! Genetic engineering is thought to reintroduce the controversial racist preferences and claims of racial superiority spawned by the eugenics craze of the previous generation. In fact, were genetic engineering to be objectively used, every human being, regardless of race could become the best human being possible. With the possibility of so many people of all races and ethnicities walking the earth with 2 to 3 times their current potential, the old notions of racism, sexism, disability, ageism, and other "isms" would inevitably be replaced by a sense of universal egalitarianism, tolerance, and respect for individual differences.

HMO greed has drastically driven up the cost of healthcare and reduced the quality of medical treatment that would otherwise be available to most Americans, particularly the elderly, "working poor", and the impoverished who are least able to afford healthcare. It isn't logical that the addition of another level of middlemen between the care giver and the patient could result in savings and a more affordable healthcare delivery system. If the average American could afford $2,000 annually for medical treatment, and the HMOs charge subscribers $1,500 annually for insurance premiums, $500 per person for annual deductibles, and another $500 for annual co-pays for visits and medicines, how's that helping to deliver more affordable healthcare services to patients? Meanwhile HMO clerks and accountants routinely deny its members needed medical care because it constitutes added expenses against the profits of their CEOs. Where are the government regulatory agencies when you really need them to fix this broken healthcare system? What politicians are routinely being wined and dined by HMO lobbyists, who then vote on regulations and laws that benefit HMOs at the expense of tax paying Americans? Let's look at the voting records of our so-called government representatives to determine the conflict of interests.

Equal access to services is not possible in our greed driven capitalistic system that has no social conscience and is predicated on the profit motive to charge the highest amount that the market will bear. People's health needs, adequate and proper medical treatment, and saving lives becomes secondary to the "de facto" class system that is based upon one's ability to access affordable and decent health care. As the population ages and more people fall out of the middle class to fill the ranks of the working poor, society is faced with solving the basic philosophical hypocrisy, which claims life to be priceless. Certainly there is a price on life. If one can afford reputable healthcare insurance, their chances of living a life with minimal suffering greatly increases over that experienced by those who have little or no access to affordable healthcare, because healthcare has become unaffordable for one-third of all Americans. Where's the justice? Does a wealthy person have a greater right to life than a poor person, who may work equally as hard or even harder for a living? Let's outlaw HMOs, unless they are non-profit organizations such as Kaiser-Permanente, who build hospitals, hire competent doctors and nurses, and provide its members with the highest quality of care that money can buy. Let's close down the for-profit greed-centered HMOs which have driven up the price of healthcare beyond affordability for a large segment of Americans.

2. Environmental Protection

Atmospheric pollution knows no boundaries. Acid rain falls across the Canadian-US borders from American industries. The jet stream takes chemical pollutants downwind across continents and particulate pollution from combustion engines eventually fall back on plants, soil, water, animals, roadways, and buildings, which are washed into the oceans and lakes with the next downpour. Ozone depletion from cow manure methane, vehicle AC Freon, and other industrial emissions may become irreversible if global development and pollution increases and remains unchecked. Any series of large volcanic explosions or nuclear warfare will be felt on a global basis, because we are all breathing the same air that has been recycled from the time of the great dinosaurs. Our atmosphere is a closed system, and we all breath health-threatening contaminants when we don't take effective measures to protect our life sustaining air supply.

Rivers, lakes, oceans are ecosystems that provide not only the potable water we need to remain alive, but is the environment for countless species of fish, plants, microorganism, and other forms of living things. When we pollute our water supply through industrial, agricultural, residential, and recreational wastes, we contaminate both our drinking water and the life that lives in the liquid dimension. The popularity of filtered and bottled water attests to the fact that people are often afraid to drink tap water due to its impurities.

Landfills are not only becoming dangers to our subterranean fresh water tables where many cities draw their drinking water, but they remain another increasing source of methane, which if not recycled is released into the atmosphere. Landfills become the resting place for unknown types and quantities of toxic materials, from mercury to oil and medical radioactive wastes that illegally find its way into trash bins. Landfills are rapidly becoming cheap land for the construction of residential subdivisions, city parks and golf courses, and where there's money to be made, bureaucrats will usually find justification to bend or ignore health and safety laws in favor of development and tax collection. Some day, residential tracts or children's playground which are built upon reclaimed landfills may spontaneously burst into flames from the methane buildup, or there will be great increases in the number of unusual child cancer cases and the public uproar will result in lawyers making more money before homes are bulldozed into the landfill and people's lives become displaced and ruined.

Agricultural lands are now producing yields far beyond its natural ability due to genetic modifications of plants and the chemical replenishment of topsoil. The problem of top soil erosion from wind and rain, inadequate or improper crop rotation, insufficient time for land to remain fallow, and the elimination of indigenous plants which reinvigorate the soil will steadily decrease the arid acreage required to feed the bludgeoning global human population. Inefficient irrigations methods wastes billions of acre feet of fresh water, and the run off into streams, rivers and lakes contain pesticides and other chemicals that are harmful to both human and animal life. Scientists may be soon called upon to make new soil from rock or from volcanic magma to replenish the world's topsoil. As we now drill for oil, someday we may have to drill for magma once most of the world's topsoil washes into the oceans.

Global warming and depletion of the ozone layer over Antarctica and most of the Artic appears to be accelerating; but since few humans can survive in those areas anyway, too bad on them. The beneficial effects of the natural ozone layer as a shield against UV light is thought to protect humans, particularly light-skinned people, against the harmful effects of sunlight, which can increase melanomas of the skin. The fear lies in scientific extrapolations that shows the ozone depletion to be accelerating, which may in the not too distant future expose large portions of the southern and northern hemispheres to excess UV rays, and in addition contribute to global warming as greater quantities of sunlight would reach the lower atmosphere as the ozone layer vanishes. Certain climatic consequences of global warming portends the sinking of great seaport cities such as New York and the complete disappearance of many islands and atolls, such as Tahiti, Bora Bora, and parts of Hawaii. Projections have been made that claim the rise in the oceans depth by upwards of 10 feet over the next century. And that means good bye to Malibu beach and multimillion dollar views.

Endangered species have become a hot topic of controversy between developers who don't care what has to die to allow them to profit from new construction, and bleeding liberals whose environmental agenda can sometimes become extreme, unreasonable and impractical. In general, ecosystems are in a dynamic balance between all life forms, from bacteria to plants, insects, and animal species. In any particular environment, there is likely to be found thousands of species of plants, insects and animals. Development reduces the size of an ecosystem, and removes portions that may have detrimental effects on the natural codependent food chain. Endangered species, which once thrived, are forced into smaller habitats, which are then threatened by further development. But to stop all development due to one or two little known species can be an extreme and impractical position.

Environmentalists must demonstrate why any endangered species would be incapable of adjusting to developmental pressures before all development is automatically stopped, particularly on private lands. Perhaps developers can provide funds to relocate endangered species to similar habitat or breeding grounds on protected public lands. And if the introduction of an endangered species into habitats that allow them to flourish, but which eventually challenges the populations of competing species, then consider the consequences as a balance in the Darwinian world, of the survival of the fittest. At least the endangered species will no longer be endangered.

Wildlife diversity enriches our lives. Imagine a world that is devoid of all wild animals, and their progeny only survive in zoos! We would live in a world filled with pigeons that poop on your roofs, sidewalks and vehicles; domesticated cats and dogs; livestock bred for slaughter houses; and sea gulls that feed off open landfills. What a world that will be for our grandchildren! Global poaching has already placed many of the world's majestic wildlife on the endangered list, and in many cases, the results will be irreversible. Each year, the world loses thousands of species of living things and along with them, possible cures for diseases and food sources for indigenous populations who can neither afford or desire to become modernized and westernized. Imagine someday once most wildlife has become extinct, only robots and virtual reality, which would make videogame players happy, will surround our lives but would that be life anymore?

Ice caps are melting away. The glacial landmass at both poles is receding on the average of a kilometer per year. Large chucks of Antarctica the size of small towns fall off its ice shelves and become shipping hazards in the southern hemisphere. When the poles melt away, the oceans will rise and there will be uncertain climatic changes, such as increased frequency and severity of hurricanes and other horrible cataclysmic events.

Space debris is becoming a threat to space travel, whether military, scientific or future commercial explorations. NORAD is barely able to track the 40,000 identified pieces of space junk from the size of marbles to basketballs. Blasting off on a future rocket plane trip to a foreign land may come with dangers from ballistic space junk that travels in excess of 17,000 miles per hour, which is far faster than a speeding bullet, able to penetrate the thin skins of space vehicles and tender flesh of human space travelers. Why is it that human beings are so effective in polluting any environment, from land to water, to air, and now space itself! Nothing is sacred anymore, not even the heavens.

3.   Agricultural Reforms

Topsoil erosion threatens to decimate the world's food supply. Vigorous planning and agricultural land management must recycle and interchange agricultural and grazing lands to extend the availability of arid soil. Proper crop mixes, alternating crop species, and introducing beneficial insects and animals to replenish topsoil nutrients is essential to preserving our agricultural lands. Natural topsoil preserving plants along with should be planted and alternated with croplands to improve top soil retention and recovery. If top soil erosion continues unabated worldwide, scientists may have to invent methods to recycle trash, demolished homes and animal/human waste to restore top soil or people and livestock will eventually consume protein and vitamin fortified synthetic foods that will be manufactured from pulverized wood pulp, weeds, insects and animal parts that are flavorized and textured to mimic vegetables and meats. Yummy!

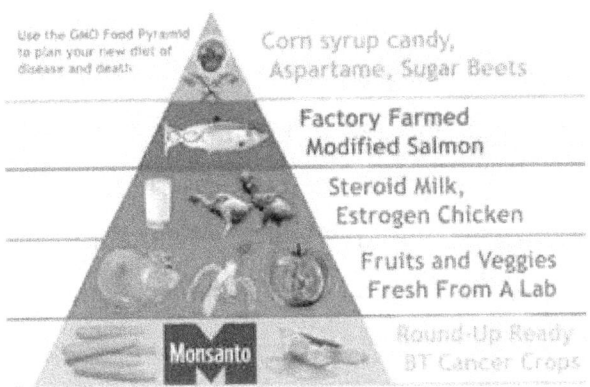

Water consumption in developed nations is wastefully obscene. Although fresh water use and consumption by people, particularly in cities account for approximately ten percent of water use, over 90 percent of that goes down the drains and toilets for hygienic purposes. Should the world's weather change dramatically or enter into lengthy periods of drought, not only will agriculture be threatened, but people will be forced to decide between bathing or drinking water. Extrapolating the human population growth rate into the next 200 to 500 years, it is clear that insufficient amount of annual rainfall at current rates will be able to sustain the requirement of humanity. Scientists will likely develop water treatment and reclamation technologies, which will be supplemented by oceanic desalinization to make up for the shortfall of rain water; however, distribution will be uneven and costly. New methods of waste disposal and hygiene will need to be developed that do not require the use of water. Hands will be irradiated and blown clean with disinfectants and disposable scented antibacterial towels and wipes would replace showers. Toileting will involve biodegradable tissue that will be collected and recycled with excretion to be used as fertilizer and topsoil replenishment. Water will be rationed, costly, and made only available for cooking and drinking needs. Car washes will be required to use recycled and/or reclaimed sewer water or subject to fines.

Genetically modified crops to better withstand natural pests are rapidly replacing pesticide usage. The increased use of cross-species and cross-phylum gene splicing may eventually have unintended consequences on both the environment and on human reaction to cellular uncertain and unpredictable genetic changes. It is not beyond the realm of possibility that genes taken from certain bacteria or insects may create new food borne diseases that become pandemic and are drug resistant. Anything is possible.

Genetic modifications of plants and animals portends the eventual genetic modification the human genome, first for improving "natural" immunity and life span extension, but acceptance for eugenic purposes will become sufficient justification for childbearing. The push for knowledge, species improvement and human evolution will push the scientific envelope to perfect cloning and species enhancement techniques. As societies become more tolerant, experiments with cross species genetic engineering will create new human species such as *Homo canis*. Science fiction or future reality? Only time will tell.

4.   **Population Control**

Abortion has become a hot political issue pitting pro-life religious zealots against secular fanatics who insist on women's rights above all. A reasonable approach to abortion should be based upon scientific evidence of the beginning and viability of independent life and not on issues of the existence of a hypothetical soul or solely upon women's supposed rights to determine their reproductive destinies. At what point of development can a fetus survive outside of a woman's womb, independent of any artificial means? That is the measure of the viability and the beginning of life, just as surely as terminally ill and aged people naturally die at the point their own bodies no longer sustain them. No person has the right to terminate the life of another, not even a fetus who if not aborted in the later months of pregnancy can survive independently outside of the woman's womb, without even the application of modern medical life preserving technology. End term and late term abortions are euthanasia at the least, and murder at the worse. Instead, the fetus should be taken out C-section, and if it survives, give it up for adoption. If not, then it was not a viable life at that point.

As in most real world predicaments, there is no true right or wrong because different personal, cultural, moral and political values prevail. Abortion should be subject to relative judgment in each independent situation, where the issues of independent viability of life should be the primary determinant factor after all other issues relating to the physical, psychological, emotional, mental and financial health of the mothers are considered and resolve as pre-conditions to the state's granting approval for abortion. Abortion should not be taken lightly and as a whimsical consequence of poor judgment and sexual activity.

Legal limits must be explored to determine what are the upper limits vs. optimal distribution of population that an environment can effectively integrate to maintain balance and homeostasis. If a nation, or state, or local jurisdiction is unable to sustain populations above certain numbers, then those who desire offspring must be limited a maximum number of childbirths permissible for that particular environment. If they desire more offspring than a particular environment can support, they have the option to move to another area that needs, seeks, or permits additional population.

A blanket 1 child policy such as in China is not an effective one size fits all solution, as in rural agricultural environments; a higher number of offspring may be essential to subsistence and survival. However, in urban areas where overcrowding and quality of life issues abound, rational and proportional limitations on the number of permissible childbirths should be instituted to insure the viability of the ecosystem and economy to prevent poverty and starvation.

Environmental impact should be a determining factor on the limits to human population and industrial development. Each human mouth that must be fed for 70 to 80 years places a deficit and strain on the natural resources of a region. It's natural environment decays from human pollution of air, water, development, urbanization, manufacturing and human waste products from hygiene and consumerism. An optimal balance must be sought between human population expansion and the destruction of the natural ecology of any region to prevent the destruction and decay that is typical of large urban concrete and asphalt jungles such as Los Angeles, which is terribly detrimental to its human inhabitants, aside from its toxicity to natural fowl, fauna, and plants.

In the book, *Population Bomb*, as the human population grows as a geometric ratio as compared to the world's natural resources, within a few hundred years, the world's resources, potable water, arid farmlands, and clean air will be insufficient to support the world population. The amount of rainfall that is collected and required by farmlands, industry, and human nutritional and hygienic needs would theoretically be maximized and tapped out when the human population approaches an upper limit of between 100 and 300 billion people, a number that could be attainable at current population growth rates easily by the next millennium, even projecting with current actual growth rates of 2.5% of births over mortality.

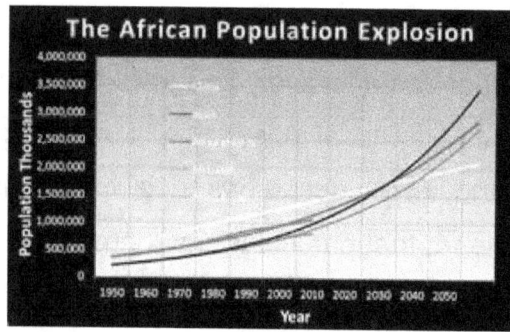

Currently, world population is about 7.5 billion, and at a average growth rate of 2.5% per year, it will exceed 25% in 10 years, 250% in 100 years, and 2500% in 1,000 years (the numbers would increase faster due to the effect of numerical compounding, but this examples uses simple arithmetic to make a simple point). 2500% x 7.5 billion equals 185.3 billion people in a thousand years – at the beginning of the next millennium in the year 3000. But why worry about a thousand years into the future? Certainly the Egyptians have survived on earth since the times of the great pyramids, over 7,000 years ago, but in a geological time frame, a thousand years is but a day. Those who live in cities and are stuck in the arduous traffic congestions can imagine survival if their cities became 25 times more densely populated. But why wait until 3005? Within 10 years, the world population will increase by 25%, reaching over 8 billion and by the end of this century will exceed 16 billion – almost 3 times the mouths to feed and wastes to pollute the environment, not to mention the accelerating depletion of the world's known reserves of oil – now estimated to become depleted by 2050. What then? If you were to place a bet in Las Vegas on the probability of human beings surviving into the next millennium, the "mob" would probably give you odds of 1000:1.

5.   Religious Tolerance

Extremism is a natural human response to a feeling of powerlessness and exploitation. While often disguised under the banner of religious, ethnic, racial, or nationalistic banners, it is rebellion against the existing order or structure that institutionalizes exploitation and human misery for the disenfranchised groups that result in their extreme behaviors and destructive retaliation. When individuals and groups believe they have nothing of value to lose but their own lives (which encompasses their religion, culture, values and whatnot), then to validate their own lives and those of similar persuasions and identification, they feel greatly empowered by extremist ideologies, identifications, thoughts, and actions. They justify this basic need to satisfy the ego (self valuation) by attributing extremism to the need to push off the yoke of oppression by dominating outsiders, exploiters and enemies whose actions denigrate and disrespect the fundamental values of the collective ego shared by other extremists.

Traditional intolerance and hatred has existed from the beginning of human existence, which pitted individuals against predators, then tribes against tribes, and nations against nations even into modern times. Humans fear what they do not know or understand, hence they are intolerant of the unknown. This principle of the human psyche extends to intolerance between various religions, races, ethnic groups, nations, political parties, economic and social classes/castes and people's fundamental philosophical constructs. It's the natural order, just as certainly as in the wild animal kingdoms where the struggle to segregate, protect, prey and fight are the facts of daily survival.

Use of violence as a survival mechanism abounds in nature where the larger prey on the smaller – and the stronger make meals of the weaker. In large part, this propensity toward violence has driven the human species and continues to define cultural dominance. The history of mankind is filled with conquest by one group over another, however unlike the animal kingdom, men have wantonly use violence for reasons of greed and power consolidation rather than for basic survival needs. It could be concluded that human expansion and subjugation of the world to human domination could not have occurred were it not for the natural violent propensity inherited in the human genome.

Hypocrisy abounds because almost all "civilized" people, culture and nations denounce violence as barbaric inhumane behavior, yet governments send their soldiers to die for banners depicting cultural and nationalistic idealism, while in fact the powerful hands that stir up the drum beating for violence and war are generally seeking to increase their own wealth and power by using the powerless citizenry to do their dirty work. That is why one man's terrorist is another man's hero, and the winners write the history books that brainwashes the subsequent generations to accept the justifications for the violent acts of their predecessors.

6.   Capitalism Reformation

Limit on greed is essential to prevent the destructive consequences of unrelenting and unconscionable greed at any cost. Simple arithmetic shows it takes more than one person to make a village. Technology now permits a greatly accelerated concentration and control of wealth and natural/human resources into the hands of a few. Currently, roughly 10% of the world's population either owns or controls 90% of the world's wealth, resources and peoples, with the top 1% as rulers of 50%. At the current rate of wealth consolidation, the world economy and geopolitical structure will be in the hands of 1,000 people within the next decade. Already, in the United States, the top 10% of one ethnic group owns a third of the wealth of the country (0.3% of the population owns 30% of the nation's wealth), and this trend is increasing at an alarming rate.

Emphasis on tangible wealth versus intangible wealth has become the overriding mantra of the culture. Leaders and the populace give lip service to higher values and spiritual salvation as they attend church services, but in their daily lives the accumulation of money, property, materialism and consumerism rules the day. Until such time as leaders of government, mass media, schools, churches and synagogues begin teaching the value of service to humanity over a generational haul, and exhibit non-contradictory actions through positive examples, then the hypocrisy of worshipping mammon instead of God will continue to prevail and social conscience will continue to be suppressed by lies, deception and self-serving greed.

Stock market reforms are well overdue. Recent revelations and prosecutions of corrupt CEO's and accounting practices are only the tip of the iceberg. It is likely that upwards of half of all companies cheat to some extent in order to manipulate their public image and financial position as a business strategy to improve their perceived market value. In order for investors, the government, and the public at large to better gauge the true performance of publicly traded corporations; all financial data should be made available on a monthly basis on their corporate websites. This will cause the evaluation of stock value to become transparent to permit investors accurate data upon which to base their financial decisions.

Corporate accounting reforms are needed and will only be possible when federal and state prosecutors and tax auditors routinely review corporate books for illegal or irregular accounting procedures and practices. As long as corporate audits account for less than 1% of federal investigations, executives feel they can skirt taxes and the law by cheating, misrepresentation, stealing from investors, and the accounting shell game through creating paper companies designed to raid corporate bank accounts and deposit ill gotten gains into offshore bank havens.

Rational executive compensation plans must become the law of the land, where a reasonable formula becomes industry standard for executive pay and perks that is tied to corporate performance. It is unconscionable for CEO's to "earn" 1,000 times the pay of the rank and file, especially as their companies slide into bankruptcy (AIG) or they are ousted for poor management into severance packages worth over $100 million (example of Eisner at Disney). How does investors benefit when their dividends are significantly reduced to pay for outrageous executive compensation, retirement, and severance packages?

A good example of responsible executive compensation is illustrated. by a health food chain that caps their CEO salary at 14 times the average pay for employees. Their company has grown an average of 20% per year because their profits are poured back into improving the business and not into excessive executive pay. A rational and reasonable cap on executive compensation should be 10% of corporate net profit for all executives combined (CEO, CFO, COO etc.), which leaves 90% for dividends and reinvestment into company assets and operations.

International monetary system and banking reforms are urgently needed to insure global economic stability and a rational yet profitable world trade system. The predatory and speculative nature of the current monetary system causes uncertainty and instability because it predisposes national currencies to hedge fund attacks. In the shrinking global economic marketplace, national economies can be destroyed overnight when the IMF, World Bank, and international bankers conspire to take over vulnerable national economies and banks, especially to milk developing nations of their natural resources and commodities.

Limits on MNCs, monopolies and oligarchies are essential to prevent the push to consolidate the ownership and control of global resources into the hands of a very few, who would then be positioned to dictate global policies through their de facto control of international economies and governments. It is a well-proven adage that power corrupts, and abs olute power corrupts absolutely. The future of global development can be tempered with socially and environmentally responsible restraints, but with power in the hands of a few, development to turn profits for the few will lead to global ecological disasters.

Social responsibility and ethical considerations must be at the forefront of all human endeavors, and not as hindsight filled with blame and acrimonious accusations after the fact, such as what occurred after the Hurricane Katrina fiasco in New Orleans. In all fields, whether industrial development, science, or technology, it would be wise to first assess the potential impact of development to determine if the probable outcomes would be positive or potentially destructive. Are we advancing the future of human viability when we bring back to earth alien bacteria and viruses, or are we potentially exposing the entire human race to incurable diseases, or the extinction of species that could detrimentally change the food chain and food supplies on earth, which could eventually result in the extinction of the human race?

Who should decide to outlaw the development of weapons that could change the molecular composition of oxygen molecules in air and water to make it toxic to living things, particularly human beings? Or do we skirt the issue of social and ethical responsibility to pursue even the riskiest activities just because we can, or because we are curious. Discovery for the sake of knowledge can be a trap that would be difficult to extricate or recover from, with potential end times results.

7.   **Legal System Reforms**

Equal access and representation in the courts for everyone regardless of class, race, sex, age or disability is essential in a democracy that values fairness and equal opportunity for all of its citizens. Unfortunately, it is evident that the ability to hire a competent attorney with advantageous legal network connections to judges and prosecutors can be beneficial. Unlike public defenders who provide legal defense to the poor, paid attorneys are willing to work as much as a client is able to pay. Public defenders on the other hand need to process and resolve their assigned case load as quickly as the system permits, and consequently are prone to advise defendants to plea bargain rather than to adjudicate. It is more likely innocent people represented by public defenders end up incarcerated than wealthy people who are guilty and go free.

Internet juries chosen at random offer a more representative "jury of one's peers" than the current system of jury selection that is tainted by challenges and other jury profiling trickery by both sides of protagonists. Jury pools chosen at random should be given basic instructions on the applicable laws applicable to the cases they are being considered to adjudicate. Subsequent to familiarizing jurors to the relevant laws and issues, they must past a basic examination to validate their understanding of the relevant laws. Only upon passing the basic examination should they be allowed to become jurists. In this manner, competent jurists who understand the law and their tasks to judge defendants according to the laws instead replace the haggling between both sides that attempt to stack the jury with people sympathetic to their view.

Open courtrooms via television and Internet permits transparency and permits the general public to better understand the legal system, thereby increasing the public support for law and the legal system. Greater transparency also places the responsibility on all parties to act in a civil manner, as grandstanders would soon fall out of public pleasure and become the objects of public condemnation. The cameras should be pin hole cameras or encased in a unobtrusive manner to blend in with courtroom décor, so as to be unnoticeable. In this way, all parties become acclimated to invisible cameras in courtrooms and the process provides direct public access to the courts.

Limits on injury awards is necessary to provide a rational balance between real losses, compensation and punishment versus bankrupting defendants through disproportionate and unreasonable jury awards to plaintiffs, which only serves to encourage more outrageous and more frequent future litigation that greatly increases court case load, and extends the period of time required to deliver any semblance of justice to all parties in litigation. The maximum award to any plaintiff should be capped at the actual and future value of their loss in terms of the economic potential at the most current labor statistics summary for a person's occupation, or the actual value of the loss plus a maximum of treble damages.

For instance, a person who is a 35 year old miner earning $50,000 per year who loses his legs due to industrial negligence should be awarded 30 years (to the retirement age of 65) at $50,000 per year plus annual adjustment for inflation (presume 5% per year) or roughly $1,600,000 x 3 = $4,800,000. In this same example, were the miner to lose his life, with actuary tables for miners projecting average age at death of 70, then the calculation in this case would be for 35 years. Awards of hundreds of millions of dollars would not be permitted unless it could be proven.

The use of maximum formula awards would be reasonable, and would not require exorbitant attorney fees and percentages that are either deducted from plaintiff's awards or added on as court costs to further burden defendants, and would be sufficient to defuse greedy plaintiffs or attorneys. Referees may simply review cases without either defendants or plaintiffs taking up court space and time, and make a rational formulated award in a relatively rapid period of time.

Lower limits on attorney fees & percentages is necessary to reduce the amount of frivolous litigation that clogs up the court system. There is no reason why a plaintiff must pay an attorney one-third to upwards of almost half of any award they may receive for injury or losses that they incurred. More often than not, attorneys use paralegals to research and file cases which are usually settled at little time and expense to attorneys. Let's say a law firm pays a paralegal $30/hour for 100 hours of research, preparation, and filing in a case where the settlement is $300,000. Why should the law firm receive $100,000 or more of the settlement for $3,000 of work? Attorneys should work for ten percent, or charge a published flat hourly rate for representation. This would be transparent and fair, but name a few attorneys who would be interested only in justice and fairness and we should consider them to be heroes of the common man.

Justice and intent of the law often appear fleeting in our adversarial court system, but these values are essential to the foundation of our legal system, without which public support would soon wane and vanish. While it is a known fact that the criminal justice system uses the court to intimidate its citizenry to obtain compliance to the laws, it is the public support of the courts to deliver justice and the belief that the intent of laws are fundamentally sound and good that permits the system promoting a concept of justice to prevail over anarchy.

When incidents of innocent people being incarcerated, or the guilty going unpunished occur with greater frequency, especially in high profile cases, the public responds with disgust, disrespect, distrust and disdain for the system. When the public cannot feel confidence in the fundamental role of the courts to deliver justice (though it is not expected to be perfect), then the seeds of anarchy seep in and society becomes a more dangerous and less civil environment.

Disengagement of non-violent criminals from penal system is desirable and long overdue to prevent the corruption of otherwise law-abiding petty criminals into becoming life long violent predators. What do we know about mixing rotten apples with fresh apples? Sooner than later, the fresh apples too become rotten. This very fact is indicative of the penal system, where persons convicted of non-violent misdemeanors and minor felonies (primarily drug use or possession) are thrown in with those who have committed more serious violent offenses. If the system is not sincere in its effort to rehabilitate, then it should desist from making matters worse through integrating non-violent prisoners with violent inmates.

Legalization of minor non-addictive & harmless social drugs will remove contact between otherwise lawful citizens from criminal drug dealers and their extended network of pushing harmfully addictive drugs such as crack, cocaine, heroin, and opium. Law abiding citizens who desire to avoid criminal contact can growth their small personal "stash" of marijuana at home for occasional recreational and social indulgence. The only reason growing small amounts of hemp is illegal is to ensure drug dealers have an avenue to recruit new users to harder drugs, which permits politicians and law enforcement departments to justify their job security.

Tort reform; elimination of redundant, antiquated, irrelevant and stupid laws is needed to remove ridiculous laws that are out of step with present day realities. Each new generation develops its own sets of social and moral standards, and should be allowed the flexibility to remove laws that are no longer useful in their society, as long as the letter and intent of the U.S. Constitution is respected and maintained. Every law instituted by legislators should come with a "sunset statute of limitations" of 20 years, upon which it becomes invalid unless extended for another 20 years by the then current legislative bodies. In this way, the laws become relevant, sensible, and reflective of the needs of the current society. Otherwise, in addition to witch hunts, we'd still be burning alleged witches.

Transformation of street gangs into legitimate "self-help" non-profit associations whose nervous energies are applied to constructive efforts to improve their communities instead of their typical destructive behaviors. What incentives will encourage young men to turn away from territorial and manhood disputes with rival gangs, fighting for control of small drug dealing territories? Give them real alternatives to income producing activities that are not illegal and destructive – where they can feel a sense of pride, participation, and belonging. Non-profit organizations can be useful and productive avenues to ensure our violent prone youth have positive ways to express themselves, to earn substantial amounts of money, develop career building skills, gain practical knowledge of society and of themselves while serving the good of their communities.

Instead of the whatever street name gangs that are so popular, community named associations such as whatever street name youth development group carry a sense of pride, responsibility and useful lawful purpose. If society wants to reduce youth crime, then let's fund neighborhood youth organizations with stipulations that those who participate sign contracts to reform their lives and resist criminality. We either pay $50,000 per year and more to incarcerate each and every gang member who is caught up in violent crime, or we pay upfront to give our youth and current gang members something better to do, and produce tax paying citizens instead of being another drag and drain on society.

8.   Full Employment

Sustainable wages should be a right of every citizen because it enables citizens to survive and avoid desperate and unlawful activities just to pay bills and buy the necessities of life for themselves and their families. The primary problem with survival in modern society is the predatory practices of landlords, lending institutions, and the government whose recurring increases in the cost of rent, interest rates, and taxes keep most hard working Americans one step out of the poor house. Why is it that workers whose average annual net pay raise is less than the rate of inflation is routinely startled with rent hikes exceeding 10 percent per year, credit interest rates that far exceed usury, and taxes that cost the average workers 40 percent of their hard earned wages? Between these three greedy merchants, no wonder the middle class is quickly shrinking and the ranks of the working poor are burgeoning.

Personal assessment, career & organizational matching as pre-screening criteria will improve employee selection and retention, which improves productivity, reduces absenteeism, and increases organizational morale. The typical scenario has job seekers who have vague ideas of the type of job and environment that may fit their personalities, skills and knowledge to company culture and expectations accepting jobs that turn out to be far from the impressions they obtained in job descriptions and interviews. The reality is over 90 percent find themselves working in professions in which they are poorly fitted, particularly from personality and psychological dispositions. Consequently, these unhappy workers generally feel exploited by their superiors and work hard because they are intimidated into subservience and obedience from fear of termination. In order to assure good matches between employee and organizational personalities, scientifically based personality assessment tests should be given to prospects as a pre-requisite to hiring. This screening criteria would greatly increase the probability of matching employees to the needs of organizations in a mutually beneficial manner.

Universal access to appropriate educational and training opportunities ensures businesses will have adequately trained workers to meet the needs of modern commerce. The current system of higher education is overrated and the return is often dismal, with graduates racking up tens of thousands of dollars in student loans just to get into the work force that pays a typical net income of less than $2,000 per month. The public education system through its curriculum, teachers, and counselors indoctrinates students into the belief that a college education is an essential right of passage into society and validation of self-worth. The reality is people in society generally judge a person's value by their external accumulations and bank accounts. Education is now widely attainable in various forms that both improve personal self-worth in addition to job-related knowledge and skills. Why borrow against one's future net worth by paying a $25,000 per year tuition, and ending up over $100,000 in debt before even earning the first paycheck? Do the math. The time lost while pursuing a 4 year degree could have been productively utilized in a career, resulting in higher wages through longevity advancements. And all the while a student is not earning even the minimal $100,000 net income, but instead is getting $100,000 deeper in long-term debt. Were a student to save even $2,000 each year, instead of sinking into over $40,000/year in debt, that student could have a million dollar nest egg waiting at retirement, instead of paying $100,000 in interest payment plus the $100,000 loan principle.

Objective hiring procedures are needed to minimize interviews disguised as fair hiring practices that are primarily excuses to screen out otherwise qualified applicants based upon the personal biases and prejudices of the interviewers. Interviews should be double-blinded, where a person's race, gender, disability or attractiveness are hidden from interviewers. An objective scoring system should be applied to applicants' answers and their verified skills and experience, aptitude and attitude test scores, and other job-relevant data can be crunched by software that evaluates the probable success of any applicant without regards to interview biases.

Eliminating hidden networking cronyism, racism and sexism in hiring and promotion is necessary to ensure a meritorious system that rewards the most deserving and most productive workers. It's high time for employees to command rewards commensurate to what they know and what they do with what they know, rather than who they know and what they do for those who they know. This is good for business and provides a work environment that encourages excellence and responsibility instead of social networking and corruption.

Objective and measurable merit system in promotion and retention should be based upon actual contributions to company's goals in cost savings, increased profits, improved employee moral, decreased absenteeism and other tangible measures of company health and viability. Board of Directors should refrain from hiring cronies to head corporations, but instead should promote from within those person's whose decisions and strategies were instrumental in the attainment of corporate goals and profits. In this way, there is a clear route for advancement, which instills a sense of purpose and loyalty among employees whose vision is to have the opportunity to rise in the corporate ranks to the top job. CEO's whose decisions and actions are detrimental to a company's viability should be fired, and not given enormous sweetheart severance packages because they were cronies of the Board. Investors have the right to impose rational executive compensation packages on CEOs' whose actions affect their dividends and stock value.

9. Drug Laws Reformation

a.   Legalize minor non-addictive sports drugs such as marijuana in order to remove otherwise law-abiding citizens from having to come in contact with drug dealers who are members of organized criminal rackets and gangs. Removing citizens from dependency on racketeers also removes their exposure to hard drugs and the addictive crime cycle that comes with drug dependency. In addition, the FDA would regulate dosage and purity to ensure that harmful additives do not cause a public health risk to users.

b.   OTC legalized minor non-addictive recreational drugs where dosage is regulated to give the recreational effect while avoiding over dosage and abuse. For instance a marijuana cookie would contain enough THP to cause a one-hour high. A pill containing stimulants would last an hour. People would have to show I.D., and the OTC drugs would be entered into their database to prevent them from buying excessive supplies without a doctor's prescription. People who abused OTC drugs would be identified through their user profiles and be offered help, or their OTC privileges would be cancelled until they complete a treatment program.

c.   Federal compensation formula for victims of hazardous pharmaceuticals

d.   Minor drug use to be "ticketable infraction" of Health/Safety Code, not a crime.

e. Active pursuit of drug trafficking financiers and investment bankers

f. More effective drug rehabilitation programs for addicts in lieu of imprisonment

g. Economic enticements for foreign nations to destroy drug crops

10. Energy Consumption & Conservation

a. Development of more cost-effective alternative non-polluting energy resources

b. Energy self-sustaining homes and structures

c. Hybrid engines that transform and conserve energy

d. Improving freeway traffic pattern flow

e. Development of more efficient fuels and engines

f. Reducing dependence on oil

11. Political and Ideological

a. Ban on political contributions from special interests groups and lobbyists

b. Ban on television campaign ads

c. Equal access on federal elections Internet website
UN & US, etc. to recognize universal principles of self-determination based upon national sovereignty, race, ethnicity, and religion

d. Support for universal individual human rights comprised of freedom, liberty, and the pursuit of happiness

e. Removing enticements from Military Industrial Complex and international arms trade to create and benefit from global conflicts and warfare. It sure stinks at the top! An influx of fresh air is urgently needed

12. Public Education Policies

- Lowering of mandatory "general education" age limit to 14
- Mandatory "trade" or "career" emphasis and job training between 14-16

- Voluntary education after age 16
- Greater individual choice in the selection of coursework and specialization
- Elimination of "required courses" that are not applicable to students' career plans
- Greater use and integration of on on-line courses
- More appropriate and world-class curricula
- Universal educational standards that make sense

13. Mass Media Reform

Strict code of ethics for openness and truth in reporting

Instantaneous public feedback to studios and government agencies on

Programming

Elimination of misleading and deceptive television commercials

Break up of media conglomerates into smaller diverse independent ownerships

America is arguably the most powerful, wealthiest, and most progressive nation that the human race has ever experienced. Yet, we must recognize and deal with our imperfections, if for no other reason than to create a better society, which I personal feel should be the ultimate goal. Common people have relied on, and have necessarily depended on the elites to shoulder the load of designing and building civilizations, as long as recorded history. Now our species is faced with the increasing potential that the proliferation and future development of weapons of mass destruction may lead our human race into extinction. I believe that a true patriot is a citizen who loves his nation, cherishes the good things, and yet acknowledges the shortcomings that must be addressed to elevate the people of the land to greater purpose and potential.

How can Americans support strategies to improve society in the following ways, through necessary paradigm shifts:

1) Convince elite capitalists to implement a kinder, gentler, more responsible, and more humanitarian and environmentally sensible form of capitalism.

2) Change cultural socialization to eliminate concepts that cause inequality, exploitation, and violence, thereby creating a more civil society.

3) Create environments where every human being can pursue happiness, and who have the conscience to refrain from hurting others.

The existing reality is based upon relative truth, illusions, deceptions and lies. Honesty is usually either inappropriate or punished in all aspects of life, from interpersonal relations to criminal justice, employment, and finances. There are only two types of knowledge, absolute and relative. Absolute truth are scientific facts and observations that are predictable and proven 100% of the time, like landing a rover on Mars as a result of mathematical calculations of planetary orbits, speed, mass, gravity, and rocket propulsion, etc. From that high point of absolute facts, everything else is relative, part facts and part fiction.

And where knowledge is based upon interpersonal relationships everything is relative to the formal and informal structure, obligation, expectations, and emotional interaction and interdependency of those relationships. Consequently, it is likely we tell lies most often to those who are supposedly closest to parents, our spouses, siblings, children, and us. It is usually easier to be completely honest (to what degree humans are capable, as limited by their world view, religion, self-image, emotional needs, etc.) to strangers when there are no other motives more than idle chatter over a few beers. When people feel there is potentially something to gain or lose in a situation, the degree of relative knowledge increases and the degree of factual content decrease as an indirect proportion to the perceived level of potential gain or loss.

Since rocket science is 100% absolute truth, then interpersonal relations is generally around 75% factual. Telling one's spouse that there is no one else in the universe more beautiful is an absolute lie, and an overweight person that they are not really that fat is generous social and perceptual deception. Adding all the daily incidents of falsehoods regardless of well intentions, we usually find relationships to be based upon large degrees of fluff – bullshit distortions of knowledge, and even deliberate lies. But relative truths don't abound only in relationships, as there are two fields where knowledge is the product of illusion and not facts.

Half-truths are discovered in movie plots presented as entertainment. Half truths are presented in the Globalist-controlled news media pandered as entertainment to sell television commercial slots. The audience never gets even a tenth of the whole story, and only the sensationalistic aspects that are exaggerated to keep their attention long enough to see the next advertising commercial. But the worse case scenario for distortion of truth lies in the criminal justice and legal system, where winning is the ultimate goal, and the presentation of illusions to manipulate jury perception of the truth is the game plan.

Five fundamental flaws have evolved in the human psyche through the interaction of genetic predisposition and cultural orientation, particularly through the spread of western civilization and values. These major flaws have enabled the elites, predators, madmen, tyrants, and warmongers to rule the meek and manipulate the beliefs and actions of the ignorant. Perhaps these five human flaws were evolutionary strengths during the early stages of human evolution into communities, cultures, civilizations and more recently into nation-states, because it permitted the unification of the efforts of many toward greater accomplishments that surpass individual capacities. Or perhaps these five flaws have marred the human race and have taken us down a path to certain mutual destruction, which trends toward the event horizon appear to confirm. These five flaws are 1) value defined as winning vs. losing; 2) the global paradigm of greed and wealth building; 3) the worship of efficiency; 4) the overemphasis on productivity; and 5) the cheapening of humanity. A discussion of each of these human flaws in the context of modern times exposes the destructive nature of baser human instincts that may have benefited human survival eons ago, but now serve only to alienate, exploit, and enslave humanity to a path that leads only to eventual extinction.

Children learn early on during the social indoctrination period during school years the importance of winning vs. losing. The grading system celebrates the top ten percent as winners, and consequently the remaining 90% are losers – also rans. No wonder an alarming number of teenagers drop out of a school system that is based upon punitive measures that rob individuals their basic sense of self-worth, while attempting to force conformity. Perhaps the top 10% aren't so much winners, but are instead the highest level conformist and maintainers of social standards... who teachers often tout as our nation's future leaders. Certainly, as disproportionate number of those who succeed in the academic track join the ranks of educators, professionals, bureaucrats, managers, and law makers, whose primary motive is to enforce social order and to pass on the values of organizations that support social order. Those who maintain social norms and conform to society's laws and values receive its rewards as middle-class careerists, and those who fail to encapsulate educational indoctrination fill the ranks of criminality and marginal subgroups that lurk in the background, not sharing in social economic prosperity. Winners are those who are defined by their higher educational and economic levels, and losers are those who slide into the lower pits of society.

What if the educational system instills a sense of self-worth and encourages the development of everyone's innate desire to discover and learn? These certainly are very innate human qualities that are naturally exhibited by toddlers and young children before the educational system's punitive paradigm attempts to transform individuals into sheep and cattle. Every human being deserves the opportunity to believe in the value of their unique individual traits – personality, talents, skills, aptitudes, attitudes, and beliefs. It's a basic injustice for social institutions and government to impose a cookie cutter to our young and impressionable. It is abundantly clear that adult members of extremist groups have modeled themselves during their formative years among extremists, such as gangs, racists, and terrorists.

What if the value of the Olympic experience were to celebrate the human potential, instead of winning medals? Then all could be winners, and not just the three in any event. What is so important about standing on the top podium? Is that view of the world significantly better than that of the audience? The audience sees an individual standing on a podium, listening to his/her national anthem. The individual on the platform is blinding by a sea of unrecognizable faces and the glare of television lights and camera flashes. Who sees the true reality? Are those in the audience envious of the one on the podium? Do they feel that particular individual is a true winner for accomplishing basically worthless and inane physical feats? Certainly many in the audience who have been brainwashed and indoctrinated by the educational and marketing institutions are suckers to admire those who can achieve apparently superhuman feats that they themselves are incapable of doing. That makes those members of the audience less than winners – it makes them losers and spectators in life… not its primarily celebrated participants.

If we put so much value into the physical accomplishment of superhuman feats and setting records for human performance, then why is there so much resistance to the enhancement of human capacity and potential performance through the use of drugs and genetic engineering? If we really want to push the envelop of human development and evolution, let's apply genetics and science to enhance human potential. Would that be cheating? Certainly not. There is no such thing as fairness in this world. Ask the person who is homeless about fairness, and you will receive an honest response. Ask the rich person who inherited wealth the same question, and no doubt fairness is not an issue. If winning continues to be so highly regarded, then people should be allowed to make their own personal decisions on what they are willing to do to win, which should no more be restricted than society is willing to restrict the tactics and performance of the wealthy, who use unfair business practices to monopolize entire industries to drive out their competitors, to enable them to control the market and dictate prices, such as what has happened in the oil, defense, media, and banking industries.

If we analyze the true value of winning, it is no more than a marketing tool to validate and celebrate the few in order to increase the corporate profits of sponsors who understand the need of the masses of losers who need to identify themselves with a winning team, nation, or individuals. Winning is just another marketing gimmick, no more and no less. People should be encouraged to participate in life, and not simply to view their dreams vicariously through the accomplishment of others, who the manipulators of social values and standards have decided are good for profits. Every human being has inherent value and the potential to achieve great things within the limits of their talents and resources. Each individual possess innate talents that has the potential to give great joy to oneself and to those around them, when socially conditioned judgment is suspended.

The concept of winning versus losing no longer has a constructive role in modern society. Perhaps in primitive human cultures, the winners were those who had the physical capacity to hunt down the game that gave their tribes another week of sustenance. Perhaps in early civilizations, the winners were the heartless murderers who defeated other tribes and the defenseless; such has been recorded throughout human history in the conquest of the weak by supposed great civilizations – the Romans, Mongols, and Greeks. How many women, infants, children, aged, and defenseless had to die so these supposed great conquerors – winners – could enslave and rule over people who never needed them nor invited them into their lands?

The native tribes in the America's were seats of great primarily peaceful civilizations whose cultures and values were in consonance with the earth and the natural order. They did not place winning as the highest societal goal, but instead valued true social order that was earned through self-sacrifice for the community benefit. They realized that the survival of their tribes and people depended upon cooperation, whether in the pursuit of game or in agriculture. Could such a peaceful, non-destructive, non-exploitive and non-competitive paradigm benefit people today?

Certainly far more than the winner takes all paradigm that currently rules the human psyche of the international elites and wealthy carpetbaggers who enforce poverty on the world in order to strip it of its natural resources for the profit of the few, to the misery of the great faceless masses.

What if it's okay not to strive to be the winner? What type of society would we have? We would likely have a world filled with people who go about their lives, not concerned about winning, but naturally pursuing their personal interests without regard for winning or losing. Without a definition of winning and losing, people would simply act and try to accomplish their personal potential in activities that interest them. Golfers could feel good about shooting a round of 100 because the course, weather and companionship was wonderful and they finished the course within the number of shots set by their personal goals. But instead, people tend to fall into the trap of comparing their scores to those of others, and worse yet to those of the pros. So instead of being the winners that they are, who should not need validation, especially in inconsequential and inane tasks, they instead punish themselves with feelings of inadequacy and failure. Then why bother to partake in stupid things where the certain outcome is negative and detrimental to one's self-worth?

The danger in people rejecting the concepts of winning and losing is the empowerment of the human spirit! How would it feel to do something for the sheer joy of doing it, and not as a pursuit of a score or standard arbitrarily set by others, who have died long ago? How would this change the marketing strategy of major corporations? Would people stop watching television and all head for the ballparks, golf courses, and bowling alleys? Not likely for a generation raised on watching cartoons and television sports. To the participant, it's an achievement. To the viewer, it's entertainment. To the sponsors, it's profits. We don't need winners and losers, because the games are entertaining enough, and consequently, everyone can just be themselves without regards for winning or losing, or being superior or inferior. People can begin to respect the fact that we are all very different and have innate value as participants in the games of life.

When cultures, nations, and peoples accept the vast differences and variations that exists among individuals of all walks of life, who pursue and value different aspects of reality and religion, then perhaps the human race would stand an improved chance for continued evolution and prosperity. The winner takes all paradigm certainly will only encourage the failure of the human race. Does winning have any value besides what people make of it in their culture? In the vast universe of a hundred billion billion stars, which one is the best? Which star is a winner that stands alone above the rest? And why, if there could be such a star, would it even matter, or should it matter. Each star is uniquely different from the rest, as no two galaxies or planets are the same. As vast as each grain of sand tossed into the expansive sky, the uniqueness of each star contributes to the beauty of the night, as each individual human being has the potential to add to the beautiful phenomenon that is life itself.

The global paradigm of greed and wealth building has set nto place an insidious and far-reaching system of exploitation and global destruction unprecedented in the annals of human endeavor. In the pursuit of wealth, the ecosystem is being destroyed. In the pursuit of wealth, unique cultures have been and are being destroyed.   In the pursuit of wealth, people commit crimes and murder.

In the pursuit of wealth, nations have gone on wars of conquest. In the pursuit of wealth, a singular world government is becoming the goal of oligarchs and multinational corporations. In the pursuit of wealth, the inherent value of human beings has been relegated to that of cheap laborers and consumers, as integrated parts of the global money making machine, owned by the rich.

What is the addictive appeal of money? When is enough, enough? A person can eat only one meal at a time, be in one room in one house at a time, drive one vehicle at a time, and wear one pair of shoes at a time. Does owning and hoarding more shoes, property and material things make a person more valuable as a human being? If their wealth is built upon indentured servitude of others, low-paid marginally surviving workers who toil under horrendous conditions, or due to their manufacturing processes wildlife and habitat are destroyed, do the profits of wealth building make the wealthy better people? And why should wealth building be an admirable goal and the rich held up on high pedestals when their rise to the top was already on the bent backs of the working poor? Unfortunately, it appears the lure of money is so universal that most people, no matter where and in what nation, would be willing to sacrifice their souls for money.

The worship of efficiency is no more than human exploitation by corporate big wigs who want to maximize profits by any means possible. People are driven to work harder and longer hours, to be more efficient producers in order to minimize labor costs while maximizing productivity. Cheaper labor markets are exploited where laws do not exist to provide basic protections to workers, and the working poor in western nations can not compete to sustain their miserable low-paying jobs, not to mention the better paying jobs that are rapidly vanishing in the workplace.

Corporations are only concerned about profit margin and global competitiveness, and social responsibility counts only when charitable contributions lower their corporate tax burden. Consequently, a twisted capitalism has become the product of corporate greed and corruption, where the four money-making principles that rule CEO decision making have become maximize profits by minimizing operational costs primarily by increasing efficiency through downsizing and outsourcing to cheaper labor markets. And whenever possible, charge the highest margin the market will permit between the cost of supplies, production and consumption price.

Corporations achieve market advantage through mergers, hostile takeovers, and acquisitions that centralize the control of supplies and distribution to permit monopolistic control of the marketplace. Gaining such control is considered the hallmark of operational efficiency because the maximum price can be obtained for supplies that are controlled, or the minimum price can be paid to supplies they do not control, if they can control distribution. The object of pricing efficiency is to pay the least possible for supplies that must be purchased, charge the maximum for supplies that are owned, brokered, or sold, pay the minimum for labor and other operational costs. What happened to the socially responsible paradigm capitalism, of producing or providing products or services that serve real consumer needs (not artificial needs created through slick and deceptive marketing ploys), and charging reasonable prices where workers who produce the products can themselves afford to be the consumers of the products of their labor? Perhaps that paradigm is falling to the wayside.

The overemphasis on productivity is based upon modern euphemistic restatement and enforcement of indentured servitude, or border-lined slavery. Cheap laborers, particularly in developing nations who work for relatively little enable multi-national corporations to substitute low-pay labor markets for the higher cost labor in developed nations, thereby exacerbating the potential unemployment quandary. As robotics and technologies continue to make great leaps forward, most jobs now reliant to some degree on human participation will eventually vanish because machines will be more productive. When the power goes off, civilization will instantaneously fall back into the Stone Age, and people will degenerate into warring tribes run by feudal lords.

The cheapening of humanity has resulted from modern day globalization due to the utility value of cheap laborers defining the net worth of human beings according to their productivity rate in proportion to corporate profits. In the evolution of pre-modernity, cultures valued human life as of inherent value subject only to the whims of god(s). To each civilization, rulers and the nobility ruled their subjects in accordance to the intrinsic value of human life – that each human being was as basically as valuable as another... that life was sacred because it was created by a higher being. In our modern money driven world, the worth of people has become relegated to their purchasing power.

Why should drug addicted heirs of great family fortunes be held in higher esteem than those afflicted among the poor? Why still should irresponsible and brash kids of the elites be considered any better than those of commoners? Why are people with more money valued higher than those with less? Shouldn't a person who works hard in an honest backbreaking job to put food on his family's table be valued at least as highly as the billionaire's spoiled brat whose arrogance justifies bad temperament and low morals? Not in the world we live in. The news media and movies have made the general public into zombies, worshipers of those who are used to shape public opinion and norms, while behind the scenes the truly powerful and wealthy are hoarded their money off into secret off shore bank accounts to evade taxes.

All people have intrinsic value – that of being living, sentient beings who are capable of independent thought and actions (though often not expressed as such). Why do so many feel they need to be led? Because too many desire to lead? So periodically, people follow madmen whose own self-aggrandizement justifies their psychotic ethnic cleansing campaigns whether against Jews, Moslems, Christians, native tribes, or "savages". The ultimate fault of the human species is intolerance, without which people would be more able to live among each other in peace and mutual respect. And with tolerance, people would recognize that everyone and all life possess intrinsic value.

Ranking second on the short list of human frailties is greed. Greed is a double-edge sword that can cut stone into great civilization or cut deep into the collective soul of entire races of people and nations. While greed allows the accumulation of great amounts that are necessary to build great monuments and the dreams of inventors, too often its uses are to fund human suffering among the faceless masses. Drug dealers make fortunes as millions become permanently addicted to the destructive nature of narcotics and other street drugs. But pharmaceutical conglomerates also exploit human misery by supplying prescription drugs at high prices, often with negative health and economic side effects. Arms merchants earn billions through the black market arms trade as their agents foment conflict and warfare in third world nations, but weapons manufacturers make hundreds of billions of dollars in legitimate profits once the smaller smoldering conflicts can justify a full scale war in the Third World. And behind most of the economic activities of the world are investment bankers, who fund anything that makes a quick buck, whether it would be trading in legal or illegal drugs, legal or illegal weapons, wars or terrorism. Money makes the world go around, and in the global economy, it is the grease that keeps the economic wheels of the global elites turning. Will a "perfect world" ever be possible? Certainly the world of the 3rd millennium appears to be more progressive than that of the first century, right? The facts clearly show the world contains more hungry people now than ever before in human history, and the percentage of the poor has never been higher – all juxtaposed against the rapidly rising wealth of the top ten percent, and especially the top one tenth of one percent of the global economic elites. Don't be fooled by all the horns and whistles, the glitz and glamour and shifting mirrors. The world is not a better place than it was 2,000 years ago, and perhaps not even 5,000 years ago or 10,000 years ago. Modern humanity continues to be subject to natural calamities, tornadoes, hurricanes, floods, earthquakes, droughts and pandemic diseases. Modern humanity continues to be plagued by religious intolerance, poverty, starvation, and armed conflict that result in massive deaths. Modern humanity has the same face of ancient humanity, only with more scars, as people continue to follow madmen, tyrants, and lunatics not too distant in kind from Adolph Hitler.

If we were to define a "perfect world" as one where disease has been conquered, starvation does not exist, and everyone acts responsibly within their communities to foster tolerance and peaceful interactions, does the world have the capacity to support the development of a "perfect world"? The answer is "yes" and "no" for the following reasons:

Yes, because it is human nature to strive for a sense of belonging, while feeling their individual existence is of value to those who they love, who love them. And no.

People are naturally intolerant due to fear of the unknown and unfamiliar. People's daily lives are a constant interplay between the forces of love and fear. Do workers love their jobs or fear their bosses? Do spouses refrain from infidelity because they love each other or from fear of the consequences of getting caught in an intimate relationship with another? Do students love to learn mandatory subjects to qualify for a degree, or from fear of failure? Usually, people compromise and neither do only those things that they cherish, nor do they refrain from doing those things they loathe.

A perfect world will only be possible when people's desire for truth and love far exceeds their propensities for fear and greed (which is oftentimes an overcompensation for the fear of unpredictability). In a perfect world, variety and abundance would rule the day, as fear would become extinct. People would be motivated by a desire to seek knowledge as a pleasure of growth and development, and not for any need for validation or permission of the government to work in any career. The sheer intrinsic joy of discovery and learning are strong allies against the intimidation of fear. There is noting to fear, but the fear of fear. Certainly confronting fear and overcoming it makes us stronger people.

Is a perfect world likely? Not until world population, development, pollution, disease, and starvation are brought under control and equilibrium is established. And that is not likely to happen anytime soon, but we must not take our eyes off the target, otherwise it is never going to happen for sure.

What Would An Ideal World Be Like?

In an ideal world, which is worth striving for, every person born would have the basic entitlement to adequate:

1.	food	2.	shelter
3.	education	4.	medical care
5.	love and affection	6.	religious freedom
7.	reasonable liberties	8.	protection from violent people
9.	protection from exploitation	10.	freedom of association
11.	pursuit of personal choices	12.	sustainable employment
13.	respect and dignity	14.	freedom from intimidation & fear

How could societies offer these basic entitlements?

- Food based on nutritional standards, supplemented by governments
- Shelter based on govt./private/self-help partnership programs
- Educational goals that provide choice, emphasize functional knowledge and skills development, good citizenship and ethics, and career goals
- Medical care that is affordable, effective, and protects against catastrophe
- Love and affection from effective parents, guardians, and community
- Peaceful religious practices of any type should be allowed; violence not
- Freedoms of speech, expression, assembly and press if not destructive
- Protection from violent offenders; incarcerate and reprogram their brains
- Non-exploitation through honest, transparent, and non-corrupt practices
- Freedom to choose associates and to disapprove association
- Pursuit of personal choices and happiness as long as not harming others
- Sustainable employment at "living wages" and minimal taxation
- Respect, dignity, and civility; "do unto others as they should do to you."
- Freedom from fear and intimidation by bullies, criminals, and authorities

The historical paradigm has always been the survival of the most ruthless, predatory, and brutal people. Human evolution has hopefully raised collective consciousness to recognize that force, violence, and intimidation is barbaric and should be avoided. Unfortunately, lip service too often gives way to bad habits BUT we can all do better by first improving ourselves, then our family and friends, our communities, our nations and in the aggregate when everyone does their small parts, the entire world will benefit.

It doesn't hurt to try improving humanity through appropriate peaceful social change based upon enlightenment, cooperation, compassion, and a reasonable sharing of national and global resources with the goal of ecological preservation. Our nation and world need not be subjugated to the greed of oil barons, overcompensated multi-national CEO's, and international bankers whose cohorts manipulate sovereign debt and Wall Street investments. If we love America, we should try to improve it in anyway possible within our personal niches and networks. Some will be more effective than others, however, everyone can do their part as small or large as it may be. Otherwise, to do nothing at all will permit the greedy Globalists and international moneychangers to rewrite the history of the world, first by conquering the United States of America, then by installing a global system that serves the appetite of the international elites through the exploitation of the global village. And that would be a terrible consequence of doing nothing at all.

Author's Note:

All images were downloaded from the Internet public domain image search on both yahoo.com and google.com. The author claims no creative or financial ownership interests in any of the images utilized in this book solely for educational illustration purposes. Images may be removed from future publication at the request of the respective copyright holders.